M000308768

The Houghton Mifflin Study Skills Handbook

The Houghton Mifflin Study Skills Handbook

James F. Shepherd
Queensborough Community College,
The City University of New York

Houghton Mifflin Company   Boston
Dallas   Geneva, Illinois   Hopewell, New Jersey
Palo Alto   London

To my friends and colleagues at
Queensborough Community College

Printed in the U.S.A.

Library of Congress Catalog Card Number: 81-82169

ISBN: 0-395-31709-6

(Credits for excerpts start on page 418.)

Contents

Contents

Contents

Contents

Contents

Contents

Contents

Contents

Contents

Preface

The Houghton Mifflin Study Skills Handbook is a complete, easy-to-use guide for practical solutions to study problems. Written for students who want to earn college degrees, it is a textbook for study skills courses *and* a reliable source of help for students when they have study problems at any time during their college careers. It was written to provide students with more thorough and easy-to-understand explanations of a broader range of study skills than they can find discussed in any other book.

Organization of the handbook. The text is organized in a sequence that is appropriate for teaching study skills to full-time college students. Twenty-nine chapters are grouped in five parts:

Part One, "How to Earn a College Degree," is an orientation to college life and an explanation of the basic requirements for earning a college degree. It also explains sources of help for students who encounter academic difficulty.

Part Two, "How to Do Well in Each Course," explains basic methods for being well organized in each class and also develops specific skills, such as those for taking good class notes, participating in class discussions, increasing concentration, enlarging vocabulary, and improving reading flexibility and fluency.

Part Three, "How to Read and Study for Examinations," relates reading to the study process and explains how to underline or highlight textbooks, how to decide what is important to study, and how to learn information for tests.

Part Four, "How to Take Tests and Examinations," presents a discussion of basic test-taking procedures and complete explanations of specific strategies for answering multiple-choice, true-false, matching, sentence completion, and essay questions.

Part Five, "How to Prepare Papers and Reports," gives practical and easy-to-use suggestions for writing papers, using a library, and giving oral reports.

A table of contents, an index, a list on the inside front cover of the book, and cross-referencing within the text make the information in the handbook easily accessible. Consult the table of contents for an overview of its broad range of topics.

At the end of the handbook there is an Answer Key that shows model notes for students who use textbook excerpts to practice note-taking skills. There is also a Glossary of important terminology.

Writing style and level. The handbook is written in a conversational and supportive style that can easily be understood by almost all first-year college students and that appeals to upper-division students because of its clarity and straightforwardness. The explanations of skills are concise, but complete; when the choice was to be either concise or complete, I chose to be complete.

Excerpts from popular college textbooks are included to illustrate explanations and, if desired, to practice skills. The passages, selected from a variety of subject areas, are representative of expository materials students read in college. Characteristics of the textbook passages may be evaluated by skimming Chapter 14.

Teaching suggestions. Each chapter is written so that it may be easily understood without first having read any other chapter. Thus, instructors may sequence skills instruction to the needs of specific students or to their own preferences. However, it is logical to teach Chapter 11 through Chapter 17 in the sequence in which they are presented; these chapters explain how to read and study for examinations.

Many teachers report success introducing test-taking skills at the beginning of a term. They find almost all students immediately grasp the relevance of developing test-taking skills and that this increases their receptivity to other study skills instruction. It seems that when test-taking skills are taught first, students apprehend more readily that a major goal of study skills instruction is to help them do their best.

Skills practice. *The Houghton Mifflin Study Skills Handbook* is not a worktext or workbook, but it includes practice for skills development. Activities are integrated into most chapters to help students understand how skills are used; Chapter 14 and Chapter 19 are two good examples of this type of skills practice. Also, questions, activities, and applications are listed at the ends of chapters under the heading "Use What You've Learned." These items include suggestions for practical assignments and class discussions.

In addition, students may practice skills by applying them to chapters of the handbook. For instance, students may read, underline, make notes for, and learn the information in Chapter 8 for the purpose of answering an essay question about how concentration may be improved.

Other features of the handbook. The handbook is a handy reference that students may consult throughout their college careers when they need solutions to study problems. When they turn to the handbook, they will find methods to use, but they will also find encouragement to understand, accept, and respect their abilities.

Request of instructors. If it is important to you to have a textbook that serves your instructional objectives and helps you have a satisfying teaching experience, I request that you write me so that in revising this handbook, your specific needs can be taken into consideration. Please tell me what you like and do not like about *The Houghton Mifflin Study Skills Handbook* and what I might improve, add, or delete to make it better. If you take the time to write to me, I will take the time to thank you. Address your letter to James F. Shepherd, c/o Marketing Services, College Division, Houghton Mifflin Company, One Beacon Street, Boston, Massachusetts 02108.

Acknowledgments. I am grateful to President Kurt R. Schmeller and the faculty of Queensborough Community College for the partial leave of absence that allowed me time to complete the writing of this book. Also, I am indebted to my colleagues in the Basic Educational Skills Department; I have benefited greatly from my associations with all these talented teachers and good friends.

In addition, I thank Hal Rand for suggestions he gave me about class discussions, and Diane Steffer and Dorothy Hosey for demonstrating to me how to develop human potential.

I also appreciate the useful comments and suggestions of the following reviewers: William T. Anagnoson, Montgomery College, Takoma Park, Md.; Gerald F. Wojcik, Los Angeles Valley College, Van Nuys; and Joseph Zielinski, Tarrant County Junior College, Fort Worth.

Finally, I thank Professor Emeritus Josephine P. Ives, New York University, who read the manuscript and made many helpful suggestions that I have included in the final version. Jo Ives has played a crucial role in all stages of my intellectual and professional development for nearly fifteen years; I cannot measure my indebtedness to this great teacher and loyal friend.

J. F. S.

To the Student

The Houghton Mifflin Study Skills Handbook was written to help you do your best in college and earn a college degree. Very simply, it explains all the things that I wish somebody had explained to me when I entered college thirty years ago.

I recommend that you read the first seventeen chapters of this book as soon as you have the time. They include many practical suggestions that you can put to use immediately if you are a college student or are about to enroll in college. If you purchased this book for a course, you will find it helpful to read the first seventeen chapters before your instructor assigns them.

When you need study suggestions, consult the list on the inside front cover, the table of contents, or the index. In most instances you will find the specific help you need, and when you do not, you will usually find suggestions that you can use to think creatively about how to solve a study problem.

I wrote this book to help you, but I will never know if it does unless you tell me. Will you please write and tell me whether you find this book useful or whether there is anything I can do to make it better? If you take the time to write to me, I will take the time to thank you. Address your letter to James F. Shepherd, c/o Marketing Services, College Division, Houghton Mifflin Company, One Beacon Street, Boston, Massachusetts 02108.

It would please me greatly if *The Houghton Mifflin Study Skills Handbook* helps you have a satisfying experience in college.

J. F. S.

PART ONE

How to Earn a College Degree

Get Off to a Good Start

The first few weeks that you spend at your college or university are critical. If you get off to a good start, you will be more likely to stay in school and earn a **degree.*** It is important that you

1. have a good reason to be in school.
2. enroll in the right curriculum.
3. take interesting and satisfying courses.
4. adjust quickly to the new way of life at college.

This chapter explains how to do these things so that your college career may have the best possible beginning.

1.1   Know why you are in college

It is not easy to earn a college degree. If it were, most of the students who enroll in colleges and universities would earn degrees—but they do not. Many students leave school because they have no good reason to expend the energy that is necessary to earn a degree. Years later, they often regret that they did not give serious enough thought to how they might benefit from a college education.

The following list summarizes reasons that students often give for attending college. Read all the reasons, and then read the list a second time to select the three reasons that best

***Bold face** terms are defined in the glossary.

2

describe why you are attending college. Circle the numbers in front of the *three* reasons that you choose.

1. I want to live the best possible life.
2. I want to prepare myself for a specific occupation.
3. I want to be a well-educated person.
4. I want to increase my appreciation for the arts.
5. I want to learn to think more clearly.
6. I want to be more responsible for my own life.
7. I want to be promoted at the place where I work.
8. I want to decide what to do with my life.
9. I cannot find a job right now.
10. I don't want to go to work right now.
11. I want to please my parents.
12. I want to make new friends.
13. I like the social life at college.
14. I want to find a wife or husband.

Most students circle numbers in front of reasons 1 through 8. The first eight reasons for being in college are all ways of saying "I want to improve myself." If you chose mostly those reasons, you believe that college will make it possible for you to live a more worthwhile life.

If you believe that a college degree will help you to live a better life, your belief should motivate you to do the things that are necessary for you to achieve your goal. But, if you do *not* have this strong conviction, you also may not have the motivation that is necessary to expend the time and effort needed to acquire a college education.

Also, there are hundreds of colleges and universities in this country, but you are enrolled in only one of them. What are your reasons for studying at the school that you have selected rather than at some other school? The following list is a summary of reasons that students give for selecting a college at which to study. Read all the reasons, and then read the list a second time to select the three reasons that best describe why you have enrolled at the school that you are attending. Circle the numbers in front of the *three* reasons that you choose.

1. A counselor, friend, or relative recommended it to me.
2. It has a good reputation.
3. It is located conveniently near my home.
4. I wanted to leave home to go to school.
5. It offers the program that I want to study.
6. I have friends who are attending the school.
7. I cannot afford to go to any other school.
8. It is the only school that accepted me.

These are all good reasons for selecting a college, but if you did *not* circle reason 5 ("It offers the program that I want to study") you have probably enrolled in the wrong school. If you are not studying a program that you want very much to study, examine your college **catalogue** or **bulletin** to find a program that interests you. Studying in college will be much more meaningful to you if you are enrolled in such a program.

1.2   Select the right curriculum

Your **curriculum** is the program in which you are enrolled; you will receive a degree when you satisfactorily complete all the course work and other requirements of your curriculum. If you are a **matriculated** student (that is, if you have been accepted to study for a degree), you should have a list of the courses and other requirements for your curriculum. If you do not have a copy of this information, consult your catalogue or bulletin, or ask your counselor or adviser to give you a copy of it.

If you are not completely certain that you are enrolled in the right curriculum, you are not alone. For most students college is a time for exploring possibilities; more than half of all college students change their curriculums during their college careers.

The right curriculum for you is the one that is best suited to your interests and abilities and that will help you to achieve whatever goals you have set for yourself after you have graduated from college. Examine your curriculum and answer the following questions about it.

1. Are you interested in studying most of the courses that are required in your curriculum?
2. Do you have the abilities that are necessary to do well in most of the courses that are required in your curriculum?
3. Will a degree in your curriculum help you to achieve the goals that you have set for yourself after you graduate from college?

If the answer to all these questions is yes, then you have obviously selected the right curriculum. But if the answer to any of the three questions is no, then you should consider selecting a more appropriate curriculum.

Your interests and aptitudes.   From your previous experiences as a student you know what subjects are interesting to you. You know whether you prefer to study mathematics, science, history, or English. However, colleges and universities offer courses in many subjects that you have not studied before. As a result, you may have no way of knowing whether you are interested in studying some of the subjects that are available for you to study in college.

If you are having difficulty in deciding what curriculum interests you, or in selecting between two equally interesting curriculums, you may find it helpful to visit the counseling center on your campus. Most colleges and universities have counselors who are trained to help students understand what their interests are. They often ask students to respond to items on **interest inventories,** which are tests that measure occupational and educational interests. Students often develop a better understanding of their interests when the results of interest inventories are interpreted for them.

The curriculum that is most suitable for you must also be one for which you have good **aptitudes,** which are your talents and abilities. Sometimes students enroll in curriculums that interest them greatly but for which they must take many courses for which they have little aptitude. For example, students sometimes enroll in nursing or pre-medical programs because they are interested in serving others, but they lack the ability to do outstandingly well in chemistry, biology, and other scientific courses that are important to nursing and pre-medical curriculums. These students often become discouraged and drop out of school. But they might not drop out of college if they consider their aptitudes as well as their interests when selecting a curriculum.

If you are uncertain what your aptitudes are, counselors can help you. Counselors can interpret placement test scores or other test scores that may be in your records. And, if you request, a counselor can probably arrange for you to take additional aptitude tests.

Many students are reluctant to visit counselors to take tests that measure their interests and aptitudes. They fear that this will be embarrassing. Also, of course, test-taking is displeasing to many students. But interest inventories and aptitude tests are very different from classroom tests. Classroom tests are designed to determine how well students have mastered course work for the purpose of assigning them grades. On the other hand, interest inventories and aptitude tests, administered and interpreted by a trained counselor, are designed to help students gain a better understanding of how they might have satisfying experiences in college and later at work. If you are uncertain what your interests or aptitudes are, take advantage of the services your school provides to help you gain insight into yourself. You are an interesting person. Why not get to know yourself better?

Your goals after college. Competition for most jobs is expected to increase through the end of the century. As a result, more so than in the past, students feel the need to study curriculums in college that will equip them to be aggressive competitors for good jobs.

If you are uncertain about what occupation you want to pursue, or what courses you should take to prepare for a specific occupation, the federal government publishes books that may be helpful to you. These books are available on most campuses in the counselors' office or in the library.

If you are interested in knowing more about specific types of occupations, *The Dictionary of Occupational Titles* gives descriptions of more than 21,000 jobs. This book will be useful to you if you want to know what types of jobs are available within a specific area that interests you.

If you are equally interested in two occupations and want to prepare for the occupation that has the best job opportunities, consult *The Occupational Outlook Handbook.* Among other things, this book gives forecasts of the numbers of workers that will be needed in various occupations in the future and identifies occupations for which many workers are needed.

1.3   Enroll in the right courses

Most colleges assign students to advisers who help them plan what courses they will take each term. Advisers can be helpful because they know what courses are required in students' curriculums. Unfortunately, since your adviser will not know you very well during your first year in college, the advice that he or she gives you may be good advice for most students but not for you.

Whether you plan your **program** by yourself or with the help of an adviser, these are the questions you should ask about each course in your program during your first year of college.

1. *Does the course interest me?* Include in your program as many interesting courses as possible. If your curriculum requires you to take some courses that are very uninteresting to you, do not take those courses during your first year unless it is absolutely necessary.

2. *Am I likely to do well in the course?* Include in your program mostly courses in which you believe you will earn a good

grade. This will increase your chances for having a satisfying first year in college. Do not register for any course for which you are certain you will receive a low grade.

3. *Will the course be accepted for credit in my curriculum?* Include in your program only courses that will move you toward your goal of earning a degree. Avoid taking any course *only* because you are interested in it. Most colleges and universities offer a wide selection of courses that are interesting and that also apply toward most degree programs.

4. *If I change curriculums, will the course be accepted for credit in the other curriculum that interests me?* Most colleges have a good selection of courses that can be applied toward the completion of most degree programs. If you believe that you are likely to change curriculums, these are the types of courses that you should take. Be especially careful when registering for mathematics and science courses; these types of courses often apply only to specific curriculums.

5. *Is the course one that I must take in order to take other courses that I want to take?* Most colleges offer courses that are prerequisite to other courses. A **prerequisite** for a course is a requirement that must be completed before enrolling in the course. For example, at some colleges the prerequisite for the three-credit English Composition I course is a specified score on a placement test or satisfactory completion of a writing course that is offered for no credit or for only partial credit. If you are required or advised to take any courses of this type, it is wise to take them as early in your college career as possible because they are intended to help you do your best in school (see Section 3.5).

When you plan your program, do not create unnecessary problems for yourself by including too many courses in it. Unless you know that you are a superior student, do not plan to register for more than the average number of credits that students at your school usually carry. For example, full-time students at one college usually require eight **semesters** to earn the 120 credits that are needed for a degree. In an average semester, students at this school complete 15 credits ($120 \div 8 = 15$). However, many students at this college take fewer than 15 credits during their first semester. They take 12, 13, or 14 credits to increase their chances of earning good grades; they take extra credits in later semesters when they are more experienced students. When you plan your program, make certain that it includes no more courses than you can handle comfortably.

When you go to **registration,** be prepared to have a frustrating experience—registering for courses is an unpleasant experience at most colleges and universities. You may need to wait in long lines to register for each course, and in some instances a course that you planned to take may be closed out. Therefore, when you plan your program, include some alternative courses for which you will register in case some of the courses you want most are unavailable.

Also, at most colleges there may be several sections for some courses. A **section** for a course is a class that is taught by a specific teacher, in a specific room, at specific times. Information about courses and sections is printed in a booklet that is available to you before registration. Use these suggestions to guide you in selecting the sections in which to enroll.

1. *Select sections that are taught by teachers who have been recommended to you by students whose recommendations you trust.* If at all possible, talk with students who have taken the courses that you plan to take. Find out which teachers they prefer, and enroll in sections that are taught by those teachers.

2. *Select sections that meet at times when you are well rested and alert.* You will need to be alert to concentrate in your college classes. If you are wide awake very early in the morning, plan your program to start as early in the day as possible. But, if you are not fully awake until ten o'clock, avoid scheduling classes before that time. Also, if you are ready to take a nap at three in the afternoon, don't schedule classes after three o'clock.

3. *Select sections so that your classes meet at times that are well distributed over the days of the week.* It is sometimes possible to enroll in sections so that almost all classes meet on one

or two days a week. Students who want to work many hours while they attend college full time often plan classes to meet on one or two days, and they also often encounter serious academic difficulties (see Section 7.2). It is difficult and tiring to sit and concentrate in one class after another for several hours in a row—college classes require your complete attention. Plan your program so that no day of the week is overloaded with classes.

1.4   Adjust to college life

The first weeks of college will probably be disturbing for you—they are for most students. You will need to make new friends. You will have new teachers to adapt to; you will need to learn where classrooms are located and to find the easiest ways to travel from one place to another. You will need to schedule your classes, buy your own books, and plan when you will eat meals. Also, you may feel uncomfortable because you don't know the difference between a *bursar* and a *registrar* or a *professor* and an *instructor*. Do not be surprised if all of this disturbs you—it is disturbing. This section gives information that may help you make a more speedy adjustment to college life.

Social activities.   Your college experience will be more pleasurable if you take part in the social life on campus. The students at your school have organized clubs for all types of interests: photography, chess, yoga, skiing, poetry reading, and just about any other interest you can think of. There are clubs for students who are interested in various religions and for students who are members of various ethnic groups, such as those who are Jewish, Italian, and Chinese. Information about clubs may be printed in your college catalogue or in brochures or pamphlets that are distributed to students during **orientation.** Clubs not only provide you with opportunities to participate in activities you enjoy, they are also a means for meeting people and for making new friends.

Your student government probably also sponsors athletic events, movies, concerts, dances, and other activities that are available to you at no or very little cost. Watch student newspapers and bulletin boards for announcements of these events.

If you have difficulty learning about clubs and social activities, visit the student activities office or an office that includes the words "student affairs" or "student government" in its title. Somebody in that office will be able to give you the information that you need in order to involve yourself in campus life.

Counseling services.   The counselors on your campus may be located in a counseling center or in an office that includes the words "student services" or "student personnel" in its title. Counselors are usually highly trained specialists in providing students with help in achieving their educational and occupational goals, and in helping them to resolve their personal problems. In addition, they are usually experts in helping students with such problems as changing curriculums, dropping courses, and filing complaints about grades. If you have any problem, chances are that a counselor can either help you or tell you where you can get the help you need.

Circle the number in front of any of the following statements that describe you.

1. I need a part-time job.
2. I need a place to live.
3. I need financial assistance.
4. I have a serious physical disability.
5. I want to improve my grades.
6. I am very anxious when I take tests.
7. I do not understand the meaning of my placement test scores.
8. I want help deciding what occupation to pursue.
9. I want help deciding what curriculum to study.
10. I want to know about job opportunities available after I graduate.

11. I want to transfer to another college.
12. I am extremely displeased with one of my teachers.
13. I need somebody to care for my children.
14. I have been away from school for many years and I feel lost.
15. I feel very lonely.
16. I have a serious problem with my parents.
17. I have poor relationships with members of the opposite sex.
18. I want help to overcome my drug problem.

If you circled any of the numbers, a counselor at your school can either help you or tell you where you can go for help. You may be advised to visit another office on campus, or, if you have a problem for which your school provides no services, you may be advised to visit an agency in the community that can give you the assistance you need.

Health services.   Your college has an office that provides services if you are ill or injured. Call this office if you have a serious illness or injury that prevents you from attending classes for an extended period of time. Somebody in the office will pass this information on to your teachers so that they can make special arrangements for you. Also, if you have a physical disability or serious chronic illness, this information should be made known to the office that provides health services.

Registrar and bursar.   The **registrar** is the person on campus who oversees registering students for courses and who keeps records of the courses students take and the grades they receive. Shortly after you complete each term of study, the registrar will send you a copy of your **transcript,** which is a record of the courses you took and the grades you received. Your transcript will be used to decide whether you have satisfied all the requirements in your curriculum and should be awarded a degree. Visit the registrar's office when you have questions about your transcript or your registration in courses, and when you want an official transcript mailed to an employer or to another school.

The **bursar** is the person at a college who is responsible for money transactions. Visit the bursar's office when you have questions about tuition or fees, or when you need to pay a bill.

Terms, semesters, and quarters.   A **term** is a specified period of study that usually ends with the administration of final examinations; ordinarily a term is either a semester, a quarter, or a summer session. When a school uses the **semester system,** the school year is divided into two parts, usually a fall term and a spring term of from fifteen to sixteen weeks each. When the **quarter system** is used, the school year is divided into three parts, usually a fall, winter, and spring term of ten weeks each.

A **summer session** is a period in the summer during which students may take courses for full academic credit, but which is usually not considered a semester or quarter for the purposes of a school's business. For example, if students are told at the end of a spring term that they must raise their grades to a specified level by the end of the following term, they usually need to raise their grades by the end of the fall term—not by the end of the summer session.

A.A., B.A., M.A., Ph.D.   There are many types of **degrees** that are awarded to students who satisfactorily complete specified courses of study, but the most commonly awarded degrees are associate degrees, bachelor's degrees, master's degrees, and doctoral degrees. The **associate degrees** are usually offered by two-year and community colleges, and they are most commonly either the A.A. (Associate of Arts), the A.S. (Associate of Science), or the A.A.S. (Associate of Applied Science). The **bachelor's degrees,** offered by four-year colleges and universities, are usually the B.A. (Bachelor of Arts) and B.S. (Bachelor of Science). The **master's degrees,** also offered by some four-year colleges and most universities, are usually earned after earning a bachelor's degree. They are usually the M.A. (Master of Arts) and M.S. (Master of Science). **Doctoral degrees** are the highest degrees that are offered by colleges and universities. Some of the doctoral degrees are the M.D. (Doctor of Medicine), Ph.D. (Doctor of Philosophy), and Ed.D. (Doctor of Education).

Freshmen, sophomores, etc.   The first year of study at a college is the **freshman** year, the second year is the **sophomore** year, the third year is the **junior** year, and the fourth year is the **senior** year. In four-year schools, **lower division** refers to the first two years of study—the freshman and sophomore years. **Upper division** refers to the third and fourth years of study—the junior and senior years. **Undergraduates** are students who have not yet earned bachelor's degrees, and **graduate students** are those who have earned bachelor's degrees and are continuing college study—usually to earn master's degrees or doctoral degrees.

Professors, instructors, and lecturers.   Those who teach in colleges and universities have ranks and titles, very much like those who work in the armed services have ranks and titles. Information about the degrees your college teachers have earned and their ranks is probably printed in your college catalogue or bulletin.

Professor is the title for college teachers who hold any of the three professorial ranks: professor, associate professor, or assistant professor. Professor (sometimes called "full professor") is the highest rank a college teacher may hold; assistant professor is the lowest professorial rank. **Instructor** is the rank that is lower than assistant professor, and at some schools this rank is reserved for teachers who work part-time. The term **lecturer** is not used consistently from school to school; it may indicate a rank lower than instructor or it may be reserved to designate distinguished visiting teachers.

Address your teachers according to their preferences. Teachers of any rank may have earned a doctoral degree and prefer to be addressed as "Doctor." When instructors or lecturers have not earned doctoral degrees, they are usually addressed as

"Mr.," "Miss," "Mrs.," or "Ms." All teachers who hold a professorial rank may be addressed as "Professor," and they may prefer this form of address even if they have earned a doctoral degree. In some instances teachers request students to address them by their first names. If a teacher says, "Don't call me Professor Abernathy, call me Tim," he'll like it if you call him Tim.

The president and deans.   The **president** is the chief administrative officer of a college or university—the person who has ultimate responsibility for all aspects of the functioning of the school. **Deans** are members of the administration who are in charge of specified areas of the school's activities such as dean of students, dean of faculty, dean of instruction, and dean of administration, or dean of a **school** or **division** within a college or university. The registrar and bursar are members of the administration of a school, and the administration of a college also often includes such specialists as the following: lawyer, architect, accountant, auditor, purchasing agent, personnel officer, superintendent of buildings and grounds, director of safety and security, and director of institutional research and testing.

Use What You've Learned

1. Write the answers to these two questions: Why have you decided to attend college? Why have you decided to study at the school in which you are enrolled rather than at some other school?

2. Explain why your curriculum, or some other curriculum, is suitable to your interests, your aptitudes, and your occupational plans.

3. What are your agreements or disagreements with the suggestions that are given for planning programs (Section 1.3)?

4. Find out what clubs there are on your campus and select three clubs that you might like to join.

5. What major social events will there be on your campus during the next six weeks?

6. At your school, what is the name of the office to visit in order to talk with a counselor? Where is the office located? Give three reasons you might want to talk with a counselor.

7. At your school, where are the offices of the registrar and bursar located? Where are the health services, financial aid, student activities, and job placement offices located?

8. What are the names, titles, and ranks of all your teachers?

Maintain Good Academic Standing

A t many high schools, students are passed from one grade to another no matter what grades they earn; but in colleges students who do not earn satisfactory grades are put on **probation**. When students on probation fail to raise their grades sufficiently, or fail to meet other requirements, they lose matriculated status and are not permitted to register for courses. This chapter will help you learn what you must do to maintain good academic standing at your school.

2.1   The importance of grades

Are grades important? Some students become angry, depressed, or even physically ill when they receive a B+ instead of an A or an 88 instead of a 95. Those who have reactions of this sort probably place too much importance on grades (see Section 8.8).

However, there is no doubt that grades are important. The grades that you earn for your courses become a permanent part of your transcript, which is the official record of the courses that you took in college. When you apply for a job or for admittance to another school, you will be requested to have your registrar forward a copy of your transcript. Your grades will be used to help decide whether you should be hired as a worker or admitted as a student. You are likely to have an advantage over other equally qualified applicants if your grades are better than those of your competitors.

What grades should you try to earn? Only you can answer that question. But why not work to earn the very best grades you are capable of earning? Why not be the very best student that you can be? If you are the best student you can be, you *will* earn the best grades that you are capable of earning.

2.2 Minimum grade requirements

All colleges have a method for determining students' average course grades. The most commonly used method is called the **grade point average,** which is a number that usually ranges from 0.00 to 4.00, with 4.00 being equivalent to 100. To understand the importance of a satisfactory grade point average, consult your catalogue or bulletin to find and write the answers to the following questions.

1. Most colleges require a minimum grade point average (GPA) of 2.00 for graduation. What is the minimum average course grade you must have to graduate from your school?

_____

2. Many colleges also require minimum grades in specified courses. For example, in some four-year colleges, students do not receive credit toward graduation for specified courses in which they receive a grade lower than C (2.00). If your school has a similar policy, state it on the following lines.

_____

_____

3. Some schools permit students to have lower minimum GPAs in the first term or two than are essential later. For example, at one school students must maintain a minimum GPA of 1.75 until they have completed eighteen credits. After completing eighteen credits, they must have a minimum GPA

of 2.00. If your school has a similar policy, state it on the following lines.

_____

_____

_____

4. All schools have penalties for students who fail to maintain minimum GPA requirements. What are the penalties for students at your school who fail to maintain the GPA requirements?

_____

_____

_____

5. At some schools, grades in addition to F are given a value of 0.00 for the computation of the GPA. For example, at one school the grade of WU (Unofficial Withdrawal) is given to students who are excessively absent. This WU grade has a value of 0.00; it counts the same as an F for the purpose of the GPA. If there are any grades in addition to F that have a GPA value of 0.00 at your school, list those grades on the following line.

_____

The answers that you wrote for the five questions summarize some very important information. A high proportion of the students who fail in college fail because they did not have this information when it would have been helpful to them.

The grades you earn in college are important. If your grades are low, you will not earn a college degree. If your grades are good, you may earn a degree and reap the benefits of being a

Figure 2a **The Usual Correspondences Between Letter Grades and Number Grades.**

Letter grades	Number grades
A	96–100
A–	90–95
B+	87–89
B	84–86
B–	80–83
C+	77–79
C	74–76
C–	70–73
D+	67–69
D	64–66
D–	60–63
F	0–59

college graduate. Even if you do not graduate from college, the good grades you earn will give you a competitive advantage when you seek employment.

2.3   Number grades and letter grades

The grades that you receive on tests, quizzes, reports, and other projects will be used to determine your course grades, and your course grades will be used to compute your grade point average.

The work students do for courses may be graded with **number grades,** such as 74 and 86, or with **letter grades,** such as C and B. At the end of a term, most schools require teachers to submit a letter grade for each student. Figure 2a is a table that shows the commonly used correspondences between number grades and letter grades. Notice, for example, in Figure 2a that the number grade of 87 is equivalent to a letter grade of B+.

Study your college catalogue to learn what correspondences between number grades and letter grades are used at your school. There are sometimes important differences among schools. For example, a few schools offer the grade of A+ and some schools do not use the grade of D−.

It is important for you to know the meanings of the grades that you receive for your tests, quizzes, papers, and other course work. For example, if you take a course in which you have one or two grades in the high 70s but mostly grades in the mid-80s, you should know that you are doing work in the C+ to B range and that your final grade should probably be about B−. If the teacher gives you a C or C−, you should complain.

2.4   Course grades

Most colleges and universities require teachers to judge students' work in courses and to report for each student one of the letter grades that are listed in the first column of Figure 2a.

Many teachers assign final grades by determining students' average grades on tests, quizzes, reports, and other course work. Following are examples of three of the many different methods teachers use to find students' averages.

1. They may compute the average for all scores. If a student has the grades 71, 76, 79, 80, 87, and 88, a teacher may add the scores (481) and divide the sum by the total number of scores (6) to find the average, which is 80 and equivalent to a letter grade of B− (see Figure 2a).

2. They may give double value for one score—often the score on a final examination. If a student has the grades of 80 for a term paper, 75 for a midterm examination, and 78 for a final examination, the 78 would be doubled (156) and added to the 80 and 75. The resulting sum (311) would be divided by 4 (rather than 3) to find the average, which is 77.75 and equivalent to a letter grade of C+ (see Figure 2a).

3. They may use a point system. For example, one instructor

makes it possible for her students to earn a maximum of 1,000 points—300 points for tests (two tests each have a value of 150 points), 200 points for quizzes (four quizzes each have a value of 50 points), 300 points for the final examination, and 200 points for a term paper. She divides students' total points by 10 to determine their course grades. If a student earns 740 points, she would divide 740 by 10 to find the average of 74, which is equivalent to a letter grade of C (see Figure 2a).

However, not all teachers are this systematic in deciding students' final grades. The following beliefs may influence the grades that teachers give.

1. Some teachers believe that the grades students should receive are simply the grades that, in their opinions, students should receive. They give students the grades that they *feel* are appropriate. They often give higher grades to students whom they find appealing and lower grades to students who are displeasing to them for some reason.

2. Some teachers believe that any student who attends class should receive a grade of at least a B. They give very few Cs, Ds, or Fs.

3. Some teachers believe that practically no student should receive an A and that very few should receive Bs. They give mostly Cs, Ds, and Fs.

4. Some teachers believe that for every class they teach there should be the same proportions of As, Bs, Cs, Ds, and Fs, and that most students should receive Cs. If a teacher who uses this grading policy has 30 students in a class, he may decide before assigning grades that he will give three As, five Bs, fourteen Cs, five Ds, and three Fs. The three students with the three highest averages will receive As, the five students with the next five highest averages will receive Bs, and so on.

5. Some teachers believe that students should always be given the benefit of the doubt. If they give several tests, they may eliminate the lowest test score before computing students' final

grades. Or, they may give students the next higher grade than the one indicated by averages; for example, if a student has an average of 89, which indicates a grade of B+, the teacher may give an A− rather than a B+.

Each of your teachers has his or her own method for determining final course grades. It is important for you to understand the method that each of your teachers uses because the grades that you receive for your courses will be used to compute your grade point average (see also Section 4.2).

2.5   The grade point average (GPA)

At most colleges and universities, students' average course grades are expressed as a grade point average, or GPA, which is a number that ranges from 0.00 to 4.00. This section explains the two systems that are most commonly used to compute the GPA. Consult your college catalogue to determine the method that is used at your school to compute average course grades, and learn that method.

Students' course grades are usually letter grades of the type listed in the first column of Figure 2b. To compute grade point averages, letter grades must first be converted to numbers called **grade point values.** Figure 2b shows two systems that are widely used to assign numerical values to letter grades. Observe in Figure 2b that when System 1 is used, letter grades have the same value whether they are accompanied by a plus or minus (for example, B+, B, and B− all have a value of 3.00). But, when System 2 is used, letter grades have a larger value when they are accompanied by a plus and a smaller value when they are accompanied by a minus (for example, B has a value of 3.00, but B+ has a value of 3.30 and B− has a value of 2.70).

After letter grades have been converted to numerical values, multiplication and addition are done so that the grade point average can be computed by dividing total grade points by total **credits.** Figure 2c illustrates how GPAs are computed using

Figure 2b **Two Systems for Assigning Grade Point Values to Letter Grades.**

	Grade point values	
Letter grades	**System 1**	**System 2**
A	4.00	4.00
A−		3.70
B+		3.30
B	3.00	3.00
B−		2.70
C+		2.30
C	2.00	2.00
C−		1.70
D+		1.30
D	1.00	1.00
D−		0.70
F	0.00	0.00

System 1 and System 2. Notice in Figure 2c that System 2 results in a lower grade point average than System 1 because letter grades accompanied by a minus have a smaller grade point value when System 2 is used.

No matter what method is used at your school to compute average course grades, the method works to the advantage of students who earn good grades and to the disadvantage of students who earn poor grades. If you have a good grade point average, you can do poorly in a course and still maintain good academic standing, but if you have a low grade point average, it will be extremely difficult for you to raise your average. For example, a student who completes fifteen credits in her first semester with a grade point average of 2.80 needs to receive a grade point average as low as 1.20 for fifteen credits in her second semester to bring her GPA *down* to 2.00. Fortunately, students who have B− averages in their first semesters seldom

Figure 2c **Two Systems for Computing the Grade Point Average.**

System 1

Grades	Numerical values		Credits		GPA points
B	3.00	×	2	=	6.00
B−	3.00	×	3	=	9.00
C	2.00	×	3	=	6.00
C−	2.00	×	4	=	8.00
C−	2.00	×	3	=	6.00
			15		35.00

$$\frac{35.00}{15} = 2.33 \text{ GPA}$$

System 2

Grades	Numerical values		Credits		GPA points
B	3.00	×	2	=	6.00
B−	2.70	×	3	=	8.10
C	2.00	×	3	=	6.00
C−	1.70	×	4	=	6.80
C−	1.70	×	3	=	5.10
			15		32.00

$$\frac{32.00}{15} = 2.13 \text{ GPA}$$

have D averages in their second semesters. On the other hand, a student who completes fifteen credits in his first semester with a grade point average of 1.60 needs to receive a grade point average of at least 2.40 for fifteen credits in his second semester to bring his GPA *up* to 2.00. Unfortunately, students who have D+ averages in their first semesters seldom have C+ averages in their second semesters.

Use What You've Learned

1. Survey some of your classmates to determine if they know the answers to the questions in Section 2.2. If they do not know the answers, do you believe it is important that they know them?

2. Learn the correspondences between number grades and letter grades that are used at your school. Then, when you receive number grades on tests and papers you will know what letter grades they represent.

3. What are the grade point values that are assigned to letter grades at your school to compute the grade point average?

4. Explain the method that each of your teachers will use to decide your final course grades for the courses you are taking.

5. Estimate the grades you will receive for the courses you are taking this term and use the grades to compute the grade point average you estimate you will have at the end of the term. Set up the problem in the format that is illustrated in Figure 2c.

Get Help When You Need It

Even the best students have difficulties with some of their courses. Personal problems, illness, lack of appropriate academic preparation, or an instructor who is not very helpful may interfere with a student's ability to do well in a course. This chapter explains some of the ways you can get help when you need it.

3.1 Use this handbook

If you have difficulty with a course, the first thing to do is analyze whether you are using good study procedures. With the difficult course in mind, circle the numbers in front of any of the following statements that describe you in relation to that course. Read the portions of this book that are indicated in the statements that you select.

1. I'm not sure that I know all the course requirements (Section 4.1).
2. I've been absent from some class meetings (Section 4.4).
3. I didn't turn in an assignment on the day it was due (Section 4.5).
4. I am behind in my work for the course (Section 4.6).
5. I don't take good class notes (Chapter 5).
6. I don't participate in class discussions (Chapter 6).
7. I don't schedule the times that I will study for the course (Chapter 7).
8. I have difficulty concentrating when I study (Chapter 8).

9. I'm trying to learn by reading and rereading my textbook (Chapter 11 through Chapter 14).

10. I'm not certain what I'm supposed to learn (Chapter 15).

11. I learn things, but then I forget them (Chapter 16 and Chapter 17).

12. I don't do as well as I should when I take tests (Chapter 18 through Chapter 23).

13. I have difficulty preparing written assignments (Chapter 24 through Chapter 28).

Also, use the lists on the inside covers, the table of contents, and the index for this handbook to find help in solving specific problems that are preventing you from doing your best in the courses you take.

3.2 Talk with your teachers

When you have difficulty in a course, discuss this with your teacher. Instructors usually have office hours during which they hold conferences with students. Make an appointment for a conference with the teacher.

Go to each teacher for help even when you have a teacher whom you believe will not be helpful. One of my students came to me for help with a course he was taking with another teacher. I gave him the help I could and advised him to have a conference with the teacher of his course. He told me that he didn't want to talk with her because she was a stern-looking little woman whom he had never seen smile. But he did schedule a conference with her during which she reminded him that he could attend review sessions that she offered outside regularly scheduled class time. He attended the review sessions and did well in the course.

A young woman who lived off campus with her family was having problems with her mother. Each morning she and her mother would have a bitter argument about her boyfriend. As a result, she arrived at her nine o'clock typing class too upset to type accurately—she was failing the course. When she explained her problem to her teacher, she was invited to attend a class that he taught later in the day. With the change of class hour, the young woman did well in her typing class.

A middle-aged woman who had returned to college to study to be a nurse was totally confused in her chemistry course because her laboratory sessions were taught by an inexperienced and unhelpful laboratory assistant. She discussed her problem with her chemistry teacher and was advised to sit in on laboratory sessions taught by a more experienced assistant. Instead of attending one chemistry lab each week, she attended two, but she did well in her chemistry course.

I could give you dozens of other examples of how teachers have helped students solve learning problems. On some campuses there are study groups for students who are having difficulty with the same course. Teachers usually know if there are study groups, tutoring, or other types of help available, and they can often think of solutions to problems that might not occur to you.

3.3   Consult other helpful persons

Counselors are usually aware of all the sources of academic help that are available on a campus, and, if they are not, they can offer suggestions about where to look for help. They may suggest that you visit the office of the department that offers the course that is giving you difficulty, an office of academic skills, a learning center, a tutorial service, or some other department or service on the campus.

If you have been assigned to an adviser to help you plan your programs, you may find that this person will take a special interest in any learning problem that you have. Your adviser, or any teacher with whom you feel comfortable, may be able to give you suggestions that might not occur to you. In your search for help, don't overlook anybody who might have access to the information you need. You may find, as I have, that departmental secretaries are frequently knowledgeable about services on campus and that they are often sympathetic to students' problems.

Finally, and very important, talk with other students who have already studied the subject that gives you difficulty. Make friends with second-, third-, and fourth-year students who are enrolled in your curriculum. They are an invaluable source of information for you. If you have difficulty discussing problems with a teacher, counselor, or adviser, a fellow student may be your best source of help when you have a study problem.

3.4 Use study guides and course outlines

In some of your courses you may be assigned textbooks that are extremely difficult for you to understand. If this should happen, you will need to find another book on the same subject that you can read and understand more easily. The book you need may be in your college library or in a local library, or it may be a **study guide** or **course outline** that you can purchase.

Study guides and course outlines briefly summarize the information that is usually included in the standard textbooks for a subject. Some teachers strongly object to the use of guides and outlines, but there is no good reason for this objection. Study guides and course outlines are designed to help students learn subject matter that they want or need to learn. There is no reason for a teacher to object when students learn the things that they want or need to learn.

A study guide or course outline is available for most popular college courses. You may need to visit several bookstores to find all the guides that are available for a particular subject. Examine as many guides and outlines as you can to make certain that you purchase the best one for your purposes. Compare the table of contents in a guide to the table of contents in your textbook— they will not be identical, but they should be similar. Then, read a portion of the guide that corresponds to information that you found difficult to understand in your textbook. After you have examined all the guides and outlines that are available, select the one that is most understandable and useful to you.

3.5   Improve your learning skills

Very few people read, study, write, and solve mathematical problems as well as they are capable. As a result, colleges usually test students' reading, writing, and mathematics skills when they apply for admission. If test scores indicate that it is advisable, students are required or advised to improve their abilities in learning skills. This instruction is likely to be provided in courses that are offered by an English department, mathematics department, academic skills department, learning center, or skills laboratory. The courses are usually taught by regular faculty members, but at some colleges **tutors** instruct individuals or small groups of students.

If you are required or advised to improve learning skills, take full advantage of whatever instruction is offered at your school. The faculty of your school believes that this instruction will help you do your best in college and earn a degree.

When this instruction is offered for no credit, or for partial credit, students often believe that this is either because they will learn nothing or because the courses are extremely easy. However, learning-skills courses are usually not easy because they require students to master skills that they did not master earlier in their schooling. You may need to work as hard in these courses as you do in courses that you take for full credit.

Some students complain when they are asked to take special reading, writing, or mathematics instruction. Often the complaints don't make much sense because when they are analyzed they state: "I do not want to receive the help that the faculty of my college wants me to have so that I will do well in school." However, from time to time the complaints are legitimate. For example, students' test scores may be invalid because they were ill the day they took placement tests. If you believe that you have been incorrectly advised to improve learning skills, discuss this with the person on your campus who can re-evaluate your abilities. He or she may be in the office of testing, learning center, counseling office, English department, mathematics department, or academic skills department.

3.6 Use W, INC, and pass/fail grades

Most colleges and universities offer grades that can be helpful to students when they encounter academic difficulty—the withdrawal grade and the incomplete grade. Some schools also offer the pass/fail grade to help students protect good grade point averages.

The **withdrawal grade,** or W grade, is provided for students who must unexpectedly leave school, for students who discover that they are taking more courses than they can handle successfully, and for students who find themselves in a course that is giving them serious difficulty. The W grade is usually not computed into grade point averages and therefore it usually does not lower or raise grade point averages. However, there are usually strict limitations on the time period during which W grades may be requested. Study your catalogue to determine if W grades are available at your school. If they are, state how the W grade is used and describe the restrictions on this grade at your school.

_____

_____

_____

_____

If it is ever possible for you to protect your grade point average by requesting a W grade rather than receiving an F in a course, you should definitely request a W. It is also usually wiser to request a W than to receive a low grade, such as a D. The only time it is advisable to accept a D in a course is when you take an especially difficult course that is not part of your major subject area.

Also, most colleges offer the possibility of taking an **incomplete grade,** or INC grade. The INC grade is usually offered so that students who are doing satisfactory work in a course may have additional time to complete a term paper or some other project that was not finished at the time final grades were reported. When the past-due project is completed and delivered to the instructor, a final course grade is computed and entered on the student's transcript. However, there are usually dead-lines after which past-due work will not be accepted, and in many instances when work is not turned in before the deadline, INC grades are automatically converted to Fs. Study your cat-alogue or bulletin to determine if the INC grade is available at your school. If it is, describe its purpose and what happens to an INC grade when required work is not completed before a deadline.

_____

_____

_____

_____

It is best to request an INC grade only when it is absolutely necessary. An alarmingly high proportion of students who receive INC grades never complete the past-due work they were supposed to complete.

Finally, some schools offer the possibility of taking a small number of courses for a **pass/fail grade.** Students declare before they enroll in a course that they want to take it on a pass/fail basis. If they do satisfactory work they receive a pass, which does not raise or lower their grade point averages; but if they do unsatisfactory work they receive a fail, which counts as an F in computing the grade point average. When this option is available, it is usually used by students who have high grade point averages and who want to take a course in which they believe they may earn a C grade that would lower their grade point averages. Study your college catalogue or bulletin to determine if the pass/fail grade is available at your school. If it is, describe how the grade is used.

_____

_____

_____

_____

Use What You've Learned

1. Use the list in Section 3.1, the table of contents, and the index of this book to identify the skills that you want to improve to do your best in college.

2. Explain why you would *or* would not discuss learning problems in your courses with the teachers of your courses. Consider each teacher individually.

3. Identify a counselor, adviser, and teacher (other than a teacher of one of your courses) with whom you would feel comfortable discussing a problem you have with one of your courses.

4. List the names of all the second-, third-, or fourth-year students you know who are enrolled in the same curriculum that you have and with whom you could discuss a learning problem.

5. Use the method described in Section 3.4 to select a study guide or course outline for the course that is giving you the most difficulty.

6. Learn the information that you wrote in Section 3.6.

PART TWO

How to Do Well in Each Course

Be a
Well-organized Student

College is more likely to be a satisfying experience for you if you are well organized. You must be well organized to achieve your worthwhile goals and also to have time for entertaining friends; engaging in sports; and going to movies, dances, concerts, and parties. If you are not well organized, you will not have the time available to enjoy a full and rewarding life.

This chapter explains how to be well organized for each course you take. Chapter 7 describes how to schedule your free time to do the studying that is necessary for your courses.

4.1 Know all course requirements

The basic information that you need to organize yourself for success in college is the requirements for each of your courses. If this is your first term in college, you may not yet know all the various types of requirements that college instructors have. The following list of questions indicates the types of requirements that you can expect; use the questions as a checklist for each course you take. When you know the answers to all of the following questions, you will have a good idea of what you are required to do in your courses.

1. What books and other materials must you purchase?
2. What books or other materials must you take to class meetings?
3. What are the topics for each class meeting?

4. Should you read about lecture and discussion topics before you attend each class?

5. Must you take notes for the course?

6. Must you participate in class discussions?

7. Are you required to read materials in addition to the books you purchase? If so, what are the materials and where are they located?

8. Must you attend a laboratory? If so, where is the laboratory located and when must you attend it?

9. Must you have conferences with the teacher? If so, where and when must you attend conferences?

10. Are you required to write a paper or report?
    a. What format must you use?
    b. How many pages long must the paper be?
    c. When is the paper due?

11. Must you do homework assignments? If so, how many assignments must you complete and when are they due?

12. Are you required to give an oral report?
    a. What format must you use?
    b. How many minutes long must it be?
    c. When must the presentation be given?

13. Must you attend concerts, visit museums, or go on field trips to hospitals, governmental agencies, or other institutions? If so, when and where must you do these things?

14. How many tests must you take?
    a. On what days will the tests be given?
    b. What topics and materials will be covered on each test?
    c. What types of questions (multiple-choice, true-false, essay, and so forth) must you answer?

Some teachers have very few requirements, but others will require you to do most of the things that are suggested in this checklist. Ask these questions about each course you take and you will have the information that you need to be well organized.

4.2   Understand how course grades are computed

Knowing how the grade for a course will be computed will guide you to do the things that you need to do to earn a good grade. Some of your teachers will explain to you exactly how they will determine your final course grades, but others will be vague about the methods that they will use (see Section 2.4). If you ask teachers how they determine final course grades and they are unable or unwilling to explain their methods, you should at least learn from them the answers to the following questions:

1. If you turn in assignments late, will you receive a lower grade for the assignment than you would have received if you had turned it in on the day it was due?
2. If you are absent from classes or late to classes, will this lower your course grade?
3. If you fail to turn in homework assignments, will this lower your course grade?
4. If you are absent the day a test is given, will you be given an opportunity to take a make-up test? If not, what grade will you be given for the test you missed? If make-up tests are given, are they more difficult than regular tests?
5. Will your final grade be based in part on your participation in class discussions?
6. Will your final grade be based in part on your attendance in a laboratory or at conferences with the teacher?

Learn as much as you can about your teachers' grading practices. This will help you understand how to do your best in each course and to make the best use of your study time.

4.3   Take a notebook to each class

Of the several types of notebooks that are available, most students prefer spiral notebooks that measure 8½ by 11 inches. The advantage of spiral notebooks is that they are easy to use on small desk tops, and the 8½-by-11-inch size is preferred because it is large enough to organize notes so that most if not all the information on a topic is on one page rather than on several pages.

The major disadvantage of spiral notebooks is that they usually do not provide a place for keeping papers that are distributed by teachers. Only a few manufacturers put pockets on the inside covers of spiral notebooks—these pockets are convenient places for keeping important papers that might otherwise be lost. If your notebooks do not have pockets, staple important papers your teachers distribute to the inside covers of your notebooks. Important papers include sheets that explain course requirements, **syllabuses** that list topics for each class meeting, descriptions of how to satisfactorily complete major term projects, and suggestions about what to review in preparation for tests.

The major purpose for taking a notebook to each class is to have a place in which to record notes for lectures and class discussions (see Chapter 5 and Chapter 6). In addition to class notes, your notebooks should contain information about assignments, tests, instructors, and classmates.

1. Information about *assignments* should explain exactly what they are, how they are to be done, and when they are due.

2. Information about *tests* should include exactly what materials and topics will be covered on each test and the dates that the tests will be given.

3. Information about *instructors* should include their names, office locations, office telephone numbers, and the times that they are available in their offices.

4. Information about *classmates* should be the names, addresses, and telephone numbers of at least two people in each class whom you can contact in case you must be absent from a class (see Section 4.4).

If you have no preference for where you keep these records, consider keeping them on the last pages of your notebooks. Turn a notebook so the spiral is to your right, open the cover, and write the information about your instructor and two class-mates at the top of the very last page in the notebook. Then, as information about assignments and tests is given, list it on the page. When that page is filled, continue on subsequent pages, moving toward the front of the notebook. By using this method you will not waste any pages, and information about an instruc-tor, classmates, assignments, and tests for a course will be in a convenient place.

4.4   Attend all class meetings

You are one hundred percent responsible for everything that happens in each of your classes, even if you are absent. If you are absent from classes, you need friends who will obtain for you copies of materials that teachers distribute, who will inform you about assignments and tests that are announced, and who will allow you to copy their class notes (see Section 4.3 and Section 5.8).

The primary purpose of classes in college is to provide you with information and experiences that are difficult, or impos-sible, for you to acquire by reading or any other method. If you want to do well in college, you must attend all your classes faithfully. Students who resent that they must go to classes should not be in college; the need to go to classes will be a con-stant source of misery to them.

The following list includes some advice about what to do and what not to do if you must be absent from a class.

1. Do not be absent from any class.
2. If you must be absent for *any* reason, be willing to accept whatever consequences result because you were absent.
3. Inform the health services office at your school immediately if you have an accident or serious illness that prevents you

from attending classes for an extended period. Somebody in that office will pass this information on to your teachers. If your teachers do not make special arrangements for you, you may need to withdraw from your courses (see Section 3.6).

4. Do not give your teachers fictitious reasons for your absences (they will know that you are lying).

5. Do not tell a teacher that an absence is "excused" because you were ill or some similar reason. This concept has no meaning at most colleges and universities (see the second suggestion in this list).

6. Do not ask teachers how many cuts you are allowed in their classes (they will know that you are irresponsible).

7. Believe any teacher who tells you that you will receive a failing grade if you have a specified number of absences.

8. Do not tell any teacher that you are unprepared with an assignment or for a test because you were absent the day that the assignment or test was announced (see the first paragraph of this section).

9. Following an absence, do not ask a teacher if you missed anything (the answer is yes).

10. Following an absence, do ask teachers if they have any suggestions that would be helpful to you because you were absent.

Also, beware of any teachers who tell students that they do not need to attend classes. These are often teachers who ask many test questions that are based on things they say in class. If you are absent, you will not know what they said and you will do poorly in their courses.

Some students have responsibilities or emotional problems that prevent them from attending classes; others have physical complaints that keep them away from school. Draw a circle around the number of any of the following statements that describe you.

1. I miss classes because of my job.
2. I miss classes because I am responsible for taking care of others.
3. I miss classes because I have problems with my family or with a special friend.
4. I miss classes because I use alcohol or other drugs.
5. I miss classes because I hang out with friends.
6. I miss classes because I am sick much of the time.
7. I miss classes because sometimes I just don't feel like going.

If you drew a circle around any of the numbers, you have a problem that is likely to prevent you from doing well in college. You should seek the help of a counselor, go to school part-time, change your job, or discontinue your education until your circumstances are more favorable or you have regained your health.

Also, arrive at classes on time. There are good reasons why a student might be late to class once or twice during a term, but the habit of consistently arriving late for a class is usually due to a personality problem. Consistent lateness usually indicates a person who is starved for attention, self-centered, disorganized, immature, inconsiderate, or hostile. Students who consistently arrive at a class late communicate one of these unpleasant messages about themselves to their teacher and to their classmates.

4.5   Turn in assignments when they are due

Teachers expect students to turn in assignments on the days that they are due—not on some later day. There are so many students who do not understand the importance of turning in assignments on time that many instructors lower the grades for assignments that are turned in late. Some teachers deduct a whole letter grade for each week that a paper is overdue. For example, if an A paper is turned in one week late it is graded B rather than A; after two weeks it is graded C, and so on.

If you cannot be in class to deliver an assignment on the day that it is due, place the paper in the teacher's mailbox before the time it is due. Or, if you are unable to deliver the paper, have a friend deliver it for you.

If you are required to write a research paper or some other major paper, plan ahead to make certain that you allow yourself enough time to complete the project. Suggestions for writing reports and papers are given in Chapter 24 through Chapter 28. In Chapter 24, pay special attention to the discussion about the need to prepare a work schedule (Section 24.2).

4.6   Keep up with course work

Experienced college students know how to catch up in a course if they fall behind. However, if you are *not* an experienced college student, you will probably be overwhelmed if you should fall behind in a course. College terms start out slowly, gradually get busier and busier, and reach a peak of activity at final examination time. If you fall behind in the work for a course, you will find yourself trying to catch up at the time you are very busy with all of your other courses. Don't fall behind—keep up to date with course work.

This is especially important when you take courses for which information and skills learned early in a course are needed to learn information and skills later in the course. Mathematics, science, and foreign language courses are among those that fit this description, and this is a major reason these courses are difficult for many students. When you study, ask yourself this question: "Do I need to learn this information or skill to learn other information or skills later in the course?" If the answer to this question is yes, learn the information or skill immediately and review it often. You will be at a serious disadvantage unless you learn the things you need to learn as you go along and keep them fresh in your mind by reviewing them.

Also, in many of the courses you take, each test will cover everything that you have learned up to the time of each test. For example, the first test may cover everything in Chapters 1 through 6 in the textbook, the second test may cover everything in Chapters 1 through 13, and the final examination may cover everything in the entire textbook. When teachers give these types of tests, you are likely to have difficulty doing well on the tests unless you constantly keep up to date with course work and review frequently (see also Section 8.6 and Section 8.7).

Use What You've Learned

1. Describe the requirements for the most demanding course that you are taking.

2. In which of your courses will your grade be lowered if you turn in assignments late, are excessively absent or late, fail to participate in discussions, are absent from a laboratory, or are absent from conferences?

3. Which of your teachers do not give make-up tests, and which ones give make-up tests that are more difficult than the tests given on regularly scheduled test days?

4. What are your agreements or disagreements with the suggestions about notebooks that are given in Section 4.3?

5. What are your agreements or disagreements with the information about absences and latenesses that is given in Section 4.4?

Take Good
Lecture Notes

G ood class notes will often be your single best source of help for understanding course material and for deciding what information you should give special attention to when you prepare for tests. They usually contain records of

1. important information that is not printed in course reading material.

2. clues about what information should be learned to do well on tests.

3. explanations of difficult information that appears in required course reading materials.

It is impossible to overstate the importance of taking complete and well-organized class notes.

5.1 Use good note-taking procedures

Use the following procedures to take well-organized notes of the type illustrated in Figure 5a.

1. *Use lined paper that measures 8½ by 11 inches* (see Section 4.3).

2. *Write a heading that includes the name or number of the course, the instructor's name, the date, and the topic of the lecture.* This will put you in the proper frame of mind for note taking, and the information can be used later to make certain you have notes for each class meeting.

3. *Organize notes so that major points stand out clearly.* In

Figure 5a An Example of Well-organized Class Notes.

Study Skills 101, 9/8/84   Shepherd

How to Take Lecture Notes

Seven Characteristics of good notes
1. Written on 8½ - by 11-inch notebook paper
2. Heading includes name or number of course, teacher's name, date, and lecture topic
3. Major points stand out clearly
4. Details are neatly listed under major points
5. Include examples teachers give
6. Don't try to repeat teachers' words exactly
7. Include things written on the board

How to improve listening
- Eliminate environmental distractions (EX) Don't sit near window or near annoying classmates.
- Eliminate physical distractions
  1. Dress so you're not too warm or cold
  2. Eat so you won't be hungry
  3. Visit rest room before class
- Eliminate internal distractions (EX) Don't think about what you'll do after class

Speakers' clues to major points in lectures
- May pause before or after a major point
- May repeat a major point
- May raise or lower voice for major point
- May state major point and number of details (EX) "Seven characteristics of good notes"
- May write important points on board to be copied.

Figure 5a, the three major points are written to the left side of the page and they are underlined.

4. *List details under the major points in an orderly fashion.*

5. *Include examples in your notes.* In Figure 5a, examples are indicated by the circled letters *EX*.

6. *Summarize what teachers say rather than try to write everything that they say word for word.*

7. *Copy into your notes information that is written on the chalkboard.*

This chapter explains how to use these procedures.

5.2   Be properly prepared for lectures

Take a notebook and a pen or pencil to all of your classes. Suggestions for notebooks are given in Section 4.3.

Proper preparation for class also often includes having read before class the portions of textbooks that are related to lecture topics. Many teachers list the topics of their lectures in a **syllabus,** which they distribute to students so they will know what portions of textbooks to read before each class meeting. Other teachers plan their lectures with the expectation that students will not have read information about lecture topics before class; they often lecture with the intention that they will provide information that will be helpful to students when they read the textbook or other required material.

When you have no difficulty understanding lectures, you may find it sufficient to use the methods described in Chapter 12 and Chapter 13 to preview and skim materials about lecture topics before classes. But, when lectures are difficult for you to understand or when you leave lectures confused, bewildered, and lost, you know that you must read and study in preparation for the lectures. You may even need to follow the suggestion given in Section 3.4 and purchase a study guide to read before you attend the classes for some of your courses.

5.3   Concentrate during lectures

Select seats in your classes that make it possible for you to
see and hear your teachers without disturbance. The best seats
for this purpose are usually the ones in the center and front of
rooms because they provide clear, uninterrupted views of teachers. Avoid seats next to annoying classmates and near windows
that give views of activities going on outside the classrooms.

Being too warm or too cold, being hungry, or needing to go
to the restroom are sources of physical discomfort that can dis-
tract you from concentrating.

1. Dress so that you can remove clothing if a room is too
   warm or add clothing if a room is too cold.
2. Carry snacks to eat between classes if you do not have time
   to eat a proper meal before a class.
3. Go to the rest room before class.

Also, you will not be able to concentrate during lectures if
you are worrying or thinking about something that happened
before class began or something that will happen after class is
finished. If you find yourself in a class thinking about something other than the lecture, use the suggestions that are given
in this chapter to refocus your attention on taking good class
notes.

5.4   Listen for clues to major points

To take notes in which major points stand out clearly and in
which details are neatly listed under major points, you must
focus your attention during lectures to listen for the major
points and the details that support them. Some teachers directly
state their major points by using phrases such as "Now I'm
going to discuss . . ." and "My next topic is. . . ." Also, lecturers
often use pauses, repetition, or changes in the loudness with
which they speak to emphasize the major points in lectures.

1. A *pause* in speech is a period of time during which nothing is spoken. If your teachers pause while lecturing, this is likely to be a clue that you should write down what was said just before the pause or what will be said just after the pause.

2. When your teachers *repeat* information, this is usually a definite clue that you should record the repeated information in your notes.

3. A *change in the loudness* of a teacher's voice may indicate that an important statement is being given. Some teachers speak more loudly when they state major points, while others speak more softly when they make statements that you should include in your notes.

When you take class notes, listen carefully for direct statements of major points and for pauses, repetition, and changes of loudness that are often clues that something especially important is being stated.

5.5   Listen for clues to supporting details

Helpful lecturers often include statements of exactly how many details should be listed under major points in class notes. For example, they make statements such as these:

There are *four types* of conflicts people experience.
There are *three reasons* we entered World War II.
There are *five advantages* of exercising daily.

When teachers state major points in these ways, it is clear exactly how many details should be listed under them. In other instances teachers make it clear that they are going to give a list of details, but they do not state the exact number of details in the list. For example, if a teacher says, "I'm going to talk about the important advantages of exercise," you should write as a major point in your notes "Advantages of exercise" and prepare to write a list of advantages. But you will not know how many details (advantages) there are in the list until the complete list has been given.

5.6   Copy what is written on the chalkboard

Anything that is written on a chalkboard may be used as the basis for a test question. Copy into your notes everything that is written on chalkboards and mark the information so that it will stand out in your notes and not be overlooked when you prepare for tests.

1. When teachers write tables, charts, diagrams, or formulas on a chalkboard, copy them into your notes unless you are given a good reason why you should not copy them. For example, if your teacher says, "You do not need to copy this diagram into your notes because it is printed on page 239 of your textbook," you know you do not need to copy it. However, write in your notes "Study the diagram on page 239," and mark this statement as being very important.

2. Terminology written on a chalkboard should be copied and marked for special attention. For example, if a teacher in a business course writes *entrepreneur, laissez-faire,* or *oligopoly* on the chalkboard, these words should be copied and marked for special attention when studying.

3. Persons' names and dates that are written on a chalkboard should also be copied and marked as important. In high school you may have been expected to know about famous people and about dates of important occurrences only for history courses. But in college you may be expected to know the people who have made important contributions to any subject that you study, and you may be expected to know the dates of important events in any subject.

Develop the habit of including in your notes everything that is written on chalkboards, and mark everything that you copy from a board for special attention when you study for tests (see also Section 15.1).

5.7   Increase your note-taking speed

It is not possible to take lecture notes that include everything that teachers say. Good lecture notes summarize what teachers say; they are not a word-for-word record of teachers' statements. In Section 16.6 and Section 28.4 there are descriptions of how to summarize various types of written information; those methods may also be used to summarize information that is presented in lectures. When you take class notes, practice summarizing what teachers say in your own words.

Also, if you analyze your handwriting, you may find that you can write class notes using a simplified form of handwriting that uses fewer lines, curves, and flourishes than you ordinarily use. The following statement is written in a student's usual handwriting.

Practice writing using fewer lines and flourishes.

This is the same statement written by the same person, but using a simplified form of handwriting.

Practice writing using fewer lines and flourishes.

In addition, use abbreviations for common words and for words that occur frequently during lectures. The word *and* may be represented by &, and the word *with* may be represented by *w/* (for example, "w/speed" means "with speed"). Make your own abbreviations for words that appear frequently in your courses. You might use *eq* for *equation, psych* for *psychology,* and *chem* for *chemistry.* The best abbreviations for your notes are the ones that you devise and understand. Also, don't worry about spelling every word correctly; you may correct misspelled words after class (see Section 5.9).

5.8   Be certain that your notes are complete

If you are aware that you have missed information during a lecture, leave a blank space in your notes and, when the time is appropriate, raise your hand and ask the question that will help you make your notes complete. If it is impractical to ask a question during a lecture, make your notes complete after class by (1) talking with the teacher, (2) talking with a classmate who takes good notes, or (3) studying your required course reading materials.

If absence should cause you to miss the notes for an entire class meeting, read the suggestions that are given in Section 4.4 before you discuss this problem with a teacher. To have a complete set of notes, you will need to handcopy or photocopy the notes that were taken by one of your classmates. However, the notes that are taken by your fellow students are not likely to be very useful to you when you study. Your classmates take the kinds of notes that are useful to them; you take the kinds of notes that are useful to you. This is one reason you should attend all your classes.

5.9   Review your notes soon after you take them

Notes that you take in September may contain information that you will need to know when you take a test in November. If you do not understand your notes in September, you will not understand them in November when you prepare for a test. Therefore, during the first free time you have following a lecture, reread your notes to make certain that they are easy for you to understand and that they are complete. While the lecture is still fresh in your mind, change your notes in any ways that make them more understandable to you. Correct misspelled words, fill in missing words, and, if you are unable to understand any part of your notes or if your notes are incomplete, put a question mark in the left margin next to the unclear or incomplete portion. Then, at the first opportunity, make your notes clear or complete by (1) talking with the teacher, (2) talking with a classmate who takes good notes, or (3) studying your required course reading materials.

5.10   Study your notes before you take tests

It is almost always essential to study lecture notes when you prepare for tests. Many teachers include questions on their tests that can be answered correctly only by students who take good class notes and who study their notes thoroughly before tests. Especially beware of teachers who give very disorganized lectures or who give lectures for which you need to take very few notes. Often these are the teachers who include a large proportion of questions on their tests that are based on information that they gave in class. Suggestions for studying lecture notes are given in Section 15.1 and Section 17.3

Use What You've Learned

1. Use the suggestions in Section 5.2 to prepare yourself to benefit as much as possible from lectures.

2. The next time you lose your concentration during a lecture, investigate whether you are too warm or too cold, hungry, or need to go to the rest room. You may find that physical discomfort is distracting you so that you cannot concentrate.

3. Use the following criteria to decide which of your teachers help you take well-organized class notes:

a. Which of your teachers directly state the major points in their lectures so that you have no difficulty knowing what their major points are?

b. Which of your teachers use pauses, repetition, or changes in loudness of their voices to help you find their major points?

c. Which of your teachers frequently state major points using phrases that make it clear to you exactly how many details you should list under major points?

4. When you copy something that is written on a chalkboard, place a star or some other symbol next to the copied material in the left margin of your notes, and give the information special attention when you study for tests. After you take tests, study the tests and your notes to determine whether some test questions were based on information that was written on chalkboards.

5. During lectures, practice writing using fewer lines, curves, and flourishes than you ordinarily use. Devise some abbreviations that help you to take notes more quickly in each of your courses.

6. After you take tests, study your lecture notes to determine how many of the questions were based on information that was given by your teachers in class.

Participate in Class Discussions

The lecture method of teaching is usually used by teachers who want to communicate factual information and by teachers who have very large classes. The class discussion method of teaching, on the other hand, is usually preferred by teachers who want small classes of students to analyze and evaluate points of view, theoretical models, controversial opinions, contrasting methodologies, and similar types of subject matter. Class discussions may also be about a concert students attended, a museum they visited, or any other experience that they shared. The suggestions in this chapter are for discussions about information that students have read, but they may be adapted for effective participation in any type of discussion.

6.1 Characteristics of class discussions

A basic characteristic of class discussions is that students do as much talking or more talking than the teacher. However, a class discussion is not simply an opportunity for one or two students to say whatever comes into their minds, and it is not a verbal free-for-all. Following are the characteristics of well-planned class discussions:

1. The chairs in the classroom are arranged so that every person in the room can easily see the faces of the other people in the room.
2. The topic for the discussion is clearly stated, usually in the form of a question, so that there is no doubt about the goal

of the discussion. For example, if the question is "Has the prestige of a college degree declined in the past ten years?" it is clear that the goal is to discuss the facts that lead to the conclusion that the prestige of a college education has *or* has not declined.

3. The statements that are made and the questions that are asked are all directly related to the discussion topic.

4. From time to time a student or the teacher summarizes the comments that have been made and may explain how some of the comments are interrelated.

5. All, or almost all, students make statements or ask questions.

6. The discussion results in a fuller understanding of the information that is relevant to answer the question that was the topic of the discussion.

Most of these characteristics need to be present for a class to have a serious and meaningful discussion.

A class discussion is an exchange of ideas that seeks to explore the advantages and disadvantages, strengths and weaknesses, appropriateness and inappropriateness, truthfulness and untruthfulness, or pros and cons of a topic. All information, facts, opinions, and experiences that pertain to understanding the topic may be brought forth in discussing it. Business discussions usually have the purpose of arriving at a decision, such as how to spend money or whom to hire for a job. But class discussions usually do *not* have the purpose of arriving at a decision; the purpose of class discussions is usually to develop more complete understanding of discussion topics without arriving at conclusions with which all discussion participants agree.

The point of a discussion is to understand the topic of discussion more fully, not to argue or persuade others what is the truth, what they should or should not believe, or what they should or should not do. A class discussion is not an argument. In an argument, one hears statements such as "You're wrong," "Will you be quiet and listen to me," "That's stupid," and

"You're a liar." Statements of this type are inappropriate during a serious discussion. Those who discuss topics seriously are more likely to make statements such as "Let's look at it this way... ," "I understand your point, but I don't fully agree because ... ," "I'm not certain that the evidence is as conclusive as you make it seem because ... ," and "I came to a different conclusion when I read that passage. ..."

6.2   Preparing for class discussions

Class discussions require students to collect information about discussion topics before they go to class, usually by studying required reading materials. To make intelligent contributions to discussions, you must prepare yourself.

Read about the discussion topic.   Prepare for class discussions by reading and making notes on all required reading material that is related to the discussion topic. Underline the important statements in the material, and make notes just as though you were preparing for a test (see Chapter 11 through Chapter 14).

Make a list of the important facts or opinions.   If the purpose of the discussion is to develop understanding of the facts that are related to an issue, list the facts so that you can refer to them during the discussion. For example, in preparing to discuss whether the prestige of a college education has declined over the past ten years, list the facts that support and that do not support the conclusion that there has been a decline in prestige. If the discussion topic is about an opinion, list the opinions and the reasons the opinions are held. For example, if the question is "Should those who murder others be put to death?" you will find the opinions that (1) murderers should always be put to death, (2) murderers should be put to death under certain circumstances, and (3) murderers should never be put to death. Under each opinion, list the reasons it is held.

Make a list of your questions. As you read the required material, make a list of your questions about any information that is unclear or confusing to you. You may use your questions to make worthwhile contributions to discussions. Also, any answers you receive to your questions during discussions will be helpful to you when you prepare for tests.

6.3   Overcoming fear of discussions

If you are afraid to talk in front of a group, you are not alone—most people have this fear. Few students feel completely comfortable when they participate in class discussions.

One reason that students are nervous when they speak during discussions is that they worry about the impression they will make rather than concentrate on what they will say. They want to present a good appearance, but their undue concern for what others will think about them causes them to freeze up, speak with a trembling voice, forget what they want to say, and express their thoughts poorly. The fear of speaking before a group is not easy to overcome—many never conquer this fear. But, if you are extremely nervous during class discussions, you may become more comfortable if you are thoroughly prepared for discussions and keep the following thoughts in mind:

1. It is normal for you to be nervous when you speak in front of a group—most of your classmates are nervous too.

2. When you speak in class, concentrate on what you want to say and not on how you appear to others. If you concentrate on what you want to say you will speak more intelligently and look better to others.

3. By participating in discussions now you will gain experience that will help you be more comfortable during discussions in the future.

Many of the most desirable jobs in our society require the ability to be an effective participant in group discussions for the purpose of making policy, management, and other types of decisions. When you practice participating in class discussions, you develop skills that will be useful to you in your other courses and, perhaps, in your work.

Another reason that students do not like to participate in discussions is that they fear they will be criticized or ridiculed for what they say. You do not need to fear this if you are well prepared for discussions, follow the suggestions in the next section, and accept the fact that your teachers are expected to correct and teach you.

6.4   Participating in discussions

Go to discussion classes armed with notes, questions, and a determination that you will overcome any fear you have of participating in discussions. In almost all discussion classes there are two or three students who love to hear themselves talk. Skillful teachers use these individuals to get discussions started. Listen carefully to everything that is said. Each time a new point is introduced, think what comment you would make if you were called on. When you are ready to make a contribution to a discussion, try using one of these strategies:

1. If somebody says something that you do not fully understand, ask for a more complete explanation.
2. If somebody gives information on a topic and you have additional information about the same topic, offer the information.
3. If somebody asks a question that you can answer, give the answer.
4. When it is appropriate, ask one of the questions in the list that you prepared while you were reading about the discussion topic.

When you participate in a discussion, you do not need to do a great deal of talking. It is usually better to say too little than to say too much. Make statements and ask questions that are directly related to the points under discussion and that keep the discussion moving toward the goal that has been established.

You are likely to grow weary of some students in your discussion classes who try to dominate conversations by talking too much and by always trying to put in the last word on every point that is made. This is inappropriate behavior during a discussion. Teachers may ask students who talk too much to give others a chance to speak, and they may also correct students who engage in any of the following inappropriate behaviors:

1. Make statements or ask questions that reveal they have not read the required material about the discussion topic.
2. Consistently state their own opinions and experiences without referring to information in required reading material.
3. Make statements or ask questions that reveal they were not paying attention while others were speaking.
4. Interrupt others while they are speaking.
5. Do anything that is distracting while others are speaking.
6. Speak so softly that it is difficult to hear what they say.
7. Engage in arguments with others.
8. Make unkind statements to others.

It is appropriate for teachers to request students to refrain from these types of behaviors during discussions. However, it is not likely that you will ever be criticized during a discussion if you prepare properly, listen carefully to what others say, stick to the topic of the discussion, and treat others kindly.

6.5   Taking notes during discussions

The notes you take during discussion classes will not be as detailed as the notes you take during lecture classes, but they are equally as important as lecture notes. They should include an outline of the major points of the discussion and a summary of any new information that you learned during the discussion.

Use the same note-taking methods that are suggested in Chapter 5, and study discussion notes in the same way you study lecture notes (see Section 15.1 and Section 17.3).

Use What You've Learned

1. Use the suggestions in this chapter to prepare for and participate in a class discussion, and then state your agreements *and* disagreements with the suggestions.

2. Do you have classes in which students do a great deal of talking, but in which discussion is *not* guided by most of the characteristics that are listed in Section 6.1? If so, what is your opinion of the instructional value of those discussions?

3. Do you have classmates in any of your discussion classes who exhibit any of the eight inappropriate behaviors that are identified in Section 6.4? If so, what are your opinions of those individuals?

4. When a teacher of one of your discussion classes discourages students from engaging in any of the eight inappropriate behaviors that are identified in Section 6.4, what is your opinion of the teacher? If these behaviors occur in a class of yours and the teacher does not discourage them, what is your opinion of the teacher?

Schedule Time for Studying

A minimum of fifteen to twenty hours a week of studying is required for full-time students to earn satisfactory grades at most colleges and universities. In a typical semester you may read five or six textbooks that have a total of more than 2000 pages and you may write a paper or complete some other major project for each course you take. If you do not set aside the amount of time that is needed for studying, your grades will be lower than they should be—you may fail courses and be forced to drop out of college.

There are no study halls in colleges, and most college students do not have parents who monitor them when they study. If you are going to spend the time studying that is necessary for you to do well in college, you will need to schedule your study time. Figure 7a illustrates a method that you may use to prepare a study schedule. Following are the basic procedures for using a form of the type in Figure 7a to schedule study time.

1. Cross out all the hours during which you cannot study because you are attending class, working, or engaging in other activities.

2. Determine how many free hours you have available for studying by adding up the hours in the schedule that you did not cross out.

3. Decide exactly which subjects you will study during your free time periods each week.

Notice in Figure 7a that after the student crossed out the times that he cannot study he had thirty-one free hours left that

Figure 7a **An Example of How to Schedule Time for Studying.**

	MON	TUE	WED	THU	FRI	SAT	SUN
8–9	Chemistry	✕	Chemistry	✕	English	✕	✕
9–10	English	✕	Chemistry	✕	Psychology	✕	✕
10–11	✕	Math	✕	Math	Chemistry	✕	✕
11–12	✕	✕	✕	✕	Chemistry	✕	✕
12–1	✕	✕	History	✕	✕	✕	✕
1–2	History	✕	History	✕	✕	✕	✕
2–3	✕	✕	✕	English	Free	✕	Free
3–4	✕	English	✕	Psychology	Free	✕	Free
4–5	Psychology	Psychology	Math	Free	✕	✕	Free
5–6	✕	✕	✕	✕	✕	✕	✕
6–7	✕	✕	✕	✕	✕	✕	✕
7–8	✕	Chemistry	✕	Math	✕	✕	✕
8–9	✕	History	✕	Free	✕	✕	✕
9–10	✕	Free	✕	Free	✕	✕	✕
10–11	✕	✕	✕	✕	✕	✕	✕

he can use for studying. He scheduled twenty-two of these hours for the study of specific subjects. He will use the other nine hours for his pleasure, or he may decide to use some of them to do more studying. In addition, he will revise his schedule several times during the term. For example, he set aside 12:00 P.M. until 2:00 P.M. on Wednesdays to study history, but some weeks he may use this time to write a paper for his English course or to study for a test in his chemistry course.

The rest of this chapter explains, in detail, how to prepare a study schedule.

7.1   Decide how much you want to study

You are the only one who knows what kinds of grades you want to receive for your courses, and you must know what grades you want to earn to decide how much time you need to set aside for studying. If you have well-developed reading and study skills and your goal is to earn Cs in most of your courses, you probably will not need to spend much time studying. On the other hand, if you want to earn As and Bs in courses that are difficult for you, you are not likely to achieve your goal unless you spend a great deal of time studying.

If you want to learn how much time you need to study to earn good grades, spend more time studying than you think you need to. A general guide is to spend twice as much time studying outside of class as you spend attending class meetings. For example, if you are taking a course that meets for three hours each week, set aside six hours each week to study for the course. This is more time than most students spend studying, but students who devote this much time to studying usually earn good grades.

On a piece of paper, list the courses that you are taking this term. Next to each course, write the grade that you want to earn. Then estimate how many hours you will need to study each week for each course to earn the grade you want. Add up the number of hours that you need for studying each course and write the number on the line in the following sentence.

I need to study _____ hours each week to earn the grades I want.

7.2 Determine how much time you have for studying

Use the form in Figure 7b to analyze how many hours you have available each week that you can use for studying. Cross out the time periods during which you are engaged in activities such as the following:

1. Attending class
2. Eating meals
3. Sleeping
4. Dressing and grooming
5. Traveling
6. Working
7. Socializing and dating
8. Attending meetings
9. Helping with household responsibilities
10. Relaxing (watching TV, and so forth)

Be certain to cross out enough time for each activity. For example, if it takes you an hour each morning to get dressed and eat breakfast, cross out an hour, not a half hour. Also, be certain that you allow enough time for meals, visits with friends, and the relaxation that is necessary for your enjoyment of life and your mental health. If you have a favorite television program that you watch every Thursday evening from nine until ten, be certain to draw lines through that hour in the schedule. You are not likely to study while your favorite television program is on.

After you have crossed out all the hours that you cannot or

Figure 7b **Make a Form like This to Schedule When You Will Study.**

	MON	TUE	WED	THU	FRI	SAT	SUN
8–9							
9–10							
10–11							
11–12							
12–1							
1–2							
2–3							
3–4							
4–5							
5–6							
6–7							
7–8							
8–9							
9–10							
10–11							

will not use for studying, add up the hours you did *not* cross out and place this number on the line in the following sentence.

I have _____ hours each week that I can use for studying.

If you wrote a number that is less than the number you wrote in the sentence at the end of Section 7.1, figure out how you can make more time available for studying.

For example, students often have insufficient time for studying because they are working at jobs that require too much of their time. Following are some of the solutions to this problem:

1. Seek financial aid so that there is less need to work.
2. Attend college part-time in the evening, rather than full-time during the day.
3. Work a great deal in the summer and very little, or not at all, during the school year.
4. If it takes a great deal of time to travel to and from work, find a job in a place that requires less travel time.
5. If late or early work hours are the problem, find a job with more suitable hours.
6. If the purpose of working is to enjoy a luxury, such as an expensive automobile, consider doing without the luxury.

If you have insufficient time available for studying, seek help from the counseling office at your school. A counselor may help you find a solution that you may not think of.

7.3   Schedule the times that you will study

To decide what subjects you will study at various times, you need to analyze what conditions help you study most efficiently. People who spend their lives writing and studying find that they write and study best when they have a special time and place for these activities. Their study places need to have all the essential equipment for their work, they need to be quiet and free of distractions, and they need to be furnished with a well-lit table or desk and an appropriate chair. However, complete quiet may be distracting to you—you may prefer the sound of soft music in the background while you study. Also, you may find that you are extremely lonely when you study unless you are with a companion or in a library surrounded by other students. Use the following questions to analyze the conditions that are helpful to you when you study.

1. Do you concentrate best in the morning, in the middle of the day, in the afternoon, or in the evening?
2. Do you study best at the place where you live, in a library, in an empty classroom, in a student lounge, or outdoors?
3. Do you study best alone, with a partner, with a special friend, with a small group, or in a library surrounded by other students?
4. Do you study best with complete quiet, with soft background music, or with a great deal of noise in the background?

Observe the conditions that help you study best and use what you learn to plan when you will study your most difficult subjects. For example, if you find that you study best in the evening at the place where you live, this is the time and place that you should study your most challenging subjects.

Also, consider these suggestions before you schedule the times that you will study for specific courses.

1. Free periods of at least one hour before classes are good times to study information about lecture or discussion topics in the classes that follow the free periods (see Section 5.2 and Section 6.2).
2. Free periods after classes are the best times to review lecture or discussion notes that you took during classes just before the free periods (see Section 5.9 and Section 6.5).
3. Concentrated periods of an hour or more are needed for challenging activities such as learning how to solve a new type of mathematical problem or writing the draft of a four-page paper.

4. Many brief periods of about thirty minutes, spaced over as many days as possible, are best for reciting or reviewing information and for practicing skills that you are learning (see Section 11.5 and Chapter 17).

5. Brief periods of thirty minutes or less may be used to do some of the work for a project, such as deciding what will be the major points in a two-page paper for an English course.

Also, it is a good plan to schedule study sessions so that they are followed by something that is enjoyable to do (see Section 8.9).

The concept of scheduling time is annoying to some students; they believe that planning how they will use their time will take all the fun and spontaneity out of their lives. But this is not true. Good use of time is what makes it possible to achieve worthwhile goals and to live a full and productive life. If you analyze the ways that you use your unplanned time, you are likely to discover that much of it is spent in very uninteresting and unproductive ways. If you plan to use your time in the ways that you want to use it, you will gain greater control over your life and you will increase your well-being.

Use What You've Learned

1. Use the procedure that is described in Section 7.2 to determine how many hours you have available each week for studying. If the number is less than the number of hours you need to earn the grades you want, figure out how you can make more time available for studying.

2. Use the four questions that are listed in Section 7.3 to observe what conditions help you to study best. After making these observations for one week, explain under what conditions you should study for your most challenging courses.

3. For two weeks, keep a diary of exactly what you do with your unplanned time. How much of the time was spent in uninteresting or unproductive ways?

4. The author states that "good use of time is what makes it possible to achieve worthwhile goals and to live a full and productive life." Explain why you agree or disagree with this statement.

5. Why have you decided that you will *or* will not make a schedule for the times that you will study for each of your courses?

Increase
Your Concentration

To make the best use of your study time, you must be able to concentrate on studying during almost all the time that you set aside for this purpose. Yet, chances are that you are unable to concentrate for long periods of time.

The inability to concentrate for extended periods is the most common study problem that plagues students. A surprisingly large proportion of students report that their minds begin to wander after as few as five minutes of reading; students very commonly complain that their minds drift off after only ten or fifteen minutes of studying.

No matter how poorly or how well you are able to concentrate, this chapter explains methods that you may use to increase your span of concentration.

8.1 Keep records of how long you concentrate

When you sit down to read or study, write the time you start on a piece of paper. Then, if your mind starts to wander, make a record of the time that this happens. For example, if you finish reading a page in a health education or English textbook and realize that you do not understand anything that you read on the page, this is an indication that you have lost your concentration. Keep records of how long you are able to concentrate on studying before your mind starts drifting off to other thoughts.

When you lose your concentration, spend a few minutes doing something else. If it was a daydream that interrupted you, enjoy your daydream. You might walk around the room, look out the window, or drink some water. When you are ready to study again, make a record of the time you start, and use some of the suggestions that are given in this chapter to try to concentrate longer. If you use this procedure, you are likely to notice that your span of concentration will double, or even triple, in a very few days.

8.2   Decide that you will study

If your mind drifts off while you are studying, you are no longer studying. You may be thinking of something that happened earlier in the day, something that is worrying you, or something that you would rather be doing; but you are not studying. This is a waste of your study time.

Don't waste your study time. Make the conscious decision to use your study time to study rather than to do something else. Decide that you are going to spend the time learning the things that you want to learn rather than to spend it daydreaming, listening to music, watching television, or talking with a friend. Unless you make this choice, you will resent the time you spend studying, and you will probably feel that studying is a punishment. If you feel that you are being punished when you study, your thoughts will be on your suffering; when you think about your suffering, you cannot concentrate on reading or studying.

8.3   Set goals that you will achieve

Whenever you study, have a clear idea of exactly what you will try to accomplish. Look over your assignments, list the things that need to be done, and then do the things that need to be done most urgently. For example, one student started a study session by making this list of assignments that needed to be completed.

1. Rewrite paper for English.
2. Solve fifteen problems for math.

3. Read Chapter 9 in sociology text.
4. Prepare for quiz in chemistry.

As she studied the list she realized that the paper was due for English class the next morning and that the chemistry quiz was the following afternoon, but the sociology and math classes did not meet until later in the week. It was clear what she needed to do first.

Learn to estimate the amount of time you need to study various subjects so that you can set realistic goals for your study sessions. For example, you can estimate how much time you need to read each of your textbooks. When you read a textbook, write the time that you start reading in pencil at the place where you begin. After you have finished reading, write the time in pencil at the place where you stop. Count the pages you read, and estimate how long it took you to read them. If you do this a few times with each of your books, you will soon be able to estimate how much time you need to read ten, twenty, thirty, or forty pages in each of them. If you discover that you read and underline your psychology textbook at the rate of ten pages an hour, you know it is realistic to set the goal of studying a fifteen-page chapter in an hour and a half.

You can also use this information to make the best use of your study time. If you find that you are studying your psychology textbook at the rate of seven pages an hour, you know that you are not making the best possible use of your study time. You may decide to speed up your studying to the rate that you know you are able to do, or you may decide to turn your attention to some other study task that you are more in the mood to do (also see Chapter 10).

8.4   Read and study actively

If you read and study to accomplish specific goals, your mind will be so busy achieving your objectives that it will be difficult for you to lose your concentration. Reading involves such activities as finding the overall organization of written material, locating the major points, and understanding the implications of writers' statements. Studying includes selecting what will be learned, underlining statements in books, and making notes on information that will be learned. When your mind is engaged in activities such as these, it simply cannot think about other things. Methods for reading and studying are explained in Chapter 11 through Chapter 17. If you read and study using the suggestions in those chapters, your mind will be so busy doing what it should be doing that it will be less likely to wander.

8.5   Do easy and routine tasks first

It helps to start study sessions by doing something that is routine, easy, or especially interesting. The young woman who needed to rewrite a paper for her English class and to prepare for a chemistry quiz decided that the easier and more enjoyable of these two tasks was the rewriting of the paper. She had already done most of the work on the paper; all she needed to do was proofread it, make a few minor changes, and copy it neatly. She did all this in about thirty minutes and the satisfaction of completing this task put her in the right frame of mind to study for her chemistry quiz.

Another way to become involved in a study session is to review things that have been studied previously. For example, before trying to learn how to solve a new kind of problem for a mathematics course, it is helpful to spend a few minutes solving the types of problems that you already know how to solve. This provides for the review practice that you need and it is also likely to warm you up for learning how to solve the new type of problem. The same is true when studying a foreign language. A study session might begin by reviewing vocabulary that you have learned previously; this review is necessary and it will ease you into studying new material.

8.6   Do large tasks one small task at a time

Sometimes it is difficult to concentrate on studying because the task that needs to be accomplished is so large that it seems overwhelming. For example, if you have a thick textbook for a difficult course, you may be stymied by the thought of learning everything in the book by the end of the term. Or, if you have a twenty-five-page research paper to write, you may wonder if you'll ever be able to complete the project. Thoughts such as these interfere with concentration.

If these types of thoughts interfere with your ability to concentrate, keep in mind that large tasks are completed by doing many small tasks, one at a time. The information in a textbook is learned one chapter at a time, and the information in each chapter is learned one step at a time (see Chapter 11 through Chapter 17). Also, a twenty-five-page research paper is written one step at a time using a schedule of the type that is described in Section 24.2.

You cannot learn all the information in a textbook at once or write a twenty-five-page research paper in two days. These, and all other large projects, are completed by accomplishing a series of manageable tasks that result in achieving the final goal. The remaining chapters in this handbook explain what those manageable tasks are and how they are done.

8.7   Accept that you must do unpleasant tasks

Some students find it difficult to concentrate while studying subjects or completing assignments that they do not enjoy or that they find difficult. When you put off studying a subject because you do not like it, you are not going to like the subject any more when you are hopelessly behind and overwhelmed by too much to learn in too little time. If you put off writing a term paper because you find writing difficult, it will not be easier for you to write the paper when you start it three days before it is due.

It is not easy to develop the desire to work enthusiastically at unpleasant tasks—it requires you to accept that to achieve your worthwhile goals you may need to do some things that are distasteful or difficult. If you want to hold a well-paying and responsible job, enjoy a satisfying married life, or achieve any other worthwhile goal you may need to do many things that you would not choose to do *except* that you have these goals that you want very much to achieve. Similarly, if your goal is to earn a college degree, you must accept that to have the benefits of a college education you may have to do things that you would prefer not to do *except* that this goal is very important to you.

Analyze what things you must do this term that you find unpleasant or difficult. Then, decide if you want a college education enough so that you will do those things even though you prefer not to do them. If you do, start work on those unpleasant and difficult tasks today knowing that each task you complete is moving you closer to an important goal that you have set for yourself.

8.8   Reduce your anxiety

Anxiety is a feeling of uneasiness or uncertainty that is often induced by worry about what will happen in the future. When anxiety interferes with students' ability to concentrate while studying, it is often worry about whether they will be able to learn the things that they need to learn or whether they will earn good grades.

Will I learn what I need to learn?   One way to avoid this source of anxiety is to keep up to date with course work (see Section 4.6). When students fall behind in studying for a course, they often find that when they finally get around to studying they are unable to study efficiently because they are worrying whether they will be able to learn the things that they need to learn in the little time that they have to learn them. This worry interferes with their ability to concentrate on doing the reading and studying that needs to be done.

Other students worry whether they will be able to learn particular subject matter because they feel that they are incapable of learning it. If this causes you to worry, ask yourself this question: "Why do I feel that I cannot learn this subject when I know that people *just like me* learn it, and do well in it?" If you answer this question, you may discover that the only thing that is preventing you from learning the subject is your erroneous belief that you cannot learn it. Or, you may find that your difficulty is that you are not devoting as much time to the study of the subject as you need to. Ask yourself: "Could I learn this subject if I spent more time studying?" If the answer is yes, give the subject the additional time it requires (see Section 7.1) and use some of the methods that are described in Chapter 3 to help you learn the challenging subject matter. If you do these things, you are likely to have the satisfaction of learning something that you thought you could not learn. You may discover that you can do things that you thought you could not do. If you learn things that you thought you could not learn, your opinion of yourself will improve.

Will I earn excellent grades?   Another source of interfering anxiety for some students is the desperate need to do outstandingly well in every course. These are students who are likely to become angry, depressed, or even physically ill when they receive a B+ instead of an A. If you have this concern, you may be creating unnecessary unhappiness for yourself. Keep in mind that you do not need to be outstanding in every course you study in college. Earning an A in every course you take in college will not make you any more lovable than you are right now. Of course, if you are majoring in business and earn low grades in business courses you have a serious problem. But if you are majoring in business, you do not need to do outstandingly well in all the courses outside of your specialization to do well in college. Also, you do not need to be exceptional in all your courses to enjoy them. For example, you may have a singing voice that nobody would pay to hear and yet you may derive great pleasure when you sing to yourself in the shower; you may not be a very good tennis player and yet you may derive great enjoyment from the game. The same is true of the subjects that you study in college. Allow yourself to enjoy all the subjects that you study, even the ones in which you do not excel. Section 18.1 gives additional suggestions for coping with anxiety.

8.9   Reward yourself for studying

My favorite method for increasing concentration is to know that study sessions will be followed by something pleasant to do. For example, you may find that it is much more pleasant to spend Saturday afternoon studying if you know that in the evening you will go to a party or to a movie. Plan the activities of your life so that work is followed by something that you enjoy doing. If you want to talk with a friend on the telephone, decide that you will study for an hour and then call your friend. If a copy of your favorite magazine arrives in the mail, decide that you will study for two hours and then read the magazine.

The hours that you spend studying are also likely to be more productive when you plan to include plenty of good times in your life. If you know that you only have three hours to study one day because you've scheduled some fun for yourself, you may be inspired to make the very best use of the three hours that you have set aside for studying.

Use What You've Learned

1. Use the procedure that is described in Section 8.1 to determine how long you are usually able to concentrate on reading and studying before your mind drifts off to other thoughts.

2. Use the suggestions in this chapter to help you increase the length of time that you are able to concentrate. After your span of concentration has doubled, determine which of the methods described in the chapter were most helpful to you.

3. What are the most distasteful or difficult tasks that you must do this term? Is your desire to have a college education strong enough for you to complete those tasks as best you can even though you prefer not to do them?

4. What is your opinion of the value of the suggestions that are given in this chapter?

5. If friends of yours tell you that they have difficulty concentrating when they study, what suggestions would you give them to help them improve their ability to concentrate?

Improve
Your Vocabulary

There are more than 500,000 words in the English language, but it is estimated that well-educated Americans make practical use of less than six percent of them. When you study for your college courses, you must expect that any of the thousands of words that you have never seen or heard before may be used in the books you read or the lectures you hear. You will need to learn the meanings of many words in college and you will need strategies that you can use to determine the meanings of unfamiliar words.

This chapter explains how to add new words to your vocabulary and how to find the meanings of words

1. by studying the passages in which unfamiliar words appear.
2. by analyzing words into prefixes, base words, and other elements.
3. by consulting glossaries, indexes, and dictionaries.

Use the suggestions in this chapter to start enlarging your vocabulary today.

9.1 Systematically learn new words

There are paperback vocabulary books that list words of the type that are in the vocabularies of well-educated people—words such as *quixotic, maudlin, mercurial, bucolic,* and *dour.* These books usually discuss the meanings of words and provide exercises for learning them. There may be value in purchasing and studying a book of this type, but a far more practical way for you to increase your vocabulary is to

1. learn the words that you *need* to learn for the courses you are taking.
2. learn the words that you encounter while reading that you *want* to include in your vocabulary.

This section explains methods for adding these types of words to your vocabulary.

Words you need to learn.   Each college subject has its own terminology. The **terminology,** or terms, for a subject are the words or phrases that are used with specific meanings when the subject is discussed. For example, *depression* is a term used with different meanings in the study of business, psychology, and meteorology. In business it refers to a period of low employment, wages, and prices. In psychology, *depression* refers to feelings of hopelessness and inadequacy, and in meteorology it refers to a condition that is associated with low barometric pressure. Sometimes terms are phrases of two or more words. For example, the phrase *fruits of a crime* is a term used in criminology to refer to anything that comes into a criminal's possession as the result of a crime.

Very often more than half of the questions on college tests are about the meanings of terminology, or they cannot be answered correctly without knowing the meanings of terminology. Fortunately, when you learn the terms you need to learn for college courses, you will also usually add words to your vocabulary that are of the type found in the vocabularies of well-educated people. After all, most well-educated people studied subjects of the types that you are studying and will study during the course of your college career.

Figure 9a lists examples of words that students learn when they study psychology, history, and ecology. Similar lists may be made for all other college subjects. The words in Figure 9a are the types of words that well-educated people use in conversation or that they know when they read or hear them. Study

Figure 9a **Examples of Words Learned While Studying College Subjects.**

Psychology	History	Ecology
affiliation	abdicate	aesthetics
altruism	abstract	aggression
ambivalence	autonomy	archaeology
catharsis	alliance	celibacy
cognition	aristocracy	coefficient
concurrent	bureaucracy	condensation
contingency	concessions	consequences
correlation	conservatism	decompose
covert	consolidation	demographic
criterion	culmination	diversity
denotative	defeatism	ecosystem
divergent	evacuation	exploitation
eclecticism	exploitation	exponential
empathy	ideologies	habitat
equilibrium	illegitimacy	hierarchical
fallacy	kinship	implementation
fraternal	parliamentary	inequities
gestalt	provisional	innovation
humanistic	reconciliation	interdependencies
induced	repatriation	opportunistic
inhibition	repressive	quantitative
integrity	restoration	regeneration
introspection	revisionism	simulation
latency	skepticism	sludge
lethargy	solidarity	socioeconomic
maturation	sovereignty	stabilization
paradoxical	stalemate	sterile
perception	suffrage	stratification
placebo	tariffs	subsidiary
prognosis	totalitarian	succession
somatic	unification	suppression
stereotypes	utopian	triage

Figure 9b **Notes for Learning a Word That Needs to Be Learned for a College Course.**

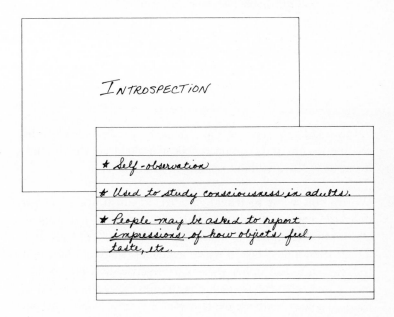

the words in Figure 9a to understand the types of words you will be adding to your vocabulary as a result of studying college subjects. You may already know some meanings for many of the words in the lists, but it is not likely that you can give accurate definitions for most of the words in the senses that they are used in psychology, history, and ecology.

Make notes to learn the meanings of words and terms for your college courses. Figure 9b is the notes a student made so she could learn the meaning of *introspection,* which is explained in the following passage from a psychology textbook.

Introspection

The structuralists studied the states of consciousness as experienced by normal adults using the method of *introspection*—literally, "self-observation." Individuals reported their

conscious experiences to the researcher. For example, subjects would be given a stimulus object, such as a substance to
place on the tip of the tongue or a piece of sculpture to touch,
and would be asked to relate their impressions. The
researcher wanted a description not of an object but rather
of all a person's impressions about an object as they were
passing through the individual's consciousness. The emphasis would be on such qualities as pressure, warmth or cold-
ness, or tactile sensations.

Information in notes of the type in Figure 9b is learned by
reciting it—the information is repeated aloud or silently until
it can be recalled without reading it (Chapter 17).

Words you want to learn.   Figure 9c illustrates a method
that you may use to keep records of words that you want to
learn, but do not need to learn to do well on college tests. It is
a page from a notebook in which a student recorded words that
she wanted to add to her vocabulary. Notice that she included
tactile in her notebook; *tactile* is the next-to-the-last word in
the psychology textbook explanation of *introspection*. She put
this word in her vocabulary notebook because she wanted to
learn its meaning but she believed she would not be tested on
the meaning of the word by her psychology instructor.

Also notice in Figure 9c that there are two checks in front of
the word *succinct* and one check in front of the word *tertiary*.
The two checks in front of *succinct* indicate that the student
encountered this word twice in her reading after she entered it
in her notebook, and the single check in front of *tertiary* indicates the word was encountered once again after it was recorded
in the notebook. When the student puts a second check in front
of a word in her notebook, she makes a card of the type in Figure 9b and learns the meaning of the word in the same way she
learns the meanings of words she needs to learn for her courses
(Chapter 17).

Use the methods that are described in this section to system-
atically add new words to your vocabulary.

**Figure 9c Part of a Page in a Notebook in
Which a Student Lists Words That She Wants
to Add to Her Vocabulary.**

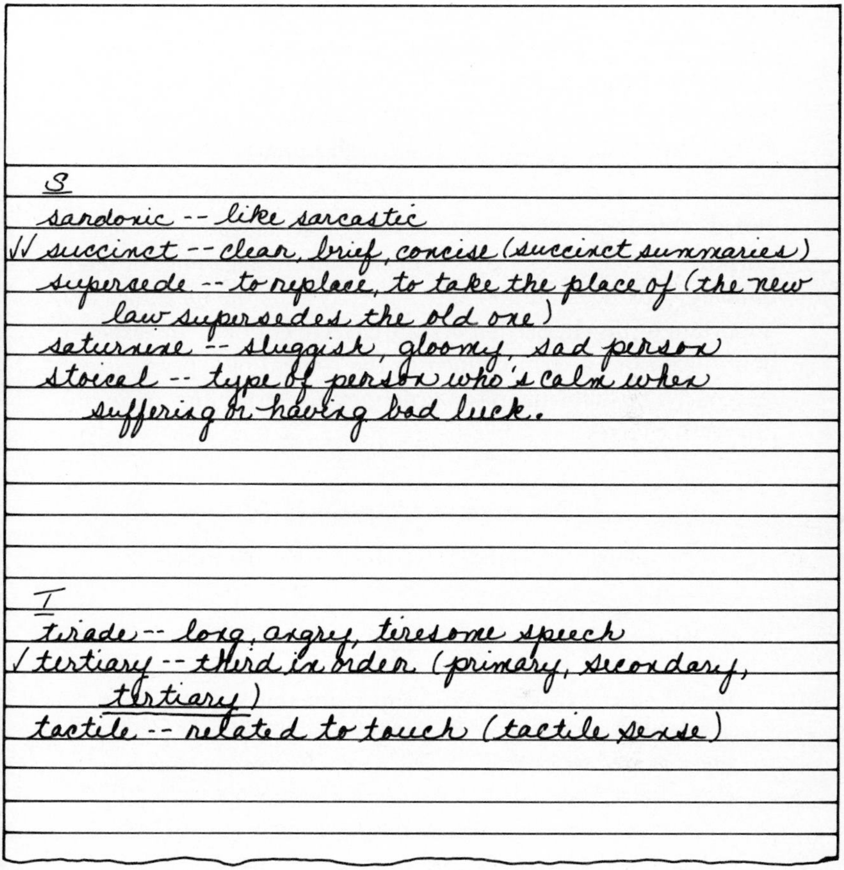

S

sardonic -- like sarcastic

√ succinct -- clear, brief, concise (succinct summaries)

supersede -- to replace, to take the place of (the new
law supersedes the old one)

saturnine -- sluggish, gloomy, sad person)

stoical -- type of person who's calm when
suffering or having bad luck.

T

tirade -- long, angry, tiresome speech

√ tertiary -- third in order (primary, secondary,
tertiary)

tactile -- related to touch (tactile sense)

9.2   Find word meanings in context

A **context** is a sentence, paragraph, or longer unit of writing that may reveal the meaning of an unfamiliar word. The meanings of words are sometimes directly stated in contexts, and at other times it is possible to infer the meanings of unfamiliar words by examining the contexts in which they appear. When you use contexts to determine word meanings, you do not need to interrupt your reading to consult a dictionary.

Word meanings stated in context.   Since one of the primary purposes of college textbooks is to explain the meanings of terminology, textbook authors often directly state the meanings of important terms. In Section 9.1 the excerpt entitled "Introspection" illustrates a term defined in the context of a psychology textbook. The following passage defines two terms that are used in speech courses.

Narration and Exposition

The content of speeches is often either narration or exposition.

Narration is simply the telling of a story—the giving of an account of what happened. When you tell the story of a movie you saw, describe what happened to you during a day at school or on a date, or give an account of events in your life, you are using narration. We never outgrow our appreciation for a good story, so the speaker who develops the ability to recount events in an interesting way has a powerful tool for captivating audiences.

Exposition differs from narration in that its primary intention is to provide an explanation. When you explain to somebody how to get from one place to another, tell people why you did something, or pass on knowledge of how to do something, you are using exposition. In exposition we make things we know plain or understandable to others who do not know or understand them. In speech making a great deal of exposition would probably be used in speeches about safe

driving, good places to hike, interesting things to do for free,
or ways to behave when being interviewed for a job.

This passage defines *narration* and *exposition* and explains the
differences between them.

Writers of the exposition in newspapers, magazines, and college textbooks frequently define the meanings of words that are
important to know to fully understand the topics that they
explain. Sometimes the definitions are long and complete—even
longer than those illustrated for *introspection, narration,* and
exposition. In other instances, though, the definitions are brief
and set off in a sentence by the use of parentheses, a dash, commas, or some other punctuation. In the following sentence, the
meaning of *abiotic* is set off by parentheses.

Let us consider the vital role that is played by the *abiotic*
(nonliving) elements in nature.

A dash is used to set off the meaning of *entrepreneur* at the end
of the following sentence:

Most of the people who have become millionaires in the
past few years are *entrepreneurs*—at their own risk, they
organized and managed businesses.

The meaning of *agape* is set off using commas in the following
sentence:

Agape, or unselfish love for another, is the ideal of the
Christian tradition.

When a sentence contains a word that is unfamiliar to you,
examine it to see if it also contains parentheses, a dash, commas,
or some other type of punctuation. If it does, the punctuation
may be there to set off the meaning of the unfamiliar word.

Word meanings inferred from context.   If the meaning of
an unfamiliar word is not directly stated in a passage, it may
be possible to infer its meaning. When you **infer** the meaning
of a word from its context, you use statements surrounding the

word to form an opinion about its meaning. For example, if you do not know the meaning of *incarcerated,* you should be able to infer its meaning from the following sentence:

> Those who are found guilty of murder are usually *incarcerated* for longer periods of time than those who are found guilty of robbery.

You know that the usual fate of those who are found guilty of murder or robbery is to be imprisoned or jailed. You also know that murderers are usually confined for longer periods of time than robbers. Thus, you are likely to infer correctly that those who are *incarcerated* are locked up in a jail, prison, or penitentiary.

Similarly, if you do not know the meaning of *interred* you should be able to infer its meaning from the following sentence:

> The remains of the dead are usually either cremated or *interred.*

You know that when people in our society die, their remains are usually either burned (cremated) or buried in the earth. Thus, you are likely to infer correctly that *interred* means "buried in the earth."

Sometimes the meaning of a word may be inferred from an example or a series of examples in a context. Examples in the following sentence may be used to infer the meaning of *folkways.*

> Some of the *folkways* in our society are to eat three meals a day, to wear shoes that match, and to keep our bodies free of odors that may be offensive to others.

Folkways is a term used by sociologists. The examples in the sentence, such as "eat three meals a day," make it possible to infer correctly that *folkways* refers to the behaviors that are common to members of a social group.

In many instances the information that can be used to infer the meaning of an unfamiliar word appears in a sentence or sentences that comes before or after the sentence that contains the word. If you are uncertain of the meaning of *precise discriminations* in the first sentence of the following passage, you may infer the meaning of this phrase from the information in the other sentences of the paragraph.

A Sex Difference

Women supposedly make more precise discriminations in naming colors than men do. For example, show someone a drapery or rug that is a brilliant bluish-red. If the speaker is a woman, she might say, "That's fuchsia." A man might say, shrugging, "It's red," or even, "It's purple." In the wall-paint section of a large department store one day, two women and a man were examining paint chips. The man with them drummed his fingers restlessly on the counter as the first woman, pairing various color chips with a scrap of carpet material, asked, "Is that ecru?" "No, I'd say it's beige," the second woman offered. The man responded with amusement, "Sure coulda' fooled me. It looks like dirty white," then added with a chuckle, "or tattle-tale gray!"

The meaning of the phrase *precise discriminations* may be inferred from the information that women are likely to name a color using a specific descriptive word such as *fuchsia* rather than some general word such as *red,* that a man might use. Women may also discuss differences between ecru and beige—differences that a man may not observe. It may be inferred from these explanations that to make *precise discriminations* is to state definite and distinct differences—in this instance, when naming colors.

The last sentence in the following passage includes the word *overzealous.* If you are uncertain of the meaning of this word, you are likely to infer its meaning if you read and understand the other statements in the passage.

Puritans and Sex

Contrary to popular belief, the Puritans did not regard sex as evil, but as a glorious necessity decreed by the Lord. And for this reason they preferred to keep sex within marriage. They viewed marriage as an institution sanctified by God. Sex was, so to speak, a way to glorify God when it was practiced within the proper setting of marriage. A number of devoted Puritans were thus understandably moved to give advice on sexual relationships between husband and wife, a move that occasionally backfired. Operating on the premise that sexual relationships on Sunday took away from one's concern for the primary relationship with God, and also under the erroneous medical assumption that children were born on the same day of the week that they were conceived, one overzealous minister firmly and repeatedly made it clear—no sex on Sunday—until that bright Sunday morning when his wife presented him with twins.

What is an *overzealous* minister? He is the type of person who is devoted firmly and repeatedly to making it clear to husbands and wives that they should have no sex on Sunday. Those who devotedly, firmly, and repeatedly state their beliefs are intense and enthusiastic about their beliefs. To be overzealous is to be extremely intense and enthusiastic about a belief or cause.

When you encounter an unfamiliar word, study the context to determine if its meaning is directly stated or if its meaning can be inferred.

9.3   Analyze derivatives

Thousands of English words belong to a class of words called derivatives. For our purposes, **derivatives** are words that contain a base word and at least one prefix or one suffix. For example, *disappear, appearance,* and *disappearance* are all derivatives with the base word *appear; disappear* contains the prefix *dis-,* but no suffix; *appearance* contains the suffix *-ance,* but no prefix; and *disappearance* contains both a prefix and a suffix.

When you are unable to determine the meanings of words by studying contexts, you may be able to determine their meanings by analyzing their parts. Sociologists are currently using the word *deinstitutionalization,* which is a derivative comprised of the prefix *de-,* the base word *institute,* and the suffix combination *-ionalization. Deinstitutionalization* is the policy of removing people from institutions and placing them in communities; for example, many people who used to live in mental hospitals now live in communities—they have been *deinstitutionalized.*

There are thousands of derivatives in the English language, and it should usually be possible for you to determine the meaning of a derivative when it contains a base word whose meaning you know.

Base words.   The following thirty-six derivatives all contain the base word *adapt.* If you know the meaning of *adapt,* you know something about the meanings of all the words in the list.

*adapt*edness	*adapt*able	*adapt*ability
*adapt*ableness	*adapt*ation	*adapt*ational
*adapt*ationally	*adapt*er	*adapt*ive
*adapt*ively	*adapt*iveness	mal*adapt*ation
mal*adapt*ed	mal*adapt*ive	mis*adapt*ation
non*adapt*ability	non*adapt*able	non*adapt*ing
non*adapt*ation	non*adapt*ational	non*adapt*ive
non*adapt*er	pre*adapt*	pre*adapt*able
pre*adapt*ation	re*adapt*	re*adapt*ability
re*adapt*able	re*adapt*ation	re*adapt*ive
re*adapt*iveness	un*adapt*able	un*adapt*ableness
un*adapt*ive	un*adapt*ively	un*adapt*iveness

Base words are English words that carry the main meanings of derivatives. *Adapt,* which means "to make suitable" or "to adjust," is the main meaning of all thirty-six words in the list. It is not uncommon for an English word to be the base word in ten, fifteen, twenty, or more derivatives. When you know the meaning of a base word, you often know the main meaning of a dozen or more other words.

When you analyze derivatives to find base words, keep in

mind that base words sometimes undergo changes in their spellings when suffixes are added to them. The two most common spelling changes are the dropping of a final *e* and the changing of a final *y* to *i*. For example, the base words in *disputable* and *maturity* are *dispute* and *mature,* and the base words in *certification* and *harmonious* are *certify* and *harmony.*

Also, since base words carry the main meanings in derivatives, base words have meanings that are directly related to the meanings of their derivatives. For example, the base word in *unimprovable* is *improve,* not *prove.* The meaning of *improve,* "to make better," is directly related to the meaning of *unimprovable*—"cannot be made better." But the meaning of *prove,* "to show to be true," is not directly related to the meaning of *unimprovable.*

Also, of course, you need to know a word to identify it as a base word in a derivative. You would have difficulty finding the base words in *incestuousness, hierarchical,* or *prenuptial* unless you know the words *incest, hierarchy,* and *nuptial.*

Prefixes.   Figure 9d lists the twenty-three prefixes that frequently appear in derivatives. **Prefixes** are word parts that appear in front of base words in derivatives and that usually provide important information about the meanings of derivatives. For example, you must know the meaning of *mal-* as well as the meaning of *adapt* in order to determine the meaning of *maladapted. Mal-* means "bad" or "badly."

> Because he dislikes loud music, John is *maladapted* for his job as a waiter in a discothèque.

The meaning of *mal-* and *adapt* may be used to determine that John is "badly suited"—maladapted—for working in a discothèque.

If you are uncertain of the meanings of any of the prefixes that are listed in Figure 9d, learn their meanings. The prefixes in the list have reliable meanings that you can use to determine the meanings of thousands of derivatives.

Figure 9d **The Meanings of Common Prefixes.**

Prefix	Meaning	Example
anti-	against	*Anti*labor organizations are *against* labor.
de-	remove	To *de*frost is to *remove* frost.
dis-	opposite of	To *dis*please is to do the *opposite of* please.
ex-	former	An *ex*-teacher is a *former* teacher.
extra-	beyond	*Extra*sensory perception is perception that is *beyond* what is experienced by the senses.
hyper-	overly	*Hyper*active children are *overly* active.
il-	not	That which is *il*logical is *not* logical.
im-	not	That which is *im*perfect is *not* perfect.
in-	not	An *in*direct route is *not* a direct route.
inter-	between	*Inter*state buses travel *between* states.
intra-	within	*Intra*state buses travel only *within* a state.
ir-	not	*Ir*responsible people are *not* responsible.
mal-	bad(ly)	A *mal*functioning car functions *badly*.
mis-	wrong(ly)	To *mis*spell is to spell *wrongly*.
non-	not	*Non*alcoholic beverages do *not* contain alcohol.
post-	after	*Post*war events occur *after* a war.
pre-	before	*Pre*war events occur *before* a war.
pro-	for	*Pro*labor organizations are *for* labor.
pseudo-	false(ly)	A *pseudo*science is a *false* science.
re-	again	To *re*heat food is to heat it *again*.
semi-	partly	*Semi*nude people are *partly* nude.
trans-	across	*Trans*continental trains travel *across* a continent.
un-	not	Those who are *un*happy are *not* happy.

Suffixes.   There are approximately one hundred different suffixes found in derivatives. **Suffixes** are word parts that appear at the ends of derivatives and that usually identify a word's part of speech without giving important information about its meaning. For example, the suffix *-able* indicates that *adaptable* is an adjective and the suffix *-ation* indicates that *adaptation* is a noun, but these suffixes do not convey important information about the meanings of *adaptable* or *adaptation*.

She can *adapt* to difficult situations.

She is *adaptable* to difficult situations.

She can make *adaptations* to difficult situations.

The three sentences contain different words, but they all convey nearly the same meaning.

While it is important to know the meanings of all the prefixes in Figure 9d, it is not important to learn the meanings of the approximately one hundred suffixes that are found in derivatives. There are only three suffixes that are reliable indicators of the meanings of derivatives:

1. *-er,* which indicates "a person," in such words as *builder*
2. *-ist,* which indicates "a person," in such words as *organist*
3. *-less,* which indicates "without," in such words as *armless*

The suffixes *-er, -ist,* and *-less* all have other meanings, but they do not have as many different meanings as the other suffixes. For example, the suffix *-ful,* which indicates "full" in such words as *armful,* has forty other meanings as well; the suffix *-ant,* which indicates "a person" in such words as *accountant,* has fifty-nine additional meanings.*

Therefore, rather than learn dozens of meanings for each suffix, use base words and context to determine the meanings of derivatives that contain suffixes. For example,

The baby's *adaptability* to strangers is very good.

*Edward L. Thorndike, *The Teaching of English Suffixes* (New York: Teachers College Press, 1941), pp. 1–15 and 25.

The base word *adapt* and the context of the sentence may be used to understand that the baby has a remarkably good capacity to adapt to strangers. It is not necessary to know the meaning of *-ability* in *adaptability* to understand the meaning of the sentence.

9.4   Learn Latin and Greek word parts

There are several hundred Latin and Greek word parts that appear in English words. They range from the familiar *tri-,* which indicates "three" in such words as *triangle, triple,* and *tricycle,* to elements such as *-phagous,* which indicates "eats" in scientific words such as *anthropophagous* and *zoophagous.*

Most standard desk dictionaries define about five hundred Latin and Greek word parts. The elements defined in dictionaries are the ones that have stable spellings and meanings when they appear in English words. For example, the Latin element *-cide* is defined in most standard desk dictionaries.

> **–cide.** Indicates: **1.** Killer of; for example, **regicide, insecticide.**
> **2.** Murder or killing of; for example, **genocide.**   [French, from
> Latin *-cida,* killer, and *-cidium,* killing, from *caedere,* to kill. See
> **skhai-** in Appendix.*]

Cide- indicates "killer" or "killing" in such words as *infanticide, homicide, suicide, fratricide, patricide,* and *matricide.*

However, there are many Latin and Greek elements that are not defined in desk dictionaries. For example, the Latin element *facere,* which indicates "to make," is not an entry in desk dictionaries. *Facere* is an example of the ancient word parts that do not have stable spellings or meanings when they appear in English words; it is the historical source of words such as *affection, sufficient, identify, faculty, classify, terrific, satisfaction, defective,* and *profitable.*

Some vocabulary experts advise students to learn the meaning of *facere* and other Latin elements that are unstable in their spellings and meanings when they appear in English words.

However, it is far more profitable to learn the meanings of elements that are defined in desk dictionaries (such as *tri-* and *-cide*) than it is to learn the meanings of elements that writers of dictionaries do not define (such as *facere*).*

People who have large vocabularies tend to know the meanings of many Latin and Greek word parts such as those listed in Figure 9e. However, the elements in Figure 9e are usually not learned by memorization, but through a process of association. For example, if you study psychology you may learn about *hypnomania* and *heliomania*. In learning the meanings of these words you will discover that *-mania* at the ends of words indicates "an abnormal craving or attraction." You will also learn that *hypnomania* is the abnormal craving for sleep and that *heliomania* is the abnormal craving to be in the sun. In learning this you will also learn that *hypno-* at the beginnings of words indicates "sleep," as in *hypnosis,* and that *helio-* at the beginnings of words indicates "sun," as in *heliotaxis,* which is a word you will encounter if you study biology. *Heliotaxis* refers to the movement of plants in response to the sun.

Just as base words carry the main meanings in derivatives (Section 9.3), Latin and Greek word parts often carry the main meaning in scientific and technical words. For example, if you study biology, you will encounter words that end with the Greek element *-cyte,* which indicates "cell." "Cell" is the main meaning of words such as *astrocyte, leukocyte,* and *phagocyte.* The other elements in these words give additional information about their meanings. *Astro-* indicates "star," and an *astrocyte* is a star-shaped cell; *leuko-* indicates "white or colorless," and a *leukocyte* is a colorless cell; and *phago-* indicates "eating or destroying," and a *phagocyte* is a cell that eats or destroys other cells.

Knowledge of Latin and Greek elements may help you determine and learn the meanings of many of the complicated-looking words that are used in textbooks for scientific and technical

---

*James F. Shepherd, "The Relations Between Knowledge of Word Parts and Knowledge of Derivatives among College Freshmen" (Unpublished Ph.D. dissertation, New York University, 1973).

Figure 9e **Some Latin and Greek Word Parts.**

Word element	Meaning	Example
anthropo-	human	anthropomorphism
archaeo-	ancient times	archaeology
astro-, astr-	star, outer space	astronaut
audio-	hearing, sound	audiology
biblio-	book	bibliography
bio-	life	biocide
chrono-, chron-	time	chronic
-cracy	rule, government	mobocracy
geo-	earth	geology
-graph	write, written	monograph
gyno-, gyn-	women	gynecology
hetero-	different	heterochromatic
homo-	same	homocentric
hydro-, hydr-	water	hydroelectric
-logy	study, science	graphology
macro-, macr-	large	macroclimate
-mania	abnormal craving	zoomania
micro-	small	microhabitat
mono-	one	monotone
neo-	new	neoclassicism
octo-, oct-	eight	octagon
-phile	preference for	bibliophile
-phobia	abnormal fear	hydrophobia
poly-	many	polyglot
psycho-	mind	psychometric
pyro-	fire	pyrometer
sept-	seven	septet
sex-	six	sexagenarians
somato-	body	somatology
syn-	together, with	synchronic
theo-	God, gods	theologian

Figure 9f **Notes for Learning a Word That Needs to Be Learned for a Chemistry Course.**

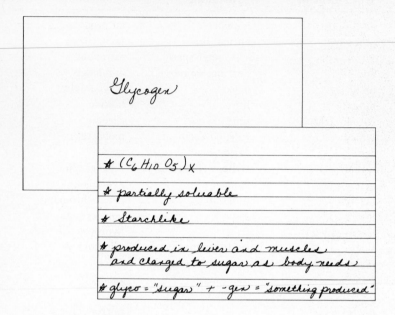

subjects. When you encounter two or three scientific words that begin or end with the same spelling, consult a standard desk dictionary (see Section 9.5) to determine if the spelling is a Latin or Greek element that is defined in the dictionary. You are likely to find information of the following type:

glyco–, glyc–. Indicates: **1.** Sugar; for example, **glycine. 2.** Glycogen; for example, **glycogenesis.** [From Greek *glukus,* sweet. See dḷku- in Appendix.*]

–gen, –gene. Indicates: **1.** That which produces; producing; for example, **oxygen. 2.** Something produced; for example, **antigen, phosgene.** [French *-gène,* from Greek *-genēs,* born. See gene- in Appendix.*]

Figure 9f illustrates notes that a student made to learn the meaning of *glycogen* for his chemistry course. Notice that the notes include meanings for the elements *glyco-* and *-gen.* When the student who made the notes in Figure 9f learned the meaning of *glycogen,* he also learned the meanings of the Greek elements *glyco-* and *-gen.* By learning the meanings of these word parts he was able to understand something of the meanings of other words in his chemistry textbook in which *glyco-* and *-gen* appear.

9.5   Consult glossaries, indexes, and dictionaries

Consult glossaries, indexes, or dictionaries to find the meanings of words that you cannot determine by studying context or word structure. When you want information about the meanings of terms that are used in your textbooks, glossaries and indexes are often more helpful than standard desk dictionaries.

Glossaries.   Many textbooks have a **glossary,** which is an alphabetical list of specialized words and their definitions. They are usually located in the backs of books, but sometimes there is a short glossary at the end of each chapter in a book. There is a glossary at the back of this handbook.

Glossaries often include definitions that are not found in standard desk dictionaries. The following excerpt from the glossary of a criminology textbook defines six terms, but of the six terms, only *polygraph* is defined in standard desk dictionaries.

> **Police agency.** A primary law enforcement agency; an agency of government whose main responsibility is to enforce criminal laws, investigate crimes, and apprehend criminals.
>
> **Polygraph.** A device used to record changes in a person's physiological state (blood pressure, respiration, etc.) during interrogation or interview to indicate when the subject is lying; often called a *lie detector.*
>
> **Prejudicial evidence.** Evidence or testimony that, although true, has the effect of unfairly or excessively influencing the emotions of the jury, usually against the defendant. Such evidence also may be called *inflammatory,* and it may be inadmissible.
>
> **Preliminary investigation.** The initial investigation of a crime, usually at the crime scene, involving collection of evidence and interviewing of the victim and/or witnesses.

Presumption of innocence. The legal principle that a person who has been accused of a crime must not be considered or treated as if the person were guilty until guilt has been determined in a proper trial. See also *preventive detention.*

Preventive detention. The use of the power of arrest to hold a suspected criminal in jail in order to prevent the person from committing additional crimes. This practice has been held to conflict with the constitutional doctrine of the *presumption of innocence* (see this term also).

Students who want to know the meanings of the terms other than *polygraph* that are defined in this glossary will *not* find them by consulting a standard desk dictionary.

Indexes.   An **index** is an alphabetical listing that states the pages on which subjects are discussed in a book. It is usually printed on the very last pages of a book, as is the index for this handbook. Indexes are invaluable reference sources for finding complete information about the meanings of words.

Definitions found by using the indexes of books are usually much more complete than definitions in glossaries. The glossary definition for *polygraph* appears in a criminology textbook, which has an index that informs readers that information about polygraphs and other lie detectors is on pages 421–423 of the book. The passage describes the voice stress analyzer as well as the polygraph and includes information about the proper and improper use of these devices.

Use the indexes of your books whenever you want to read full explanations of important terms that are explained in them.

Dictionaries.   Consult a dictionary when you are unable to find the meanings of words by referring to a glossary or index. You should own a paperback dictionary to carry with you and a desk dictionary to use at the place where you live or study.

Paperback dictionaries are handy to carry and contain the meanings, spellings, and pronunciations of most common words. But you also need a good desk dictionary because paperback dictionaries do not include all the information that college students need. Figure 9g shows excerpts from the desk edition and the paperback edition of *The American Heritage Dictionary*. Notice that the desk edition defines more words and gives more complete definitions than the paperback edition.

There are several excellent desk and paperback dictionaries available. I especially recommend *The American Heritage Dictionary of the English Language, Webster's New World Dictionary of the American Language,* and *Random House Dictionary of the English Language.* Compare these and other dictionaries and purchase the one you prefer.

A basic difficulty in using dictionaries is that since there is usually more than one meaning listed, it is often a problem to select the appropriate meaning. Desk dictionaries provide help in the form of **subject labels.** Observe in the following dictionary entry for *regression* that three of the five definitions begin with italicized words: *Psychoanalysis, Statistics,* and *Astronomy.* The italicized words are subject labels.

> **re·gres·sion** (rĭ-grĕsh'ən) *n.* **1.** Reversion; retrogression. **2.** Relapse to a less perfect or developed state. **3.** *Psychoanalysis.* Reversion to a more primitive or less mature behavior pattern. **4.** *Statistics.* The tendency for the expected value of one of two jointly correlated random variables to approach more closely the mean value of its set than the other. **5.** *Astronomy.* Retrogradation.

The subject labels inform readers that the third definition of *regression* applies to psychology, the fourth definition applies to statistics, and the fifth definition applies to astronomy. Subject labels are usually not included in paperback dictionaries; when desk dictionaries are condensed to paperback editions, subject labels and many definitions are usually left out. The following entry from a paperback dictionary includes no subject labels and it does not give the definitions for *regression* that students of statistics and astronomy need.

> **re·gres·sion** (rĭ-grĕsh'ən) *n.* **1.** Reversion; retrogression. **2.** Relapse to a less perfect or developed state.

Figure 9g **The Entries for *elm* Through *elongate*
in the Desk and Paperback Editions of
*The American Heritage Dictionary.***

Desk edition

elm (ĕlm) *n.* **1.** Any of various deciduous trees of the genus *Ulmus,* characteristically having arching or curving branches and widely planted as shade trees. **2.** The wood of any of these trees. [Middle English *elm,* Old English *elm.* See **el-²** in Appendix.*] —**elm′y** *adj.*

El Man·su·ra (ĕl măn-sŏŏr′ə). A city of southern Egypt; site of the defeat of Louis IX of France by the Mamelukes in 1250. Population, 147,000.

El·mi·ra (ĕl-mī′rə). A city of southwestern New York State; the site of Mark Twain's home and burial place. Population, 40,000.

El Mis·ti (ĕl mēs′tə). A volcano, 19,166 feet high, in southern Peru, northeast of Arequipa.

El Mor·ro National Monument (ĕl môr′ō). An area occupying 240 acres in western New Mexico, reserved to protect its cliff-dweller ruins and a sandstone rock bearing inscriptions by early Spanish and other later explorers.

El O·beid (ĕl ō-bād′). The capital of Kordofan Province, Republic of Sudan, and an important transportation and trade center. Population, 52,000.

el·o·cu·tion (ĕl′ə-kyōō′shən) *n.* **1.** The art of public speaking, emphasizing gesture and vocal production and delivery. **2.** The style or manner of public speaking. **3.** An artificial, forced manner of speaking. [Middle English *elocucion,* from Latin *ēlocūtiō,* from *ēloquī* (past participle *ēlocūtus*), to speak out : *ex-,* out + *loquī,* to; speak (see **tolkw-** in Appendix*).] —**el′o·cu′tion·ar′y** *adj.* —**el′o·cu′tion·ist** *n.*

E·lo·him (ĕ-lō′hĭm, ĕl′ō-hēm′). The Hebrew name for God most frequently encountered in the Old Testament. Compare **Yahweh.** [Hebrew *'Elōhīm,* plural of *'Elōah,* God, possibly enlarged from *'Ēl,* God.] —**E·lo′hism′** *n.*

E·lo·hist (ĕ-lō′hĭst) *n.* The author of the passages of the Hexateuch in which the name *Elohim* is used to designate God rather than the name *Yahweh.* —**El′o·his′tic** *adj.*

e·loign (ĭ-loin′) *tr.v.* **eloigned, eloigning, eloigns.** *Archaic.* To remove or carry away (property). [Middle English *eloynen,* from Old French *esloignier,* from Vulgar Latin *exlongāre* (unattested), variant of Late Latin *ēlongāre* : Latin *ex-,* away + *longē,* far away, distant, from *longus,* long (see **del-¹** in Appendix*).]

El·o·ise (ĕl′ō-wēz′, ĕl′ō-wēz′). A feminine given name. [French *Héloïse,* from Germanic. See **kailo-** in Appendix.*]

e·lon·gate (ĭ-lŏng′gāt′, ĭ-lŏng′-) *v.* **-gated, -gating, -gates.** —*tr.* To lengthen or extend. —*intr.* To grow in length. —*adj.* **1.** Lengthened; extended. **2.** Slender. [Late Latin *ēlongāre* : Latin *ex-,* out + *longus,* long (see **del-¹** in Appendix*).]

Paperback edition

elm (ĕlm) *n.* A shade tree with arching or curving branches. [< OE. See **el-².**]

el·o·cu·tion (ĕl′ə-kyōō′shən) *n.* The art of public speaking. [< L *ēloquī,* to speak out.] —**el′o·cu′tion·ist** *n.*

e·lon·gate (ĭ-lŏng′găt′, ĭ-lŏng′-) *v.* **-gated, -gating.** To lengthen; grow in length. —**e·lŏn′ga′tion** *n.*

Paperback and desk dictionaries usually have guides that explain how to use them. A guide is usually a chapter in the front of a dictionary with a title such as "Guide to the Dictionary." It is very much worthwhile for you to read the guides for your dictionaries; you will learn how to make the best use of your dictionaries, and you may discover that your dictionaries contain types of information that you do not know are in them.

Also, examine the tables of contents and all the pages at the beginnings and ends of your dictionaries. In these pages you may find a summary of symbols that are used in a subject that you are studying, an explanation of how to write more effectively, or some other information that may be valuable to you.

Use What You've Learned

1. Use the method that is explained in Section 9.1 to learn the words that you *need* to learn for the courses you are taking.

2. Use the method that is explained in Section 9.1 to learn the words that you *want* to add to your vocabulary, but do not need to learn for your courses.

3. Which of the textbooks that you are studying do *and* do not give long explanations of the meanings of terminology? List five terms that are explained in one of your textbooks in two or more paragraphs.

4. Which of the textbooks that you are studying use punctuation to set off the meanings of words in sentences? Give five examples of these types of definitions that you find in your books.

5. Give five examples of how you were able to infer the meanings of unfamiliar words by using the contexts in which you read the words.

6. Prepare a list of ten derivatives that you find in your reading that have meanings you were able to determine by using the methods described in Section 9.3.

7. If you are studying a scientific or technical subject, list six Greek or Latin elements, and their meanings, that you find in terminology used in the subject.

8. Which of your textbooks do and do not have glossaries?

9. Compare a definition for a term in a glossary of a textbook with an explanation of the same term that is found by consulting the index of the book. Which explanation is more informative?

10. If you do not own a desk dictionary of the type described in Section 9.5, purchase one.

Be a Flexible and Fluent Reader

Y ou will have a great deal of reading to do for your college courses; it will benefit you to be a flexible and fluent reader. Flexible readers read at the rates that are appropriate for the various types of materials they read; they read difficult materials slowly and easy materials quickly. Fluent readers usually read smoothly and easily with their eyes gliding across lines of print.

Most of what you read, study, and learn in college cannot be read at fast rates, but it can be read fluently and at appropriate rates. This chapter explains how to use easy reading materials to practice reading faster to become a more flexible and fluent reader. Additional skills that are associated with faster reading are explained in Chapter 12 and Chapter 13.

10.1 Flexible reading rates

Flexible readers use at least three different **reading rates:** slow, for very difficult material; moderate, for material of average difficulty; and fast, for easy material.

1. A *slow reading rate* is used to read carefully material that is very difficult to understand. Many college students use their slow reading rates when they read scientific materials.

2. A *moderate reading rate* is used to read carefully material that is of average difficulty. Many college students use their moderate reading rates when they read health education and English textbooks.

3. A *fast reading rate* is used to read easy novels, newspaper articles, magazine articles, and similar materials for pleasure. Many people use their fast reading rates when they read the sport sections or theater sections of newspapers.

Reading rates are measured by the number of words per minute that are read, and a range of words per minute is associated with each reading rate. For first-year college students, *slow reading rates* tend to range from 75 to 125 words per minute, *moderate reading rates* tend to range from 150 to 250 words per minute, and *fast reading rates* tend to range from 200 to 400 words per minute. On the average, first-year college students' reading rates are at about the midpoints of these ranges. For example, the average fast reading rate for first-year college students is about 300 words per minute, which is the midpoint between the low of 200 words per minute and the high of 400 words per minute.

In addition to slow, moderate, and fast reading rates, some skillful readers also have a *rapid reading rate* of more than 400 words per minute. One way to develop a rapid reading rate is to use the previewing and skimming skills that are explained in Chapter 12 and Chapter 13. A rapid reading rate is helpful for doing many study tasks. For example, when selecting books or articles to use in preparing papers or reports, it is a great time-saver to be able to read rapidly so that many books and articles may be examined quickly to select the ones that are most appropriate (see Section 27.4).

10.2   Deterrents to fluent reading

The most common deterrents to fluent reading are regressions, word-by-word reading, and lip movements.

Regressions.   With regard to reading, **regression** refers to the tendency for the eyes to look back at something that has already been read; this is the most common symptom of slow reading among first-year college students. The following sentence includes, in parentheses, the regressions that a student made while reading it.

> America seemed like a (like a) paradise to many Eastern Europeans (Europeans) who could (could) know little or nothing of what it was (it was) really like.

The student knew all the words in the sentence. The regressions were not caused because the words were unfamiliar to him but because of his habit of frequently going backward while reading instead of going constantly forward. As a result, whatever he reads is garbled.

By using special cameras and other equipment, researchers have found that first-year college students very commonly make more than ten regressions while reading only one hundred words. It is sometimes necessary to reread a word, sentence, or paragraph, but most regressions are symptomatic of a bad reading habit that may be broken by doing practice that is suggested later in this chapter.

Word-by-word reading.   The habit of focussing attention on one word at a time while reading is called word-by-word reading. This / sentence / is / divided / to / illustrate / the / technique / that / is / used / by / people / who / think / of / one / word / at / a / time / as / they / read. If you read in this way, you need to practice thinking in phrases as you read, just as you think in phrases when you speak. Rather than think / of sentences / as series of words, / think of them as / series of phrases, / such as / the phrases / in this sentence. Thinking in longer units will lead your mind forward to find writers' meanings more readily.

Lip movements.   If you almost always read very slowly, investigate whether you move your lips while you read. Hold your fingertips gently to your mouth as you read silently; if you detect movements of your lips, they may be preventing you from reading faster. The reason for this is that, if you move your lips while you read, you cannot read faster than you speak. The average rate of speech is less than 200 words per minute; few people can speak as rapidly as 250 words per minute.

One way to break the habit of moving your lips while reading is to hold a piece of gum or candy (preferably sugarless) toward the front of your mouth with your tongue while reading. An object held in the mouth in this way makes it more difficult to move the lips and it serves as a reminder to keep the lips still.

10.3   Practice for flexible and fluent reading

One way to improve reading fluency is to practice reading faster because this practice tends to reduce or eliminate regressions, word-by-word reading, and lip movements. It also increases flexibility because reading flexibility is measured by the difference between your fast reading rate and your slow reading rate—the greater the difference, the greater the flexibility. As your fast reading rate increases, your reading flexibility increases.

Materials for practice.   When you practice reading faster, use material (1) that contains very few words that are unfamiliar to you, (2) that is easy for you to understand, and (3) that is interesting to you. Paperback books and articles in newspapers and magazines are ideal materials for practicing reading at faster rates. Do not practice fast reading using difficult materials.

Procedures for practice.   Spend ten minutes each day reading easy and enjoyable materials as fast as you can, never stopping to let your eyes look back at words that you have already read. Read in phrases rather than word-by-word, and, if your lips move while you read, use the method that is described in Section 10.2 to break yourself of this habit. *Do not worry about understanding all you read.* The practice of reading fast will help you eliminate or reduce regressions. As a result, your comprehension will improve even if you do not work to comprehend all of what you read while you practice reading fast. The aim of the practice is to develop the habit of moving your eyes smoothly from left to right across lines of print and the habit of returning them quickly to the left sides of pages.

When you practice, you may find it helpful to pace yourself by moving your hand down each column or page. Do not place your fingers under each line of print. Rather, move your hand down the right side of a column or page at a slightly faster rate than is comfortable for you to read. Gradually increase the speed with which you move your hand and force your eyes to move as fast as your hand moves.

Your head should not move when you read, but it may be helpful from time to time to be conscious of the movement of your eyes. Every now and then attend to your eyes as they move rapidly from left to right across a line of print and fly back to the left margin to repeat the process on the following line.

Length of practice.   Each day for six weeks, spend ten minutes practicing reading fast. This will probably not require any additional time in your daily schedule because the practice can be done using books, newspaper articles, magazine articles, and other materials that you are likely to read even if you do not practice reading fast. Section 10.4 explains how to keep records of your progress during the six-week practice period. After six weeks, practice reading fast from time to time so that you do not lose the gains you make during the six-week practice period.

Mechanical aids for practice.   If there is a reading laboratory or learning center at your school, it may be equipped with mechanical aids that are designed for the practice of reading fast. One type of equipment is a device that fits over the pages of books and that can be regulated to slide down pages at various rates to force faster reading. The sliding device serves essentially the same purpose as a hand moving down the side of a column or page of print.

Another type of equipment is a specially designed filmstrip projector that projects reading selections on a screen. Projectors of this type have a control so that reading selections printed on filmstrips may be flashed on a screen at the rates readers select. Mechanical aids are not essential for practicing reading fast, but they can be helpful—especially during the early stages of practice.

Tired eyes while reading. If your eyes become strained while reading, you may need to use better lighting, or you may have a visual problem that needs to be corrected. Some clues to vision problems are watering, itchy, or burning eyes. Headaches, dizziness, or an upset stomach following reading or the need to blink, shut, or cover eyes frequently while reading also sometimes indicate a vision problem.

Either an optometrist or an ophthalmologist can test visual skills and prescribe corrective lenses or visual training. Ophthalmologists are medical doctors who treat eye diseases; optometrists cannot treat eye diseases or perform operations on eyes, but they are properly trained to test visual skills.

All students who need corrective lenses should own them and wear them. My vision problem was not detected until I was in the tenth grade because the superficial visual screening done by my schools always indicated that I did not need to have a professional eye examination. When I finally got glasses, reading and studying became more pleasurable for me, and my school work improved immediately. If you suspect that you might benefit by wearing corrective lenses, you should have a professional eye examination.

10.4   Tests for reading rates

This section explains how to measure the rates at which you read. Before you practice reading faster, use the methods that are described in this section to pretest your reading rates so that you can use your present reading rates to chart your progress. Record you reading rates under "Pretest" in the chart in Figure 10a. **Reading flexibility** in the chart refers to the difference between your fast reading rate and your slow reading rate. For

Figure 10a **A Chart for Recording Your Reading Rates.**

	PRETEST	WEEKLY RETESTS					
		1	2	3	4	5	6
Slow reading rate							
Moderate reading rate							
Fast reading rate							
Reading flexibility							

example, if your fast reading rate is 260 words per minute and your slow reading rate is 90 words per minute, your reading flexibility is 170 words per minute (260 − 90 = 170). Reading flexibility should be at least 150 words per minute; if it is less than 150 words per minute, this usually indicates that easy material is being read too slowly.

At the end of each week during which you practice reading fast, retest your reading rates and enter the rates in the chart in Figure 10a. Most students find that practice reading fast increases their slow and moderate reading rates as well as their fast reading rates.

Materials for tests.   Select (1) a textbook that is difficult for you to read, (2) a textbook that is of moderate difficulty for you to read, and (3) a book, newspaper article, or magazine article of the type that you read for pleasure. The material of the type that you read for pleasure must contain very few words that are unfamiliar to you, it must be easy for you to understand, and it must be interesting to you. Use the first book to test your slow reading rate, the second book to test your moderate reading rate, and the third book (or newspaper or magazine article) to test your fast reading rate.

Number-of-lines test.   Slow, moderate, and fast reading rates may be measured using the number-of-lines test. Select a passage from a book or article and use the following procedures to find the average number of words per line in the passage.

1. Count the number of words in 10 lines.
2. Divide this number by 10.

If there are 125 words in 10 lines of a book, divide 125 by 10 to find that the book has an average of 12.5 words per line (125 ÷ 10 = 12.5).

Test your slow and moderate reading rates by reading as you normally do, but test your fast reading rate by reading as fast as you are able. *Use a kitchen timer, or have somebody time you as you read for exactly five minutes.* At the end of five minutes use the following steps to find the number of words you read per minute.

1. Count the number of lines you read.
2. Multiply this number by the average number of words per line.
3. Divide this number by 5.

If 60 lines are read in 5 minutes and there are an average of 12.5 words per line, multiply 60 by 12.5 and divide the resulting number (750) by 5 to find the reading rate of 150 words per minute (750 ÷ 5 = 150).

Number-of-pages test.   The number-of-pages test is suitable for testing the fast reading rate using an easy book, but it is not appropriate for testing slow and moderate reading rates. The test is so easy to do that you may want to do it following each ten-minute practice session during which you use a book to practice reading fast.

First, use the following procedures to find the average number of words per page in a book.

1. Select 3 representative pages from the book.

2. Count the number of words on each of the pages.
3. Add these numbers and divide the sum by 3.

If 3 pages have 248, 259, and 286 words, add these numbers together and divide the sum (793) by 3 to find that the book has an average of 264 words per page (793 ÷ 3 = 264.3).

Use a kitchen timer, or have somebody time you as you read as fast as you can for ten minutes. At the end of ten minutes use the following steps to find the number of words you read per minute.

1. Count the number of pages you read in 10 minutes.
2. Multiply the number of pages by the average number of words per page.
3. Divide this number by 10.

If 13.25 pages are read in 10 minutes and there are 264 words per page, multiply 264 by 13.25 and divide the resulting number (3498) by 10 to find the reading rate of 350 words per minute (3498 ÷ 10 = 349.8).

The number-of-pages test makes it possible to keep daily records of reading rates on the inside cover of a book or in some other convenient place.

Retests of reading rates.   At the end of each week during which you practice reading fast, retest your reading rates and enter the rates in the chart in Figure 10a. You may not need to do special retests of your fast reading rate if you use the number-of-pages test daily or if you practice fast reading using a mechanical aid in a reading laboratory or learning center. Your daily scores for the number-of-pages test, or the rate at which you read using a mechanical device, is your fast reading rate.

10.5   Benefits of flexible and fluent reading

If you use the suggestions in this chapter and the previewing and skimming skills explained in Chapter 12 and Chapter 13, you are likely to benefit in one or more of five ways.

First, it is more enjoyable to read when reading is done smoothly rather than word-by-word or with the constant need to look back at familiar words that have already been read.

Second, reading is done with greater understanding when the eyes move constantly forward rather than when they repeatedly back up to examine words that do not need to be examined. The constant backtracking associated with regressions interferes with understanding. Regressions add words to sentences that confuse rather than clarify their meanings.

Third, practice reading at fast rates makes reading at slower rates a more comfortable experience. For example, if you find it uncomfortable to walk four miles in one hour, this will be more comfortable for you if you practice running six miles in an hour. In the same way, if you find it uncomfortable to read at a moderate rate of 175 words per minute, this will be more comfortable for you when you practice reading at the rate of 325 words per minute.

Fourth, practicing reading fast usually has the effect of increasing the slow and moderate reading rates. At the end of six weeks of practice reading fast, one student found that her slow reading rate had increased from 85 words per minute to 120 words per minute.

Fifth, when reading rates increase, more can be read in less time. The student who increased her slow reading rate from 85 to 120 words per minute had four very difficult textbooks to read. The books had a total of 2000 pages and an average of 500 words on each page. At the rate of 85 words per minute, it would have taken her 200 hours to read the four books, but at the rate of 120 words per minute she read the books in 140 hours—a saving of 60 hours.

Use What You've Learned

1. Are regressions, word-by-word reading, or lip movements preventing you from being a fluent reader? If the practice of reading fast does not help you to overcome your problem, seek the help of a reading specialist at your school or in your community.

2. If you have decided that you will *not* practice reading fast to improve your reading flexibility and fluency, why have you made this decision?

3. Use the suggestions in this chapter together with suggestions in Chapter 12 through Chapter 14 to increase your slow, moderate, and fast reading rates.

4. Use the suggestions for previewing and skimming in Chapter 12 and Chapter 13 to develop a rapid reading rate of more that 400 words per minute.

PART THREE

How to Read and Study for Examinations

11

Understand Reading and Studying

This chapter introduces the methods for reading and studying that are explained in detail in Chapter 12 through Chapter 17. Read this chapter to understand the differences between reading and studying, the ways in which reading and studying are related, and the methods that are used to read and study for examinations.

It is not uncommon in one term of college for full-time students to read five or six textbooks, other books and articles, and to write a paper or complete some other major project for each of their courses. The methods that are summarized in this chapter and that are explained in detail in Chapter 12 through Chapter 17 make it possible to learn the things that need to be learned in as little time as possible.

The methods to use when reading and studying for college tests are the same methods to use when reading and studying for any purpose, except in college you will need to learn information that you might not choose to learn if you were studying for your own purposes. For example, if you study history to do well on a history test, you will need to learn all the information that is presented in class and in required course reading materials. But, if you read and study history for your own purposes, you may read whatever history books you choose and you may skip any parts of books that do not interest you. One important difference between college-educated people and self-educated people is that college-educated people learn many things that they are not likely to have learned if they had educated themselves.

11.1   The differences between reading and studying

A fundamental misconception about reading and studying is that they are identical processes. Many students believe that information in a book should be learned by reading the book over and over again. However, while reading is an important part of studying, reading and studying are two different processes. The confusion about these two processes seems to arise out of the fact that much of what is read in college must be studied, but books and other printed material may be read without studying them.

Reading is the process that is used to understand information that is presented in writing. It involves such activities as locating major points, determining how ideas are related to one another, and drawing conclusions using information that has been read. **Studying,** on the other hand, is the process that is used to remember and recall information. It includes selecting the information that will be learned, organizing the information so that it can be learned easily, and reciting and reviewing the information until it can be recalled when it is wanted or needed.

When the goal is to do well on college tests and examinations, reading is done for the purpose of studying, and studying is done for the purpose of learning information or skills so that test questions can be answered correctly.

11.2   The best reading and study methods

The best reading and study methods for you to use are simply the ones that help you achieve easily whatever goals you have when you read and study. This handbook includes a wide variety of suggestions so that you may select from them the ones that are most useful to you in achieving your goals.

You may find that this term you need to use almost all the suggestions for studying explained in this handbook for every course you take. But next year, when you are a more skillful student, you may decide to modify your study procedures for some of your courses. Also, you may find that you need to use all the study methods for some of your courses but not for others.

Use the suggestions that are given in this handbook to develop your own efficient study procedures.

11.3   The analysis of skills

The following section in this chapter and Chapter 12 through Chapter 17 analyze the reading and study processes so that you may better understand them and know how you can use them to make the best use of the time that you set aside for reading and studying.

Analysis is the process of dividing something into its parts so that it can be better understood; a problem with analyzing skills is that the analyses are, of necessity, artificial. For example, when coaches want to train high-jumpers, they analyze the act of high jumping so that they can better teach this skill. There is a very brief period of time from the moment that high-jumpers start running, hurl themselves over bars, and land on mats. But, to train competitive high-jumpers, it is necessary to analyze the act of high jumping by artificially dividing this brief moment into various parts.

The same is true when reading and study skills are analyzed. To explain these skills they must be artificially discussed separately although they are actually often used simultaneously. The analysis of reading and study skills is further complicated by the fact that reading may be divided into parts for analysis and studying may also be divided into parts for analysis.

As you read the following section of this chapter, and Chapter 12 through Chapter 17, keep in mind that two, three, or more of the reading and study procedures described are sometimes done at the same time.

11.4   Reading and studying for examinations

Reading is done before studying; but I am going to describe how to read for the purpose of studying. Therefore, you will need to know something about the suggestions for studying to fully understand the suggestions for reading.

Studying is the process that is used to remember and recall information. The usual procedure for studying books is to underline information that will be learned, to make notes that summarize the information, and to learn the information from the notes. For example, after reading the passage in Figure 11a, a student underlined the information that he wanted to learn for a test in his psychology course. At a later time he made the notes in Figure 11b so that he could recite the information efficiently. **Reciting** is the repeating of information aloud or silently until it can be recalled without reading it; reciting is the single most important step in studying when the goal is to learn information (Chapter 17).

The demarcation between reading and studying is not clear-cut, but it is helpful to think of underlining as the first step for studying information in books. You should only underline in a book the information that you decide you will learn, and study logically begins with the decision that something will be learned.

Chapters of books are often twenty, thirty, or more pages long; but they are read, and eventually studied, one small section at a time. The remainder of this section briefly summarizes procedures for reading and studying that are explained in detail in Chapter 12 through Chapter 17.

1. Preview chapters.
2. Skim sections of chapters.
3. Read and underline with a purpose.
4. Decide what you want to study.
5. Make notes for studying.
6. Recite information you want to learn.

The first step, "Preview chapters," is explained fully in Chapter 12; the second procedure is explained in Chapter 13; and so on through the sixth step, which is explained in Chapter 17.

Figure 11a **Underline in Books the Information You Decide to Learn.**

Transfer

Who has a better chance of learning to repair an Army tank quickly—a person who has never repaired mechanical equipment or one who has had experience repairing cars and trucks? The latter person would, because he or she has had some similar experience that can be applied to this new learning task.

The principle that past learning carries over into new learning situations is called *transfer*. It means, in its broadest sense, that we bring our past experiences to bear on all our learning. Sometimes these past experiences make our current learning endeavors easier; other times, they make them harder. *Positive transfer* means that previous learning helps us in subsequent learning. Burt, for example, finds that in studying physics, his knowledge of math is of great assistance in understanding many physical laws. Janellen, an excellent typist, has an easy time *Examples* learning to operate a keypunch machine, which is very similar to a typewriter.

Negative transfer means that previous learning interferes with subsequent learning and, therefore, makes it more difficult. Because his knowledge of traditional math keeps interfering, Barry can't get used to the New Math. *Examples* Phyllis experiences a great deal of difficulty counting her change when she gets to England, where the money system is different from the one she is used to at home.

Important One of the most important variables that determines whether transfer will be positive or negative is the degree of similarity of the stimuli and responses in the two tasks. Very strong positive transfer occurs when the stimuli are similar and require identical responses. For example, *Examples* someone who has been driving a Chevy will know how to drive a Ford. Someone who speaks French very well should have an easy time learning Spanish. Negative transfer occurs when two stimuli are the same or similar, but the responses required in the two situations are different. For example, driving a car in England is difficult for people who have spent years driving in America.

Figure 11b **Use Notes to Recite the Information You Want to Learn.**

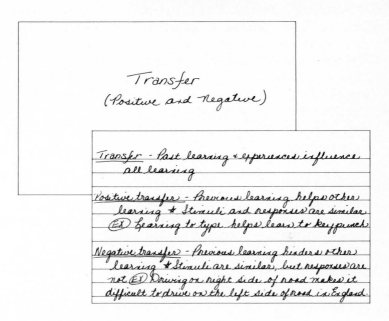

Preview chapters.   Before you read a section of a chapter, preview the chapter. **Previewing** is done by reading the preface and other material at the front of a book to learn how a chapter is related to other chapters in the book and by quickly examining introductory paragraphs, headings, figures, tables, and other features of a chapter to learn what major topics it discusses (Chapter 12). It takes only a few minutes to preview a chapter, but this is time well spent because it provides background information that increases reading comprehension.

Skim sections of chapters.   As you preview a chapter, you will find its major sections and subsections. For example, if you previewed this chapter you would have found that it is divided into five major sections. You would also have found that this section is divided into six subsections, each with its own heading ("Preview chapters," and so forth).

Skimming includes reading introductory paragraphs, headings, and words printed in special type (Chapter 13). For example, in skimming the passage in Figure 11a, one would read the heading "Transfer" and the terms *transfer, positive transfer,* and *negative transfer* where they are printed in italic type in the passage. Skimming is similar to previewing in that it provides the reader with background information that can be used to read a section of a chapter with the best possible comprehension.

Read and underline with a purpose. Information gathered while skimming a passage is used to set a purpose for reading it. A well-chosen purpose for reading aids concentration and comprehension. For example, after skimming the passage in Figure 11a, one might devise the following question to use as a purpose for reading the selection: *What is transfer and how do positive and negative transfer differ?* If the passage in Figure 11a were read for the purpose of answering this question, it would be read with good understanding.

The ability to analyze the types of information in passages increases the likelihood of setting good purposes for reading them. Therefore, Chapter 14 explains seven types of information that are commonly found in college textbooks:

1. *Definitions* of important terms (such as *studying*)
2. *Categories,* or *types,* of items (such as the types of reading rates)
3. *Methods* for doing certain things (such as the method for skimming)
4. *Sequences* in which events occur or happen (such as the sequential steps for reading and studying a chapter of a book)
5. *Causes,* or *reasons,* things are as they are (such as the reason why analyses of skills are artificial)

6. *Effects,* or *results,* of actions or events (such as the effects of the practicing of fast reading)
7. *Comparisons* or *contrasts* among items (such as the differences between reading and studying)

The ability to analyze the types of information in textbooks also facilitates underlining.

Figure 11a illustrates how a section of a textbook may be underlined. Underlining is used to guide making notes of the type in Figure 11b. If a section of a book is not underlined after it is read, notes must be made for the section before reading the section that follows. Otherwise it is necessary to reread the entire section later so that notes can be made for it. Most students find that it is easier and more efficient to underline sections of chapters before making notes for them.

It is usually necessary to read a section of a chapter through completely to underline it accurately. Guidelines for underlining are summarized in Section 14.1.

Decide what you want to study.   It is not uncommon for full-time college students to read and study five or six textbooks during a term. It is impossible, or at least very difficult, to learn all of the information in five or six thick books during the few weeks of a college term; therefore, it is essential to decide what information in a book will and will not be studied.

These decisions are made by comparing class notes to information in required course reading materials, by reviewing tests that teachers have given, by conferring with teachers' former students, and by using other strategies that are explained in Chapter 15. The students who consistently do well in most of their courses are usually the ones who have developed the talent for deciding what they should and should not learn.

Make notes for studying.   Notes for books greatly condense the amount of information that needs to be studied and they organize information so that it is easier to learn than when it is printed in books. Chapter 16 explains the value of notes, how to make well organized notes, and the advantages of making notes for books on 3 x 5 index cards.

Recite information you want to learn.   **Reciting** is the act of repeating information aloud or silently until it can be recalled without reading it. *It is the single most important step in the study process when the goal is to learn information.* Chapter 17 explains how to recite and also gives suggestions about how you may learn information that you have difficulty remembering.

11.5   Practice skills you want to acquire

For some of your courses you will need to acquire skills as well as learn information. **Skills** are abilities that are acquired as a result of training and practice, such as the skills of writing papers, solving mathematical problems, speaking foreign languages, engaging in scientific experimentation, and drafting blueprints. These and many other skills are taught in colleges and universities.

Skills are acquired through practice. If you can add, subtract, multiply, and divide accurately, this is because you have spent much time practicing these abilities. Similarly, if you want to become expert at using a computer language, analyzing the chemical components of organic materials, solving quadratic equations, or any other skill, you will need to do the practice that is necessary.

When you must acquire skills, it is especially important that you attend all class meetings (Section 4.4) and keep up to date with course work (Section 4.6). Also, unless you are blessed with aptitudes that most people do not have, you will need to schedule a great deal of time for practicing and reviewing skills (Chapter 7). Schedule frequent, short study sessions to practice and review skills that you must acquire for mathematics, science, foreign language, and similar types of courses.

Use What You've Learned

1. Which of the procedures described in Section 11.4 are ones that you use when you read and study for examinations? Give an example of how each procedure is helpful to you.

2. If there are any procedures described in Section 11.4 that you do not use when you read and study for examinations, explain what you believe may be the advantages or disadvantages of the procedures.

3. Do you agree that studying is done more efficiently by underlining books and then making notes for underlined information? If not, explain your reasoning.

4. The author states that reciting is the single most important step in the study process when the goal is to learn information. Do you agree or disagree? After you have answered this question, read Chapter 17.

Preview Chapters

Previewing is the first of the six steps that are used to read and study for college tests and examinations.

1. Preview chapters.
2. Skim sections of chapters.
3. Read and underline with a purpose.
4. Decide what you want to study.
5. Make notes for studying.
6. Recite information you want to learn.

A common assignment in college is to read, study, and learn the information in a chapter of a textbook. Most students undertake this task by turning to the first page of a chapter to read the chapter through from beginning to end. However, a chapter is read with better understanding when it is previewed before it is read.

Previewing is a process that is used to understand how a chapter is related to other chapters in a book and to learn what major topics are discussed in a chapter. It includes quickly examining introductory paragraphs, headings, figures, tables, and other features of a chapter. It only takes a few minutes to preview a chapter, but a preview provides background information that makes it possible to read with good comprehension.

12.1 Preparation for previewing chapters

Before you preview a chapter in a book, first familiarize yourself with the book by examining it to understand its basic plan and major features.

Begin by examining a **table of contents;** it provides an overview of the topics that are discussed in a book and usually summarizes the topics that are discussed in each chapter. Examine the table of contents at the front of this handbook to observe that it is organized to show the plan of this book and the major topics that are discussed in each chapter.

After you have examined the table of contents for a book, read the **introduction** or **preface.** These passages are usually located on pages that immediately follow a table of contents. Most books have either an introduction or a preface—some books have both. These give an author's explanations of why a book was written, and they often give a summary of the purpose, philosophy, or contents of a book. This handbook has no introduction, but it has a preface. If you have not already read the preface to this handbook, read it now to understand the types of information that authors include in prefaces.

Some textbooks include an introduction or preface that is especially written for students. It usually follows a general introduction or preface and may be entitled "To the Student" or "For Students." Explanations for students at the beginning of textbooks often include helpful information. If you have not already done so, read the passage entitled "To the Student," which follows the preface at the front of this handbook.

The introductory passages in books are not always interesting and informative. However, it is worthwhile to examine any passage at the beginning of a book that includes the word *introduction, preface,* or *student* in its heading. If you make it a habit to examine these passages you will find that they often provide excellent background information for understanding or studying a book.

Preparation for previewing the chapters in a book continues by examining pages at the end of the book. They may include an appendix. An **appendix** contains supplementary materials or information. When a textbook has an appendix, it is located in the back of the book, usually immediately following the last chapter.

The information in appendixes is often extremely helpful.

For instance, the appendix for a merchandising textbook lists the 26 mathematical formulas that students who study the book are expected to learn. Always examine your textbooks to determine whether they have appendixes and whether the information in the appendixes is useful to you. This handbook has no appendix.

A **glossary** is an alphabetically arranged list of important terminology and definitions (see Section 9.5). When a book has a glossary, it usually follows the last chapter or the appendix. When there is no glossary at the end of a book, there may be a short glossary at the end of each chapter in the book. There is a glossary in the back of this handbook.

An **index** is an alphabetically arranged list of the subjects that are discussed in a book. The index is always located at the very end of a book, as is the index for this handbook. Many textbooks have an *author index* or *name index* in addition to a *subject index*. When this is the case, the author index or name index is located in front of the subject index. If you look for the name of a person in an index and do not find the name listed, check to see if the book has an author index. For example, if you do not find "Sigmund Freud" listed in the index of an introductory psychology textbook, check to see if his name is listed in an author index or a name index.

You will also frequently find references or a bibliography listed at the ends of books. **References** or **bibliographies** are lists of publications and other sources that an author quotes or refers to in a book. They may be arranged alphabetically, using the last names of authors, or they may be arranged numerically in the sequence in which they are referred to or quoted in a book. When you find no list of references at the back of a book, you may find references or a bibliography at the end of each chapter in the book.

12.2   Summary of how to preview a chapter

After you have examined the major features of a book in the way described in Section 12.1, you have the preparation that is helpful to preview the chapters in the book before you read and underline them. In summary, preview a chapter by examining

1. lists at the beginning or end of the chapter that state what you are expected to learn or understand from reading and studying the chapter.
2. an introduction at the beginning of the chapter or a summary at the end of the chapter.
3. headings within the chapter that describe the major topics and subtopics that are discussed in it.
4. figures and tables in the chapter that illustrate or summarize information that is explained in it.

The following discussions explain exactly how to preview chapters before you read and underline them.

12.3   Read the lists in chapters

When the chapters in a book begin or end with lists of learning objectives or questions, these lists should be read as part of the preview. The first page or two of a chapter may present lists under headings such as "Learning Goals," "Learning Objectives," "Performance Objectives," or "Study Guides." These lists often provide hints that may be used to read chapters intelligently. Figure 12a is the first page of a chapter in a chemistry textbook; it includes a list of learning goals. The first goal in the list can be used to read and study the chapter to be able to state the similarities and differences among gases, liquids, and solids. Students who read and study the chapter using this goal and the other goals in the list are likely to learn almost everything they are expected to learn in the chapter. Each chapter in the chemistry textbook begins with a list similar to the one in Figure 12a.

Sometimes lists at the ends of chapters may be used to guide the reading of chapters. The chapters in this handbook, for example, end with lists entitled "Use What You've Learned," which usually summarize the basic understandings that are

Figure 12a **Learning Goals in a Chemistry Textbook.**

CHAPTER 14

Liquids and solids — what a state they're in!

And we see that the extracts made with water or spirit of wine (ethanol) are not of a simple and elementary nature, but masses consisting of the looser corpuscles, and finer parts of the concretes whence they are drawn; since by distillation they may be divided into more elementary substances.

Robert Boyle
THE SCEPTICAL CHYMIST, 1661

LEARNING GOALS

After you've worked your way through this chapter, you should be able to:

1. Compare and contrast the properties of gases, liquids, and solids.
2. Apply the kinetic theory to describe the behavior of liquids and solids.
3. Explain what happens as a solid changes to liquid and the liquid to gas.
4. Define and illustrate *dynamic equilibrium, equilibrium vapor pressure, evaporation,* and *boiling point.*
5. Explain the processes of distillation and fractional distillation.
6. Define the terms *condensation, distillate, distilling head,* and *condenser.*
7. Describe what is meant by *crystalline* and *amorphous solids.*
8. Discuss the three kinds of crystalline solids and the forces of attraction in each.
9. Define and give an example of (a) a crystal lattice and (b) a unit cell.

INTRODUCTION

As you know, matter falls into three categories: solids, liquids, and gases. In Chapter 11 we discussed gases. Now we'll turn our attention to liquids and solids. It was these two states of matter that the alchemists studied so extensively.

developed in chapters. Examine the chapters in the textbooks you study to determine if they conclude with lists that have headings such as "Questions," "Exercises," "Review Questions," or "Discussion Questions." Even though the questions are at the ends of chapters, it may be helpful to read them *before* reading chapters.

At the beginning or end of a chapter there may also be a list of important terminology that is explained in the chapter. The list may have a heading such as "Key Concepts," "Important Terms," or "Terms Used in This Chapter." Following is an example of lists of this type that appear at the ends of chapters in a business textbook.

Terms to Understand

Analysis	Vertical thinker
Synthesis	Lateral thinker
Problem solving	Thinking
Complementary thinking	Systematic thinker
Problem	Intuitive thinker
Cause	Creativity

When you study books that have lists of important terms in each chapter, copy the terms on a piece of paper and give them your special attention when you read and study the chapter in which they are explained.

12.4   Read introductions

Chapters of textbooks usually begin with a paragraph or group of paragraphs that briefly explain the information that is discussed in them or provide other information that is helpful for reading chapters. You have probably noticed that the first paragraphs of the chapters in this handbook give brief summaries of the information in the chapters. Introductions to chapters may be quite long, but even when they are short they can be extremely informative. Following is an introduction to a chapter in a psychology textbook.

Learning and Instruction

Henry Adams once said of children: "They know enough who know how to learn." There is much to be said for this view, for complex learning does not take place automatically. Carefully planned instruction is often helpful.

In this chapter we move beyond theory and research to consider the application of learning principles in practical situations. The central question is this: Given a certain task to be learned, such as a geography unit, how does one go about planning the learning environment?

Notice that the first sentence in the second paragraph of this short introduction explains how the chapter on learning and instruction is related to other chapters in the book. The second paragraph also informs students that they should read the chapter to answer the following question: *How can a learning environment be planned to promote the learning of a specific task?* Those who find the answers to this question as they read will have a good understanding of the information in the chapter.

Whether an introduction to a chapter is short or long, read it carefully to prepare yourself for what you will read in the chapter.

12.5   Read summaries

When there are summaries at the ends of chapters in a book, it may be helpful to read them before reading the chapters. Summaries, under the heading "Summary," at the ends of chapters are sometimes easy-to-read, short explanations of the information in chapters. When this is the case, it is helpful to read a summary for a chapter before reading the chapter.

However, summaries are also sometimes written in ways that make them difficult to understand if the chapter has not been read. This is illustrated by the following paragraph that begins a six-paragraph summary at the end of a chapter in a psychology textbook.

Summary

Motivation is what moves a person to action. *Drive* generally refers to physiological determinants of behavior, while "motivation" is a more inclusive concept, referring to all determinants of activity. *Instinct,* or behavior inherited by all members of a species, is related to drive and motivation. Studies of animal behavior have led to our recognition of *imprinting* and *species-specific behavior* as forms of instinctive behavior.

It is difficult to understand this paragraph and the other five paragraphs in the summary unless the chapter that the summary concludes has been read. Read summaries at the ends of chapters as part of a preview only when you find that they are easy to read and understand before you read the chapters they conclude.

12.6   Read headings

Continue a preview by examining the headings in the chapter; they usually summarize the topics discussed in a chapter. The headings in this handbook, for example, have been written to provide you with informative summaries of the information in each chapter. When you preview headings, you learn what topics are discussed in a chapter and what emphasis is given to each topic. The number of pages devoted to a topic often provides clues about its importance or complexity; the longer a discussion, the more important or complex it is likely to be.

By previewing headings, you also learn how major topics and subtopics in a chapter are related to one another. In most textbooks the headings for major topics are all printed in the same kind of type. For example, in this handbook the headings for major topics are all printed in the same kind of type as the heading at the beginning of this section: **12.6 Read headings.** Also, all the headings for subtopics in a book are usually printed in the same kind of type. For example, in this handbook, the major-topic heading, **11.4 Reading and studying for exami-**

nations, is followed by six subtopic headings; the first two of the subtopic headings are **Preview chapters** and **Skim sections of chapters.**

Figure 12b illustrates one of the many other ways in which headings for major topics and subtopics are shown in textbooks. Notice in Figure 12b that the heading for the major topic, "Institutional and Noninstitutional Corrections," is set off by lines that are printed above and below it, but the headings for the subtopics, "Prisons" and "Jails," have no lines printed above or below them.

Textbooks often have more than two types of headings. In many books the subtopics under major topics are discussed in subdivisions, which are indicated by a special kind of heading of their own.

Following are some ways to determine the relationships among headings in a book:

1. If headings are printed in different sizes of type, the larger the type, the more important the headings.
2. If headings are printed in the same size type but some are printed in black ink and others are printed in another color (such as red), the headings printed in the other color are more important.
3. If headings are printed in the same size type but some are printed in **boldface** and some are printed in *italics,* the headings printed in boldface are more important.
4. If headings are printed in the same size type but some are printed in ALL CAPITAL LETTERS and others are not, the headings printed in all capital letters are more important.

Analyze each book you study to understand how headings are printed to indicate major topics, subtopics, and the relationships among them. Understanding the relative importance of the headings in your books will help you when you use the methods described in Chapter 13 through Chapter 17 to skim, read, underline, study, and learn the information in them.

Figure 12b **Example of Headings in a Criminology Textbook.**

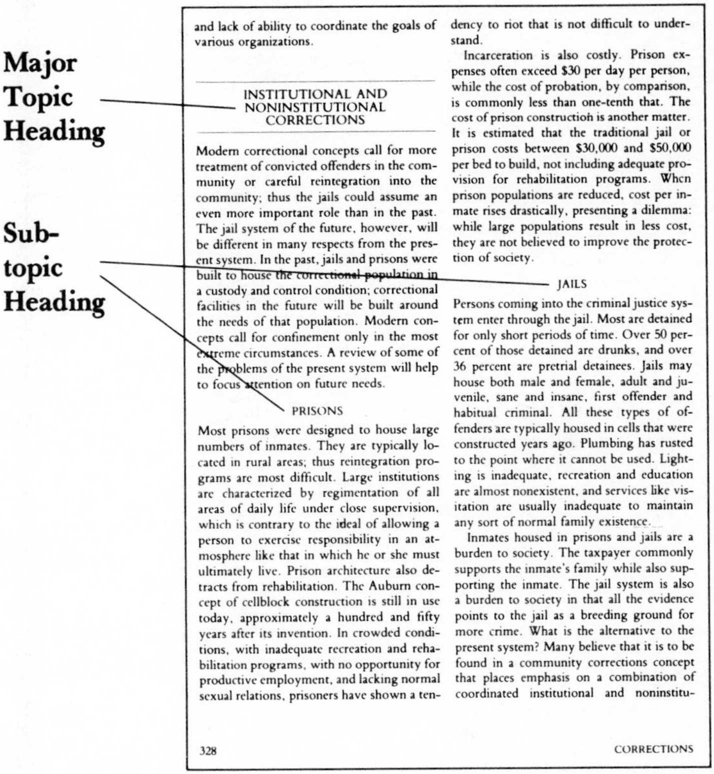

Major Topic Heading

Sub-topic Heading

and lack of ability to coordinate the goals of various organizations.

INSTITUTIONAL AND NONINSTITUTIONAL CORRECTIONS

Modern correctional concepts call for more treatment of convicted offenders in the community or careful reintegration into the community; thus the jails could assume an even more important role than in the past. The jail system of the future, however, will be different in many respects from the present system. In the past, jails and prisons were built to house the correctional population in a custody and control condition; correctional facilities in the future will be built around the needs of that population. Modern concepts call for confinement only in the most extreme circumstances. A review of some of the problems of the present system will help to focus attention on future needs.

PRISONS

Most prisons were designed to house large numbers of inmates. They are typically located in rural areas; thus reintegration programs are most difficult. Large institutions are characterized by regimentation of all areas of daily life under close supervision, which is contrary to the ideal of allowing a person to exercise responsibility in an atmosphere like that in which he or she must ultimately live. Prison architecture also detracts from rehabilitation. The Auburn concept of cellblock construction is still in use today, approximately a hundred and fifty years after its invention. In crowded conditions, with inadequate recreation and rehabilitation programs, with no opportunity for productive employment, and lacking normal sexual relations, prisoners have shown a ten-

dency to riot that is not difficult to understand.

Incarceration is also costly. Prison expenses often exceed $30 per day per person, while the cost of probation, by comparison, is commonly less than one-tenth that. The cost of prison construction is another matter. It is estimated that the traditional jail or prison costs between $30,000 and $50,000 per bed to build, not including adequate provision for rehabilitation programs. When prison populations are reduced, cost per inmate rises drastically, presenting a dilemma: while large populations result in less cost, they are not believed to improve the protection of society.

JAILS

Persons coming into the criminal justice system enter through the jail. Most are detained for only short periods of time. Over 50 percent of those detained are drunks, and over 36 percent are pretrial detainees. Jails may house both male and female, adult and juvenile, sane and insane, first offender and habitual criminal. All these types of offenders are typically housed in cells that were constructed years ago. Plumbing has rusted to the point where it cannot be used. Lighting is inadequate, recreation and education are almost nonexistent, and services like visitation are usually inadequate to maintain any sort of normal family existence.

Inmates housed in prisons and jails are a burden to society. The taxpayer commonly supports the inmate's family while also supporting the inmate. The jail system is also a burden to society in that all the evidence points to the jail as a breeding ground for more crime. What is the alternative to the present system? Many believe that it is to be found in a community corrections concept that places emphasis on a combination of coordinated institutional and noninstitu-

328

CORRECTIONS

12.7   Examine figures and tables

The photographs, drawings, diagrams, graphs, charts, and other graphic materials in textbooks are included, often at great expense, to summarize or illustrate information in the text. As you preview a chapter, examine this material and read the titles and captions for figures and tables. Figures and tables often summarize the information in a section of a chapter.

Figure 12c **The Typical Grievance Procedure.**

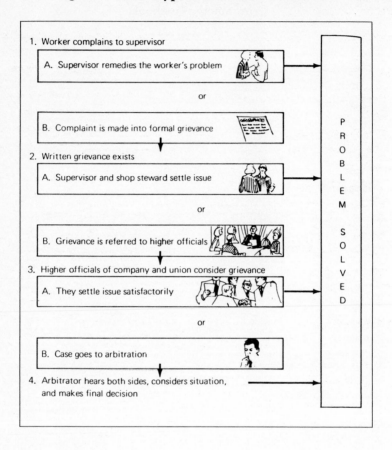

For example, Figure 12c summarizes a two-page discussion in a business textbook that explains the steps in grievance procedures when workers have problems with employers. Table 12a summarizes information about measures of central tendency that fills a large, two-column page of a psychology textbook.

Examine Figure 12c and Table 12a to observe that they both convey a great deal of information. Figure 12c gives answers to several questions, including the following:

Table 12a **Computing the Mean, Median, and Mode.**

Nine hypothetical scores on an examination

89
86
81
78
78
73
71
70
67

The *mean* (average) is obtained by adding up all of the scores and dividing by the total number of scores. If we add up these nine scores, we get a total of 693. Next, we divide by 9 (the number of scores), and we find that the mean for this group of scores is 77. The *mode* is the most frequently recurring score (78). The *median* is the middle score (78).

1. What are four ways in which a worker's grievance with an employer may be resolved?

2. What are the possible alternatives when the officials of a company and a union consider the written grievance of a worker?

Table 12a gives answers to six questions: "What is meant by the terms (1) mean, (2) median, and (3) mode?" "How are the (4) mean, (5) median, and (6) mode for a set of numbers calculated?"

If you sometimes have difficulty interpreting graphs, tables, or diagrams, Section 13.6 gives suggestions that may be helpful to you.

Use What You've Learned

1. Use the procedures that are explained in Section 12.1 to familiarize yourself with all of the books you are studying for your courses. Then answer the following questions:

a. Which of your books do *not* have tables of contents or indexes?

b. Which of your books have interesting or useful information in passages that have the word *preface, introduction,* or *student* in their headings?

c. Which of your books have appendixes that contain information that is useful or informative to you?

d. Which of your books have an author index or name index in addition to a subject index?

e. Which of your books have one glossary at the ends of them, and which have glossaries at the ends of each chapter?

f. Which of your books have one list of references or a bibliography at the ends of them, and which have lists of references at the ends of each chapter?

2. Use the procedures that are explained in Section 12.3 through Section 12.7 to preview a chapter in each of the books you are studying for your courses. Then answer the following questions:

a. Which chapters include lists of things to learn?

b. Which chapters include lists of words or terms?

c. Which chapters begin with informative introductions?

d. Which chapters end with discussions entitled "Summary"?

e. Are you able to understand how the headings in each chapter are printed to indicate major topics and subtopics?

f. Which chapters include informative pictures, tables, diagrams, graphs, or other graphic materials?

Skim Sections of Chapters

After you have previewed a chapter, prepare to read and underline the chapter by skimming it a section at a time.

1. Preview chapters.
2. **Skim sections of chapters.**
3. Read and underline with a purpose.
4. Decide what you want to study.
5. Make notes for studying.
6. Recite information you want to learn.

It is easier to read and understand the information in a long chapter when it is approached as a series of logically related sections than when it is viewed as one long succession of pages. As you preview a chapter, you examine headings that give information about the major divisions and subdivisions within the chapter. Use what you learn about major divisions and sub-divisions so that you can skim, read, and underline it one section at a time.

This chapter explains skimming techniques, but makes some references to reading and underlining because skimming is done to facilitate reading and underlining. However, the full discussions of reading and underlining are in Chapter 14.

Skimming is similar to previewing; in fact, for our purposes, **skimming** is the careful previewing of a section of a chapter before reading and underlining it. It includes reading introductory paragraphs, heading, words printed in special type, and carefully studying figures, tables, graphs, and diagrams that were examined quickly while previewing a chapter.

Figure 13a **Sections in a Chapter of a Psychology Textbook.**

Headings for major topics and subtopics	Total pages for major topics	Pages for subtopics
The Normal and Abnormal	.75	—
Frustration and Conflict	4.50	—
Frustration		1.50
Conflict		1.75
Adjustment		1.25
The Defense Mechanisms	4.75	—
Repression		.75
Projection		.75
Rationalization		.50
Reaction formation		.75
Denial		.50
Displacement		.50
Sublimation		.25
Identification		.50
Regression		.25
Historical Approaches to Behavior	2.00	—

13.1   Divide chapters into sections

The sections of chapters that you skim and then later read and underline one at a time may be as short as one paragraph and they should seldom be much longer than three pages. Figure 13a summarizes some of the headings in a chapter of a psychology textbook and the number of pages of text that follow each heading for major topics and subtopics. The major-topic headings are the ones that are printed farthest to the left: "The Normal and Abnormal," "Frustration and Conflict," and so on. The subtopic headings are indented under the major-topic headings. For example, "Frustration," "Conflict," and "Adjustment" are subtopics under the major topic "Frustration and Conflict."

Notice in Figure 13a that less than one page is devoted to the discussion of the major topic "The Normal and Abnormal." That section is short enough that it should be skimmed and then read and underlined in its entirety. However, the discussion of the major topic "The Defense Mechanisms" is almost five pages long and it is divided into nine subtopics. An efficient approach to that section of the chapter would be to skim the entire section and then to read and underline the section one subsection at a time. For example, after skimming the entire section, the information about "Repression" should be read and underlined before reading and underlining the information about "Projection."

13.2   Read introductory paragraphs

Just as chapters usually begin with introductory paragraphs, so do the sections that make up chapters. Figure 13b is a passage from a human sexuality textbook that describes the stages of pregnancy. Notice that the short introductory paragraph includes informative facts that may be used to read the passage with good understanding.

Most textbook authors begin the sections of their chapters with introductions that are intended to prepare students to read the subject matter in them. Read introductory paragraphs when you skim a section or subsection of a chapter.

13.3   Read headings

When you skim a section of a chapter, also read the headings that are printed within the section. Notice in Figure 13b that headings are used to divide the discussion about the stages of pregnancy into three subsections: first trimester, second trimester, and third trimester.

Many textbook authors include subheadings of this type to help readers quickly grasp the divisions of their discussions. Subtopic headings are used in Section 13.6 and other sections in this handbook.

Figure 13b **A Textbook Section with an Introduction and Subheadings.**

Stages of Pregnancy

A normal pregnancy can last between 240 and 300 days, with about 266 days the average length. Most literature on pregnancy divides the experience into three-month periods called *trimesters*.

First trimester During the first trimester the signs and symptoms mentioned earlier are the most noticeable physical changes. Psychologically, this is a time of emotionally admitting and "owning" the pregnancy. Most women have mixed feelings, both negative and positive, about being pregnant during this time.

Second trimester During the second trimester, the pregnancy begins to show. The weight of the uterus increases about twenty times during pregnancy, with most of this increase taking place before the twentieth week. During the fourth or fifth month fetal heartbeats can be heard through a stethoscope. The movements of the fetus can be felt during the second trimester. By late in the trimester, movements of the fetus can be seen as brief risings in the mother's abdomen. If nausea or strong feelings of needing to nap were present during the first trimester, they usually go away during the second trimester. By midpregnancy a woman's breasts, stimulated by hormones, have become ready for nursing.

Third trimester The uterus becomes larger during the third trimester, and a woman may become more uncomfortable. The stomach and other internal organs become crowded. Pressure on the bladder may again cause frequent urination. Feelings of wanting to nap may return. The baby will often be felt moving, kicking, and even hiccupping during this stage of pregnancy, sometimes with an all too strongly developed individuality.

13.4   Read words printed in special type

When you skim, also read words printed in italic type, bold-face type, or in a special color such as red, blue, or green. Words printed in special type sometimes give important clues to the major points in a section of a chapter. Read the words printed in italics in the following passage.

Types of Families

There are four basic ways families are viewed by sociologists.

A *nuclear family* consists of a married couple and their children. Most people are born into a nuclear family—their family of orientation—and then go on to establish a nuclear family of their own—their family of procreation. The only possible members of a family of orientation are a mother, father, brothers, and sisters. Your family of procreation may include your spouse, sons, and daughters.

The *extended family* is another term sociologists use to describe family relationships. Exactly who is considered a member of an extended family differs from country to country, but in the United States the extended family is usually considered to include children, parents, and other relatives who live with them in the same house or very near by.

Families may also be viewed in terms of the number of partners in a marriage. In our country we have *monogamous families*—there is only one husband and one wife in a marriage partnership. In some societies, though, there are *polygamous families* with more than two marriage partners. Polygyny is the form of polygamy in which there is one husband and two or more wives; polyandry is the form in which one wife has two or more husbands.

The terms *nuclear family, extended family, monogamous families,* and *polygamous families* are printed in italic type to help readers quickly find the four basic types of families that are described in the passage.

Throughout this handbook words are printed in boldface

type to help you find major points when you skim. The terminology printed in boldface type in this book is also defined in a glossary at the back of this handbook.

Sometimes entire sentences are printed in special type. Figure 13c is an excerpt from a four-page discussion in an education textbook. Read the sentences that are printed in italic type in Figure 13c. The complete four-page discussion identifies six guidelines for developing curriculums and all six guidelines are printed in italic type.

Often sentences printed in italic type are preceded by numbers such as *1, 2,* and *3* for additional emphasis, as in Section 13.6 and elsewhere in this handbook. When words or sentences are printed in italics, boldface, or some other special type, read them when you skim a section of a chapter.

13.5   Look for words that signal major points

Also, skim sections to find words that signal major points. The most conspicuous of these words are *first, second, third,* and *fourth,* but they also include words and phrases such as *next, furthermore, moreover, finally, in addition,* and *in conclusion.*

Notice in Figure 13c that the authors placed the words *first* and *second* conspicuously at the beginnings of the paragraphs that state the first and second guidelines for curriculums. The four-page discussion presents six guidelines using a total of thirteen paragraphs; four of the other paragraphs begin with the words *third, fourth, fifth,* and *sixth* so that each guideline can be easily identified.

The following section from a communications textbook includes words that signal the major points in the passage. Read the selection and underline the words that signal the *norms* (appropriate behaviors) that are associated with the eyes.

Eye Behavior

One of the first things many of us learn as children is that people who lie do not look straight into our eyes. There are

Figure 13c **A Textbook Section with Sentences
Printed in Italics.**

Guidelines for Curriculums

It is also not our purpose to describe in detail how to go about developing curriculum in a systematic and orderly way. We do want to discuss, however, a number of principles or guidelines that we believe to be basic to the development of a relevant and meaningful curriculum.*

First, *a curriculum should not be prepackaged, rigidly scheduled, or uniform throughout a school system. Instead, it should be flexible and geared to the unique needs of the students.* A prepackaged curriculum says, in effect, "Whether you're black, white, brown, or yellow, whether your parents earn $50,000 or $5,000 per year, whether you can read well or just barely, whether you're secure and have developed a good self-concept or not, here is what you need to learn!"

A flexible curriculum geared to the unique needs of the students says, in effect, "This curriculum is designed to help you deal in personal terms with the problems of human conduct, rather than with the requirements of various subject disciplines. We start with you, the learner, not with the content, because you are more important than the subject matter."

Second, *a curriculum should start from an "experience" base, rather than a "symbol" base.* Because symbols are abstract, they are not appropriate starting points for instruction. It is not that symbols and abstractions are unimportant—in fact, they are crucial in our society—but abstraction must be grounded in the concrete reality of the individual student's life if it is to have meaning for him or her. As Edgar Dale's famous "Cone of Experience" (Figure 8.1) illustrates, the kinds of experiences that can be provided the student vary on a continuum from the most direct to the highly abstract.

*The authors are indebted to Mario Fantini and Gerald Weinstein for elucidating these principles in their pamphlet, *Toward a Contact Curriculum* (New York: Anti-Defamation League of B'nai B'rith, 1969).

many folk tales like this one about eye behavior. As you might guess, some are based on myth, including this one. While our eye behavior communicates many things, the degree to which we are telling the truth is not one of them. And if you don't believe us, ask a good poker player like former world champion Amarillo Slim.

In our culture, eye behavior, which is technically called *oculesics,* is expected to conform to certain norms. One of the most pervasive norms concerns attention. When we communicate with a person we assume that if he or she looks us in the eyes the person is paying attention. We should realize, though, that maintaining strict eye contact is uncomfortable for some people and, as a result, is not necessarily indicative of attentiveness.

Another norm in our culture is that sustained eye contact is an invitation to communicate. Have you ever been called on in class when you did not want to be called on? Chances are you made and briefly sustained eye contact with your teacher. Most students intuitively realize this and avoid eye contact with a teacher when they are unsure about responding to the question.

Finally, eye contact in our culture commonly is associated with physical attraction. Depending on the environment, males frequently assume that if a female is looking at him, she finds him physically attractive. Lest females take this as another indication of the macho needs of males, females frequently draw an identical conclusion when being "checked" out by a male. The truth of the matter is, though, people stare. If we notice we are the primary object in another's field of vision, it does not necessarily mean the person is enamoured with our physical appearances.

In the second paragraph you should have underlined *one* at the beginning of the second sentence, and you should have underlined the first words in the third and fourth paragraphs: *another* and *finally*.

When you skim a section of a chapter, read the first few words in each paragraph looking for *first, another, next, in addition, finally,* and similar clues to the number of major points that are made about the topic discussed in the section.

Figure 13d **Numbers of Workers of Various Ages: 1970–1990.**

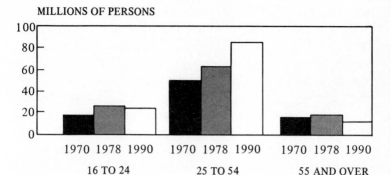

SOURCE: *Occupational Outlook Handbook,* 1980–81 Edition, U.S. Department of Labor, Bureau of Labor Statistics, Bulletin 2075.

13.6   Interpret graphs, tables, and diagrams

The skimming of a section includes carefully studying graphic material that was examined quickly while previewing. This section gives suggestions for interpreting the information in bar graphs, line graphs, tables, and diagrams. Similar procedures are used for interpreting bar graphs, line graphs, and tables: (1) understand the heading, (2) understand the labels, (3) compare the information, and (4) decide what information is important.

Bar graphs.   **Bar graphs** are usually used to show differences in amounts. Refer to the example of a bar graph in Figure 13d as you read the following explanations.

1. *Understand the heading.* A heading explains what information is represented in a graph. The heading for Figure 13d states that the information is about numbers of workers of various ages for the years 1970–1990.

2. *Understand the labels.* Labels indicate where specific information is located in a graph. The label for information that goes from bottom to top on the left of the graph states that it is about

millions of persons. The labels under the bars specify to which age group each set of three bars pertains, and also which bars represent the years 1970, 1978, and 1990.

3. *Compare the information.* Since bar graphs usually show differences in amounts, it is logical to make comparisons among differences in amounts. By comparing the three sets of bars, it can be determined that for each year there are more workers in the 25- to 54-year-old group than in the groups of younger and older workers. By comparing the bars for 1978 and 1990 for each of the three age groups, it may be learned that while the numbers of workers in the younger and older groups will decrease slightly over this twelve-year period, the number of workers in the 25- to 54-year-old group will increase dramatically—by more than twenty million workers.

4. *Decide what information is important.* Other comparisons may be made, but these comparisons make it clear that the important information in the bar graph is that there will be a dramatic increase in the number of workers in the 25- to 54-year-old group between the years 1978 and 1990, but there will be decreases in other age groups.

Line graphs.   **Line graphs** are usually used to show increases and decreases. Figure 13e is an example of a line graph; it will be used to describe the procedures that may be used to interpret information in most line graphs.

1. *Understand the heading.* The heading that follows "Figure 13e" states that the graph gives information about the percentages of persons arrested for the period 1960–1978.

2. *Understand the labels.* The labels for information that goes from bottom to top on the left and right of the graph state that it is information about percentages—in this case, percentages of arrests. The labels at the bottom of the graph state that the information there is for the years 1960 through 1978. There are also labels to indicate the age group represented by each line.

Figure 13e **Percentages of Persons Arrested: 1960–1978.**

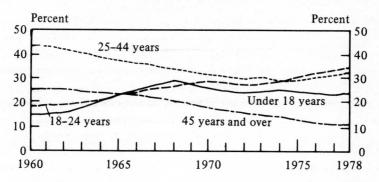

SOURCE: Chart prepared by U.S. Bureau of the Census. Data from U.S. Federal Bureau of Investigation.

3. *Compare the information.* Since line graphs usually show increases and decreases, it is logical to compare increases and decreases in percentages of arrests for the four age categories. Notice that the line for those under 18 years old shows an increase from about 15 percent of arrests in 1960 to about 23 percent of arrests in 1978, and that the line for those 18–24 years old shows an increase from about 18 percent in 1960 to about 34 percent in 1978. Compare these to the line for those 25–44 years old that shows a decrease from about 43 percent in 1960 to about 32 percent in 1978, and the line for those 45 years and over that shows a decrease from about 25 percent in 1960 to about 11 percent in 1978. In 1960, approximately 33 percent of arrests were of persons 24 years old or younger, but in 1978 approximately 57 percent of arrests were of persons 24 years old or younger.

4. *Decide what information is important.* Other comparisons may be made, but these comparisons make it clear that the important information in the graph is that, from 1960 to 1978, arrests of younger persons increased dramatically while arrests of older persons decreased markedly.

Table 13a **Life Expectancy by Age, Race, and Sex: 1977.**

Age in 1977 (years)	Expectation of life in years			
	White		Black and Other	
	Male	Female	Male	Female
At birth	70.0	77.7	64.6	73.1
10	61.3	68.8	56.6	65.0
20	51.9	59.1	47.2	55.2
30	42.7	49.4	38.6	45.8
40	33.4	39.8	30.2	36.7
50	24.7	30.7	22.7	28.3
60	17.1	22.3	16.5	21.0
70	11.1	14.8	11.4	14.5
80	6.8	8.8	8.7	11.3
85 and over	5.3	6.8	7.3	9.6

SOURCE: U.S. National Center for Health Statistics, *Vital Statistics of the United States,* annual.

Tables.   **Tables** may be used to summarize almost any type of statistical information. The procedure for interpreting the information in tables is similar to the one for interpreting information in bar graphs and line graphs. Table 13a will be used to explain the procedure.

1. *Understand the heading.* The heading for Table 13a states that it gives information about life expectancy by age, race, and sex for the year 1977.

2. *Understand the labels.* The label for information that goes from top to bottom in the left column states that it is for various ages in the year 1977. The label "Expectation of life in years" is placed over all of the other columns in the table to indicate that this is the type of information in the other four columns. The labels "White" and "Black and Other" indicate that the second and third columns pertain to "White" persons and that

the fourth and fifth columns pertain to "Black and Other" persons. The other labels indicate which columns list data for "Male" and "Female" persons.

3. *Compare the information.* The table makes many types of comparisons possible. But the most obvious comparisons are between males and females within each race, between males in both race groups, and between females in both race groups.

a. In comparing the years that "White" males are expected to live with the years that "White" females are expected to live, "White" females are expected to live longer.

b. In comparing the years that "Black and Other" males are expected to live with the years that "Black and Other" females are expected to live, "Black and Other" females are expected to live longer.

c. In comparing the years that "White" males are expected to live with the years that "Black and Other" males are expected to live, "White" males are expected to live longer (except after age 70).

d. In comparing the years that "White" females are expected to live with the years that "Black and Other" females are expected to live, "White" females are expected to live longer (except after age 80).

4. *Decide what information is most important.* Other comparisons may be made, but these comparisons make it clear that the important information presented in the table is that (1) females of a race are expected to live longer than males of the same race and (2) "White" persons of a sex are expected to live longer than "Black and Other" persons of the same sex.

Diagrams.   Textbooks often use diagrams to illustrate discussions. **Diagrams** are drawings that explain something by outlining its parts and showing the relationships among its parts or by showing the relationships of objects to one another. Figure 13f is a diagram from an astronomy textbook that can be understood easily by reading the caption for the figure and studying the diagram. Without referring to any passage in the astronomy

Figure 13f **Solar and Lunar Eclipses.**

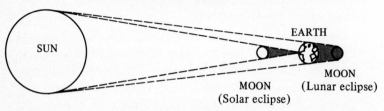

Solar eclipses occur when the earth, moon, and sun are lined up, with the moon in the middle. Lunar eclipses occur when the earth is between the sun and the moon.

textbook, it may be understood from Figure 13f that a solar eclipse is caused by the moon preventing sunlight from reaching the earth and that a lunar eclipse is caused by the earth preventing sunlight from reaching the moon.

Figure 13f illustrates that in some instances it is possible to interpret diagrams by examining them or by reading a short caption that accompanies them. However, in many instances it is necessary to read explanations in a text to understand diagrams. When you encounter a diagram that you do not fully understand, it is likely that you will understand the diagram if you refer to it as you carefully read the portion of the text that the diagram is provided to illustrate.

If you know that you have difficulty interpreting diagrams, seek the help of a teacher, tutor, or fellow student. For example, if you have difficulty interpreting diagrams in a biology textbook, ask your biology teacher to help you. If your biology teacher is unable to help you, teachers or tutors in a learning center or reading laboratory at your school may be able to provide the instruction you need. Also, a friend or classmate may be able to help you unravel the mystery of how to interpret diagrams and other types of drawings.

Use What You've Learned

1. Use the procedures that are explained in this chapter to skim sections of chapters in your books before you read and underline them.

2. Which of your books do *not* have headings that you can use to divide chapters into sections for skimming, and later reading and underlining?

3. Which of your books have sections that do *not* begin with informative introductory paragraphs?

4. Which of your books use words printed in italic type, boldface type, or in a special color such as red or blue to help you find important points made in the sections of chapters?

5. Which of your books use words such as *first, second,* and *third* or numbers such as *1, 2,* and *3* at the beginnings of sentences or paragraphs to help you find major points?

6. If you have difficulty interpreting bar graphs, line graphs, tables, or diagrams, use the suggestions given at the end of Section 13.6 to improve your ability in interpreting these kinds of displays.

Read and Underline
with a Purpose

The third step for learning information in a book is to read and then underline the information that you believe is important for you to learn.

1. Preview before you read.
2. Skim sections of chapters.
3. **Read and underline with a purpose.**
4. Decide what you want to learn.
5. Make notes for studying.
6. Recite information you want to learn.

Reading is best done for the purpose of answering a question. For example, the following question can be used as a purpose for reading this chapter: *How can I set purposes for reading that will help me read with better understanding and underline information that is important for me to learn?* If you learn the answers to this question, you will understand the information that is explained in this chapter.

Unless you are specializing in the study of literature, most of what you read in college will be exposition. **Exposition** is writing that states facts and explanations; it is the kind of writing that is found in psychology, business, biology, and most other types of college books. Exposition in these books usually gives facts or explanations about one or more of the following types of information:

1. *Definitions* of important words
2. *Categories,* or *types,* of items

3. *Methods* for doing various things
4. *Sequences* in which events occur or happen
5. *Causes,* or *reasons,* things are as they are
6. *Effects,* or *results,* of actions or events
7. *Comparisons* or *contrasts* among items

Section 14.1 describes underlining methods you may practice using materials in this chapter. Section 14.2 through Section 14.8 explain how to analyze the various types of information in your books to set appropriate purposes for reading and underlining, and Section 14.9 illustrates how the suggestions in this chapter will help you when you study for tests.

14.1   What should I underline?

Underlining is the drawing of lines under words (Figure 14a). It may be done with a pencil, but it is usually done with a ballpoint pen, and it requires the use of a straightedged instrument, such as a ruler. Few people can underline books neatly without using a straightedge as a guide. This is one reason many students prefer to highlight; books may be highlighted without using a straightedge. **Highlighting** is done by using felt-tipped pens that contain water-color ink. Yellow is the most popular color. If the passage in Figure 14a had been highlighted, yellow or some other water-color ink would have been placed over the words that are underlined.

The value of underlining is that it renders a permanent record of information to be learned. If you do not underline a section after you skim and read it, either you will need to make notes before you skim and read the following section, or you will need to reread the section completely at a later time to make the notes you need to learn the information in it efficiently (see Chapter 16 and Chapter 17). Underlining is a great time-saver for all students except those who have such highly developed note-taking skills that they can make notes for their books as they read them.

The Impact of the Civil War on the South

The immediate ravages of war most deeply affected the
South, since most of the fighting took place there with the
usual consequences. <u>Crops were destroyed, homes and
farm buildings went up in flames, cities and towns were
occupied.</u>

①

The relentless pressure of the Federal naval blockade
of Southern ports, the presence on Southern soil of Union
armies, the cutting-off of Texas and Arkansas by Grant's
campaign along the Mississippi River, the steady shrink-
ing of Southern resources chewed up by military
demands—<u>all these combined to ruin the Southern economy and make miserable the lives of the people</u>. The
transportation system broke down, shortages of many
goods developed, coffee disappeared, salt became scarce,
and inflation by 1864 led to butter selling at $25 a pound
and flour at $275 a barrel. <u>Impoverishment was the fate
of many, and disease the byproduct of poverty</u>. Women
and children tried to carry on the work of the farms and
the shops, but by 1864 the task had become too great for
many, the penalties in suffering too high.

②

Examples

③

<u>Intellectual and cultural life in the South suffered dev-
astating blows under the impact of the war</u>. Many private
plantation libraries were destroyed; the importation of
books was severely limited by the blockade; book publishing was greatly restricted by lack of paper, some of the
books published came out on coarse brown paper or even
wallpaper, and in all cases the number of copies was far
below the demand. Newspapers and periodicals were
equally hard hit, some being forced to suspend publication, others coming out on half-sheets, mere slips of paper,
or wallpaper. Except for a few isolated instances, the public school system broke down, private academies closed or
survived on a day-to-day basis, colleges closed for lack of
private or public funds. The war was clearly an economic,
social, and cultural disaster for the South. Scarcely a single aspect of life remained unaffected.

④

Examples

There are four important guidelines to keep in mind when you underline or highlight your books:

1. *Read a section before you underline or highlight it.* You will find that often what seems very important *as* you are reading a section turns out to be not very important *after* you have read the entire section.

2. *Do not underline or highlight too much.* If an entire page is marked, it is the same as if nothing were marked.

3. *Underline or highlight only information that you want to learn.* The purpose of underlining is to make a permanent record of the things you want to learn.

4. *Make the major points stand out clearly.* You want to learn the major points.

It is also sometimes helpful to write *1, 2, 3,* and so on in front of major points to help in remembering how many major points you want to learn. Also, it is sometimes possible to avoid underlining too much by writing *Example* or *EX* in the margin next to important examples. Notice in Figure 14a that major points are numbered to make the effects of the Civil War on the South stand out clearly and that *Examples* is written in the margin next to examples.

Some students do not underline books because they fear they will not be able to sell them back to a bookstore. This is usually a foolish way to economize. Textbooks are expensive, but their cost is only a tiny fraction of the cost of tuition, food, housing, transportation, clothing, and other expenses of going to college. Underlining your books is an inexpensive way for you to make certain that you will learn the things you need to learn to do well in college.

14.2   Are definitions of terms given?

A primary purpose of the textbooks for many subjects is to explain the meanings of terminology. Psychology books explain the meanings of words used in psychology, physics books explain the meanings of words used in physics, and so on. Therefore, when you skim sections of a chapter and notice that they give the meanings of terms, read the sections to understand and underline the definitions. Many questions on college tests are about the meanings of terms or they cannot be answered correctly unless the meanings of terms are known.

Notice that the three terms in the heading for the following excerpt from an English textbook are printed in boldface type in the passage to guide you as you skim, read, and underline. Skim the passage and then use the following purpose to guide you as you read it: *What are the meanings of the terms* pretension, jargon, *and* cliché? Read the passage a second time to underline the definitions of the terms.

Pretension, Jargon, and Cliché

Pretension, jargon, and cliché are roadblocks to good communication.

When writers select words for the purpose of impressing readers rather than to express thoughts clearly, we say they use **pretension.** Some writers never use a familiar word when they can use an unfamiliar one; they write "inebriated" for drunk, "perambulate" for walk, and "interred" for buried.

Jargon is somewhat like pretension, but it differs in that its purpose seems to be for obscuring, or clouding, meaning. Also sometimes called *gobbledygook,* jargon is used when a military officer refers to bombs as "antipersonnel detonating devices," an economist calls poor financial policies "inoperative fiscal procedures," or a sociologist speaks of poor families as "familial entities of the lower economic strata."

A **cliché** is a phrase that has been used so many times it has become trite—worn out, tired. Phrases such as "blushing bride," "clear as day," and "quick as a flash" have all been heard so often that they are, undeniably, clichés. Clichés block communication because they give readers the impression that writers did not try hard enough to express thoughts in their own words.

You, of course, should avoid pretension, jargon, and cliché in your writing.

When it is suggested in this handbook that you underline a passage, an explanation will be given of how the passage might be underlined. These explanations are only suggestions; the best way to underline a passage is in the way that is most meaningful to you. For "Pretension, Jargon, and Cliché," the sentences in which the words *pretension, jargon,* and *cliché* are printed in boldface type should be underlined. Also, it is advisable to underline one example for each term. In the first paragraph, you might underline "they write 'inebriated' for drunk" as an example of pretension, or you might write *Example* or *EX* in the margin next to the examples.

14.3   Are categories, or types, identified?

Categories, or **types,** are divisions created to organize facts and concepts so that they may be more easily understood. For example, to study mental illness, psychologists divide the subject into two basic categories: neurosis and psychosis. Then these two categories of illness are broken down into various types. Some of the categories of psychotics are manic-depressives, schizophrenics, and paranoids.

English textbooks identify and discuss the various literary forms, merchandising textbooks explain types of pricing strategies, and biology textbooks classify types of plants and animals. Almost all textbooks identify categories for topics they discuss.

In many instances, categories are created by **analysis,** which is the act of dividing a fact or concept into its parts so that it may be better understood. Categorization does not require that items be placed in one category and one category only. Consequently, many of the classifications you will encounter in your college textbooks do not allow for clear-cut categorization— they may overlap. Read the following introduction to a two-page discussion from a sociology textbook.

Types of Crime

The major types of crime in the United States can be conveniently classified into five main categories, although there is inevitably considerable overlap among them: juvenile delinquency, crimes without victims, white-collar crime, organized crime, and crimes against property and persons.

The author states that there is considerable overlapping among five types of crime that he will discuss. For example, when juveniles commit crimes against property, juvenile delinquency and crimes against property overlap. The five categories or types of crime are discussed separately even though actual instances of crime often have the characteristics of two or more of the types.

When you skim a section of a chapter and notice that it identifies the types of things there are, read to understand the differences among them and underline them to have a permanent record of the important information about each type or category.

Notice that in the following passage some words are printed in italic type to assist you as you skim, read, and underline. Skim the passage and then use the following purpose to guide you as you read it: *What are the types of social mobility, and how are they different from one another?* Read the passage a second time to underline the important information about each type of social mobility.

Types of Social Mobility

Social mobility can take one of three forms. *Horizontal mobility* involves a change in an individual's lifetime from one status to another that is roughly equivalent, say, from that of a plumber to that of a carpenter. *Vertical mobility* may be either upward or downward. It involves a change within the lifetime of an individual to a higher or lower status than the person had to begin with. Movement from the status of plumber to that of corporation president, or vice versa, is an example of vertical mobility. The third form of social mobility is *intergenerational mobility*. This is a change in the status of family members from one generation to the next, as when a plumber's child becomes a corporation president or vice versa. Intergenerational mobility is the most important of the three forms, because the amount of this mobility in a society tells us to what extent inequalities are being passed on from one generation to the next. If there is very little intergenerational mobility, inequality is clearly deeply built into the society, for people's life chances are being determined at the moment of birth. If there is a good deal of intergenerational mobility, people are clearly able to achieve new statuses through their own efforts, regardless of the circumstances of their births.

There is a great deal of information packed into this short passage. The following sentences should be underlined: second, third, fourth, seventh, and eighth. Also, since the author states that *intergenerational mobility* is the most important type of mobility, you may have underlined other sentences at the end of the paragraph or written the word *Important* in the margin next to the place where this term is printed. You want to learn the things that you know are most important to learn. *Example* or *EX* may be written in the margin next to the examples for each type of social mobility, and it is logical to number the types of mobility *1, 2,* and *3* as a reminder that three types of mobility must be learned.

Textbook passages often explain more than one type of information. "Types of Social Mobility" (1) identifies the *types* of social mobility there are and (2) gives *definitions* for the terms that are used to name each type of mobility. The passage is offered as an example of information about categories, or types, because the title the author selected for the passage makes it clear that he believes this is the most important kind of information in the passage.

14.4   Is a method explained?

Methods are the procedures, processes, or ways of doing something. Some textbooks are devoted almost entirely to explaining the ways things are done. For example, textbooks for mathematics courses primarily explain how to solve various kinds of mathematical problems; textbooks for foreign language courses primarily teach how to speak and write a foreign language; and textbooks for speech courses explain how to prepare and give speeches.

Books for mathematics, foreign language, and speech courses explain methods that you are actually expected to use. Other books explain methods that you are not expected to use. For example, an introductory ecology textbook may explain the methods used by demographers to measure distributions of populations of humans on the earth, but it is not likely that you will be required to measure distributions of human populations for an introductory ecology course. You will be expected to know the methods demographers use, but not to use the methods yourself.

When you skim a section of a chapter, question whether it explains a method for doing something. If it does, read the passage to understand the method and underline the passage to make a permanent record of the parts of the method that you want to learn. The following passage explains a method for controlling weight. Skim the passage and then use the following purpose to guide you as you read it: *What method may be used to control weight?* Read the passage a second time to underline the important information about the method.

A Method for Controlling Weight

A precise measurement of your caloric intake is a prerequisite to a healthful, permanent weight-control program. A calorie is a basic unit of measurement that tells you how much energy you get from food. For every 3,500 calories you get that you do not use up, you gain approximately one pound. That pound is stored in the form of fat. You can lose that pound of fat by eating less (getting fewer calories), by increased activity, or by a combination of both. For example, if your present weight is maintained by 2,800 calories each day, you would have to cut back to 2,300 calories in order to lose one pound per week, unless you also increased physical activities.

One way to calculate your calorie needs is to first determine your desired weight. Then, if you're a relatively inactive person, you multiply that weight by twelve; twelve represents the number of calories you would need each day to maintain each pound of body weight. If you engage in a moderate amount of physical activity, you need approximately fifteen calories to maintain that pound, and if you are heavily involved in daily physical activity (loading trucks, running ten miles, playing four sets of advanced tennis), you would need eighteen or more calories per pound of body weight.* Thus, if your desired weight is 160 pounds and you engage in a moderate amount of physical activity, you multiply 160 by 15, which tells you that you need 2,400 calories per day to maintain that weight.

Before you can identify what foods to eat to meet your caloric needs, you must first determine the caloric values for various foods. Food calorie charts are indispensable in choosing diet foods.

*T. Berland, "The Diet Connection," *Insider: Ford's Continuing Series of College Newspaper Supplements,* 13–30 Corporation (1977), 10–15.

The following should be underlined: In the first paragraph, the third and fifth sentences; in the second paragraph, the first, second, and third sentences, but not the information enclosed in parentheses; in the third paragraph, the first sentence or the second sentence may be underlined. *Example* or *EX* may be written in the margin next to the examples at the ends of the first and second paragraphs.

When you read about a method, it is essential to verify that you understand how the method is used. If you understand the method for controlling weight, you can answer the following questions:

1. Assuming that you do not exercise any more than you are exercising right now, how many fewer calories must you consume each week to lose weight at the rate of two pounds each week?

2. Assuming that you are moderately active, how many calories do you need to consume daily to maintain your ideal weight?

The answer to the first question is 7,000 calories. One pound is lost by consuming 3,500 fewer calories than are needed to maintain present body weight, and two pounds are lost by consuming twice that many fewer calories ($2 \times 3,500 = 7,000$). The answer to the second question is found by multiplying your ideal weight by 15. If a moderately active person's ideal weight is 150 pounds, this weight may be maintained by consuming 2,250 calories daily ($15 \times 150 = 2,250$).

14.5   Is a sequence presented?

In addition to giving definitions, identifying categories, and explaining methods, textbooks also often present information about sequences. A **sequence** is the order in which things follow each other in time, space, rank, complexity, or some other dimension. Following are descriptions of the types of sequences that are most often explained in college textbooks.

1. *Chronological order* is used to recount events in the order in which they happened in time. While studying American history, you might learn the chronological order in which our presidents were in office or the chronological order in which our country fought its major wars. This type of sequence is also sometimes called *temporal order, sequential order,* or *time order;* these three terms have the same meaning as *chronological order.*

2. *Spacial sequences* are used to explain the position of places on earth and in outer space. When you know the order of the planets in space, for example, you know that a rocket flying away from Earth must pass the orbits of Mars and Jupiter before reaching Saturn.

3. *Hierarchical order* is used to sequence items by rank or complexity. In biology, forms of life are organized in a hierar-

chical sequence, beginning with the least complex and advancing to the most complex forms. In this arrangement of animal life, the one-celled protozoa are at the bottom, and apes are very near the top of the hierarchy.

4. *Logical sequences* are used to present information or facts in a rational progression. For example, this handbook suggests that skimming, reading, underlining, and note-taking should be done in this sequence—no other sequence is as logical. It is not reasonable to underline a passage before it has been read, and it is much more appropriate to skim a passage immediately before reading it than immediately after reading it.

When you skim a section of a chapter, question whether it presents a sequence. If it does, read the passage to understand the sequence and underline the passage to make a permanent record of the sequence that you want to learn.

The heading for the following passage indicates that it explains a hierarchical sequence. Notice that an introductory paragraph and subheadings in the selection are included to assist you as you skim, read, and underline. Skim the passage and then use the following purpose to guide you as you read it: *What is the sequence in which human needs are satisfied?* Read the passage a second time to underline the important information about each need in the sequence.

Maslow's Hierarchy of Human Needs

In 1943 a psychologist by the name of Abraham Maslow proposed that people are motivated by a five-step hierarchy of needs.* . . . Maslow's message was simply this: people are constantly in need; when one need is relatively fulfilled, another emerges to take its place. He identified physiological needs, safety needs, love needs, esteem needs, and self-actualization needs and arranged them in a fixed *hierarchy of needs.* . . . According to Maslow, most individuals are not consciously aware of these needs. Nevertheless, we all proceed up the hierarchy of needs, one level at a time.

Physiological needs At the very base of the need hierarchy are physical drives. These include the need for food, water, sleep, and sex. Fulfillment of these lowest-level needs enables individuals to survive. Nothing else is important when these bodily needs cry out for fulfillment. However, the average, fairly well-adjusted individual experiences little serious deprivation of physiological needs. As Maslow has observed, "It is quite true that man lives by bread alone—when there is no bread."† But when we have plenty of bread to eat, the prospect of eating more bread is no longer a source of motivation. Other things become important.

Safety needs The next step in Maslow's need hierarchy is the area of safety needs. Once the basic physiological needs are satisfied, we want to assure our safety from the elements, enemies, and other threats. The average employee achieves a high degree of fulfillment in this area by earning a living and paying taxes. According to Maslow, prolonged deprivation of physiological and safety needs will create a seriously maladjusted individual.

Love needs A physiologically satisfied and secure person focuses next on satisfying needs for love and affection. This category of needs is a powerful motivator of human behavior. People work hard to achieve a sense of belonging with others. As with the first two levels of needs, however, relative satisfaction of love needs paves the way for the emergence of the next higher level.

Esteem needs People who view themselves as worthwhile individuals are said to possess high self-esteem. Self-respect is the key to esteem needs. Much of our self-respect and hence esteem comes from being accepted and respected by others. It is important for those who are expected to help achieve organizational objectives to have their esteem needs relatively well fulfilled. But, according to Maslow's theory, esteem needs cannot emerge if lower-level needs go unattended.

Self-actualization needs At the top of Maslow's hierarchy resides an open-ended category that he labeled self-actualization needs. It is open-ended because it relates to the need "to become more and more what one is, to become everything that one is capable of becoming."‡ One may self-actualize by striving to become the best homemaker, the best plumber, the best rock singer, or the best manager.

*See: A. H. Maslow, "A Theory of Human Motivation," *Psychological Review* 50 (July 1943), 370–396.
†Ibid., p. 375.
‡Ibid., p. 382.

The subheadings help in following the guideline "Don't underline too much." In the first paragraph, the second and third sentences should be underlined. In other paragraphs the following sentences should be underlined: "Physiological needs," second and fourth; "Safety needs," second and third; "Love needs," first; "Esteem needs," second, third, and last; and "Self-actualization needs," second and third.

"Maslow's Hierarchy of Human Needs" gives three types of information: (1) information about a *sequence,* (2) information about the *types* of needs there are, and (3) *definitions* of the terms that identify the needs.

Information about sequences is also sometimes combined with information about methods—the steps in methods are often most efficiently done in a specified sequence. For example, in Section 13.6 it is suggested that the method for interpreting information in bar graphs, line graphs, and tables should be done in a specific sequence: (1) understand the heading, (2) understand the labels, (3) compare the information, and (4) decide what information is most important. Whenever you read or learn about a method, pay attention to the sequential order in which the steps for the method are most efficiently done to achieve the purpose for which the method is used.

14.6   Are causes, or reasons, given?

Causes, or **reasons,** are explanations that help us understand why things are as they are. Reasons may be given as answers to questions that begin with the words *how* or *why.*

How did we become involved in World War II?

Why do some people become criminals?

The answers to these questions require reasons; they require statements of the circumstances that caused us to become involved in World War II and that cause some people to become criminals.

There are two basic types of reasons: facts and theories. *Facts* are things that actually happened and that are really true. The question "How did we become involved in World War II?" can be answered by stating facts—actual occurrences that caused us to fight in the war. Many times, though, explanations are provided by *theories,* which are possible but not certain explanations. For example, we cannot be certain why some people become criminals, but sociologists have formulated theories to try to understand and explain antisocial behavior.

Add causes, or reasons, to the types of information to look for as you skim, read, and underline your books: (1) definitions; (2) categories, or types; (3) methods; (4) sequences; and (5) causes, or reasons.

The following passage explains the reasons for rapid population growth in developing countries. Skim the passage and then use the following purpose to guide you as you read it: *Why are the populations of developing countries growing rapidly?* Read the passage a second time to underline the causes of population growth.

The Causes of Rapid Population Growth

Why is population increasing at such a speed in the developing nations? The main reason is the change in the ratio of births to deaths. The death rate in these societies has been sharply reduced by the introduction of modern medical techniques, but the birth rate has remained extremely high. In the early industrial societies medical techniques were improved in a slow process extending over many decades, and there was time for cultural values about family size to adjust to the changed material conditions. In the newly developing nations, however, medical knowledge has been introduced with dramatic suddenness, causing a sharp drop in death rates while the birth rates remain at or near their previous levels. Thus Algeria has a birth rate of 49 and a death rate of 15, Mexico a birth rate of 46 and a death rate of 8. As a result, the overall rate of population increase in the developing countries exceeds 2 percent—a rate sufficient to double their populations no less than ten times in 116 years.

A complicating factor is that the developing nations, unlike the early industrial societies, are facing rapid population growth at a time when they already have very large populations. The high rate of growth, operating on this large population base, therefore produces a much greater increase in absolute numbers of people than the comparable population expansions that took place in Europe and the United States in earlier years.

Why have cultural values that emphasize the desirability of large families been so slow to change? The reason is that technological innovations, such as modern medical techniques, have an obvious utility and tend to be rapidly accepted into a society. Cultural values, however, are much more conservative and tend to change only slowly. In many traditional societies a man's virility is gauged by the number of children he fathers, and most traditional societies emphasize the domestic role of the wife as mother and child rearer. These cultural patterns are not easily changed. A large family was always an asset in a rural economy in the past, and people in a tradition-bound society may have difficulty in appreciating that this situation has changed within the course of a few decades. Even today a large family may serve important functions for parents in developing societies. In countries that lack a system of social security, children provide the only guarantee that one will be looked after in old age.

Many religions, too, emphasize some version of the Judeo-Christian injunction to "be fruitful and multiply." An old

Arab proverb declares that "to have many children is to be blessed by Allah," and Islamic religion in several countries is opposed to birth control. The Catholic Church, which is particularly influential in the overpopulated continent of South America, has always opposed the use of contraceptives. To complicate matters further, many people regard high birth rates as essential for their economic or political strength. Argentina banned the use of contraceptives in 1974 as part of a planned campaign to double its population as soon as possible, in the supposed interests of economic development. In the wretchedly poor country of Bangladesh, once described by Henry Kissinger as "an international basket case," the first minister of family planning was the father of eighteen children. He was opposed to birth control in principle and his first act was to curtail family-planning programs. Bangladesh, he felt, can be politically secure only if it has as many people as its neighbor, China. Similar arguments about the political desirability of a population increase are heard all over the world—for example, among some Israelis, some white South Africans, and some black Americans. Some black radicals in the United States have maintained that American family-planning programs are directed mainly at blacks, who have a higher average birth rate than whites, and are really a form of genocide. Throughout history, in short, large families and growing nations have been considered a fundamentally good thing. This value has deeply pervaded culture and institutional arrangements, and it is not easily or rapidly changed.

In the first paragraph, the third sentence should be underlined; in the second paragraph, the first sentence; in the third paragraph, the third and fourth sentences; and in the fourth paragraph, the first sentence. *Example* or *EX* may be written next to the examples in the last paragraph. It would be good to number the reasons for population growth *1, 2, 3* and *4* to aid in remembering how many reasons there are for this phenomenon.

14.7   Are effects, or results, identified?

Effects, or **results,** are the consequences of actions, events, or circumstances. For example, some of the effects, or results, of the energy shortage have been higher prices for airline tickets, shorter automobile trips during vacation periods, and lower temperatures in homes and public buildings during winter months. One of the effects, or results, of using good reading and study procedures is that more can be learned in less time.

The following passage discusses the effects on young people of maturing earlier or later than their peers. Skim the passage and then use the following purpose to guide you as you read it: *What are the effects on young people of maturing at earlier or later ages than others?* Read the passage a second time to underline the effects.

Effects of Early and Late Maturing

Individual differences in the age of reaching puberty and the resulting differences in physical size and appearance play important roles in physical and social adjustment as well as in behavior generally, and these differences persist to some degree into the adult years. Several studies* have shown that boys who reach physical maturity early are usually accepted and treated by adults and their peers as more mature and do not need to strive for status. It was found that high school student leaders were usually those who had achieved physical maturity at a comparatively early age. In contrast, the physically late-maturing boys showed many forms of immature behavior, which may have been due in part to the tendency of others to treat them as the little boys they appeared to be and in part to their own feelings of inadequacy and inferiority. The late maturers also seemed to need to counteract their physical disadvantage by greater activity and striving for attention. They were more likely than the early maturers to be personally and socially maladjusted. When the subjects were followed up at about age 33, it was found that the adolescent handicaps and advantages associated with early or late maturing carried over into adulthood to some extent, particularly affecting psychological traits.†

Girls have similar problems. A late maturer may become anxious and shy because all her friends are wearing bras while she is still wearing undershirts. On the other hand, an early-maturing girl may have serious problems too. She may feel embarrassed and self-conscious. Because she feels that everyone is staring at her, many a young girl has developed poor posture in trying to hide her fully developed breasts. Also she may feel pressured to date before she is ready. Both male and female early maturers are usually expected by adults to act independent and grown up because they look older than they are.‡

*P. H. Mussen and M. C. Jones, "Self-conceptions, Motivations, and Interpersonal Attitudes of Late- and Early-maturing Boys," *Child Development,* 28, (1957) 243–256.

†M. D. Jones, "The Later Career of Boys Who Were Early- or Late-maturing," *Child Development,* 28, (1957) 113–128.

‡J. M. Tanner, "Physical Growth," in *Carmichael's Manual of Child Psychology,* ed. P. H. Mussen, Vol. I (New York: Wiley, 1970).

In the first paragraph, the second and fourth sentences should be underlined; you may underline other sentences also, but not too many. In the second paragraph, the second, third, and fourth sentences should be underlined, and, perhaps, the last sentence.

14.8   Are comparisons or contrasts made?

Comparisons are explanations of similarities or differences, and **contrasts** are comparisons that emphasize differences. Comparisons and contrasts are made *between* two persons, places, or things and *among* three or more persons, places, or things. The following passage compares mature love with romantic love, stating the differences between them. Skim the passage and then use the following purpose to guide you as you read it: *How is mature love different from romantic love?* Read the passage a second time to underline the comparisons between mature and romantic love.

Mature Love and Romantic Love

Romantic love is based on a sense of need or lack of completeness so that an individual desperately seeks the one perfect person who will give the love that will fill that need. In contrast, mature love proceeds, not from need, but from a sense of wholeness and a self-acceptance. Mature love honestly respects the total individuality of each person, including fears and faults as well as joys and strengths. Because mature love is based on acceptance of a total person rather than unrealistic idealization, it can increase with continuing intimacy.

A romantic lover wants to possess the loved one completely. In mature love there is no idea of possession. Each person allows the other complete freedom to grow and develop her or his potential to the fullest, even when this means they have less time to spend together. Mature lovers know that time together can be more enjoyable when each person has more interests and joy of life to bring to the relationship.

When romantic lovers are apart they may suffer real pain or "withdrawal" symptoms, because, without the other person each is incomplete. In contrast, mature lovers feel complete whether alone, together, or in the company of others.

Romantic lovers expect to feel love and passion only for each other. But mature love is a part of the love one feels for all persons. It is not expected to be exclusive. There may be a commitment that the sexual relationship will be reserved for the two partners, but loving feelings will be shared with all others.

Within a relationship based on mature love, sexual expression can reach its greatest potential. In these relationships, sex is a means of physically expressing the high degree of caring, acceptance, and intimacy of both the physical aspects and the feeling aspects of the relationship. In this setting it can reach its most complete and joyous expression.

Many relationships between couples who love each other involve elements both of romantic love and mature love. Often the earlier stages of a relationship involve many aspects of romantic love. Later stages will involve more elements of mature love, if the relationship continues beyond the early period of idealization.

In the first paragraph, you should have underlined the last sentence; in the second paragraph, the first and second sentences; in the third paragraph, both sentences; in the fourth paragraph, the first and second sentences; in the fifth paragraph, the first sentence; and in the sixth paragraph, the first sentence.

Comparisons tend to emphasize differences, or contrasts. The following passage explains differences between the upper-middle class and the lower-middle class, but it also includes important similarities. Notice that words are printed in italic type to assist you as you skim, read, and underline the passage. Skim the selection and then use the following purpose to guide you as you read it: *What are the similarities and differences between the upper-middle and lower-middle classes?* Read the passage a second time to underline the similarities and differences.

The Middle Class

The *middle class* lacks the cohesion of the upper class but has a distinctive life-style that distinguishes it from the upper and lower classes. In fact, the values of the middle class form the dominant morality of the United States. Middle-class attitudes and tastes are respected and endorsed by politicians, media, advertisers, and schools. This class also contains two fairly distinct elements.

The *upper-middle class* consists primarily of high-income business and professional families. Like the upper class, this group contains a disproportionate number of people from white, Protestant, Anglo-Saxon backgrounds. Members of the upper-middle class are highly "respectable," but they are not "society." They tend to live in comfortable suburban homes, to enjoy a stable family life, and to have a high sense of civic duty. They are very active in political life and dominate community organizations. They are concerned with personal career advancement and have very high aspirations for their children, who receive a college education as a matter of course.

The *lower-middle class* share most of the values of the upper-middle class, but they lack the educational or economic advantages that would let them enjoy the same lifestyle. This class consists of people whose diverse jobs do not involve manual labor. It includes small-business operators and sales representatives, teachers and nurses, police officers, and middle-management personnel. The lower-middle class is very concerned about respectability and "proper" behavior, about decency and the value of hard work. Members of this class, who usually must work hard to achieve and retain what they have, are often politically and economically conservative.

In the first paragraph the second and third sentences should be underlined; in the second paragraph, the first sentence; and in the third paragraph, the first sentence. The second and third paragraphs include so much information that there is a temptation to underline most of the sentences in them. However, to do so would violate the guideline "Don't underline too much." There are two possible solutions to the problem. The words *Important details* may be written in the margins next to the paragraphs so that the details will not be overlooked when making notes, or key words in the paragraphs may be underlined. For example, in the second paragraph "white, Protestant, Anglo-Saxon," "high aspirations for their children," and similar phrases may be underlined. Appropriate phrases of this type to underline in the third paragraph include "very concerned about respectability" and "economically conservative."

Information about comparisons is often combined with other types of information. The selection in Section 14.7, "Effects of Early and Late Maturing," gives effects and *compares* the effects for those who mature early with the effects for those who mature late. "The Middle Class" combines comparisons with explanations of two *categories* within the middle class: upper-middle class and lower middle-class.

14.9   How will this help me study?

When you analyze the types of information in your books, you are likely to find what is most important to understand and learn. For example, if a writer's purpose is to explain a sequence and you understand the sequence, you understand exactly what the writer intended you to understand. If you then underline and learn the steps in the sequence, you prepare yourself to answer the most logical questions that can be asked about the information.

If you can give good answers to the following questions about textbook passages in this chapter, it is likely that you can also give or select correct answers to multiple-choice, true-false, or any other type of questions that are asked about the passages.

1. *Define* the following words: pretension, jargon, and cliché.
2. Identify three *types* of social mobility and explain which type is most important.
3. Explain a *method* for planning a weight control program.
4. In correct *sequence*, discuss Maslow's hierarchy of human needs.
5. What are the *causes* of rapid population growth in developing nations?
6. What are the *effects* on young people of maturing earlier or later than others?
7. *Compare* mature love with romantic love.

When you skim, read, and underline using purposes of the kinds that are explained in this chapter, you prepare yourself to study in ways that will help you write or select the correct answers to test and examination questions.

Use What You've Learned

1. Use the methods that are explained in this chapter to read and underline the information that you want to learn in the books you are studying for your college courses.

2. Prepare a list of ten terms that are defined in a chapter of one of your textbooks.

3. Find one example of each of the following types of information in books you are studying for your courses: categories, or types; methods; sequences; causes, or reasons; effects, or results; comparisons or contrasts.

Decide What You Want to Study

Few people have the ability to learn everything on every page of five, six, or more books during the few weeks of a college term. Therefore, the fourth step in preparing for examinations is to decide what will be learned from among all the many things that could be learned.

1. Preview chapters.
2. Skim sections of chapters.
3. Read and underline with a purpose.
4. **Decide what you want to study.**
5. Make notes for studying.
6. Recite information you want to learn.

This chapter explains how to make wise decisions about what you should study and it offers some suggestions about the specific types of information that you should give special attention to when you read and study your textbooks.

15.1 Use your class notes as a guide

Most college teachers use class time to help students understand the things that are important for them to learn. As a result, the notes you take during class lectures and discussions will usually be your best source of information about what you should decide to study.

Information also in books. When there is information in class notes about topics that are also discussed in a course textbook, it is very likely that you will be asked test questions about the information. Compare class notes to your books and mark topics discussed in both of them for special attention while studying. Underline or highlight the information in your notes, and draw a star or some other symbol in the margins of your book where the information is discussed.

When students highlight their books, they sometimes mark this type of information with a special color of highlight ink. If they use yellow highlight ink when they mark books, they use pink, blue, or some other color of highlight ink to mark key terms and phrases for information in their books that is also included in class notes. This emphasizes in their books what they will definitely not overlook when they study.

Information not also in books.   Teachers often lecture on topics that are not discussed in required course reading materials or they give additional information about topics that are discussed in books. Few teachers spend class time discussing topics that they believe are unimportant or giving additional information about topics if they believe the information is irrelevant. You will find that half or more of the questions on some teachers' tests are based directly on information given in class but that is not discussed in required reading. Therefore, mark this type of information for special attention when you study.

Things written on chalkboards.   All your teachers have been students, and as students they learned that the information their teachers wrote on chalkboards was very often used as the basis for test questions. Many of your teachers assume that you have also figured out that you should copy and learn anything written on a board; many of them believe that they are announcing a test question to you whenever they write on a chalkboard.

Therefore, devise a method for marking information you copy into notes from a board so that it will stand out in your notes and not be overlooked when you study. You might draw a star or write *Important* (or *Impt.*) in the margin next to the information, or you might underline it. When you review your notes after class, you may wish to highlight the information for additional emphasis.

Always copy into your notes and mark for special attention anything that is written on a board unless a teacher gives you a very good reason why you should not. For example, if a teacher draws something on a board and says, "I will *definitely not* ask any question about this drawing on a test," then you probably do not need to copy and study the drawing. However, if a teacher writes something on a board and makes statements such as "I *probably* won't ask a question about this" or "I *don't think* I'll ask a question about this," definitely copy and study the information. College teachers seldom write things on boards unless they are important to learn, and when they prepare tests, they sometimes forget they said they "probably won't" or "don't think they will" ask questions about it. Decide you will learn everything that is written on a chalkboard unless you have a very good reason not to learn it.

Statements about what to study. Some of your teachers will make statements in class to inform you what is especially important for you to study. Following are examples of the types of things they might say:

Now this is very important.

I'm certain I'll ask a question about this.

You must be able to solve these kinds of problems.

Be sure to learn this well.

This confuses many students—don't let it confuse you.

The sequence is very important here.

Whenever teachers make statements such as these about information you put in notes, mark the information for special attention in the same way you mark things you copy from a chalkboard.

Some teachers give less guidance than others in making it clear to students what they should study. However, if you observe your teachers carefully, you will find that almost all of them give at least subtle clues about what is important to learn. Also, teachers are often helpful when students ask for their advice about what to study. When you are uncertain what you should learn for courses, make appointments with your teachers and ask them to give you suggestions about how you should focus your study. You may not always get the help you need, but you will find that many teachers will be helpful to you when you ask them for their advice.

Also, some instructors give review sessions to help students prepare for tests. During these sessions they may suggest topics that you should study or they may give lists of questions that you should prepare to answer. Always attend the review sessions your teachers give even if they are not given during regular class hours. If you learn everything that a teacher suggests you should learn during a review session, you will probably be at an advantage when you take the test. Many students do poorly on tests because they do not follow their teachers' advice about what they should study.

Unfortunately, teachers often give very general suggestions such as, "The test will cover everything in Chapter 7 through Chapter 13." If you receive this advice, your only alternative is to learn as much information in Chapter 7 through Chapter 13 as you can.

15.2   Confer with your teachers' former students

If at all possible, ask former students of your teachers how to study for your teachers' tests. Teachers' testing methods seldom change much from year to year and, as a result, students who studied with your teachers in the past have probably answered test questions very much like the ones you will answer. Students who received good grades for the courses you are taking know things that may be very useful to you, and they may be eager to explain to you the methods that they used to earn good grades.

Twenty and thirty years ago books such as this one were not available to most students. In those days students taught each other how to study. If you have friends who are good students, they know a great deal about studying that they may be willing to share with you.

15.3   Examine tests your teachers have given

Some teachers give students tests to keep. Also, at some colleges and universities samples of tests teachers gave in the past are available for students to examine in departmental offices or in some other office. Ask former students of your teachers if they have copies of tests you may examine; or if your teachers' tests are on file in an office for you to examine, go to the office and study them.

Teachers usually have very definite opinions about the types of questions that should be asked on tests; when you examine the types of questions your teachers asked on tests in the past, you learn what types of questions they will probably ask on tests that they give in the future. For example, by examining tests you may learn whether a teacher's questions are based mostly on information in required course reading materials or on information given in lectures. You may also learn whether questions require you to study many little facts or to acquire a broad understanding of major topics. If a teacher tested mostly on minute details in a textbook last year or the year before, chances are that he or she will ask questions about the same kind of information on tests this year.

15.4   Study information you think you know

One of the biggest mistakes students make when they prepare for tests is that they fail to study information that is easy for them to understand. They believe that if they understand something, they know it. But the difference between understanding and knowing is the difference between reading and studying; information is read so it can be understood and it is studied so it can be remembered and recalled.

You have no doubt understood everything that you have read

in this handbook; this book was written so that it would be easy for you to understand. But chances are that you do not *know* most of the information in this book unless you have studied it. For example, in Section 5.1 you should have had no difficulty understanding the seven characteristics of well-organized lecture notes, but chances are that you do not know the characteristics. Without looking back at Section 5.1, list the seven characteristics of well-organized lecture notes on the following lines.

1. _____

2. _____

3. _____

4. _____

5. _____

6. _____

7. _____

Unless you have studied Section 5.1, or looked back at it, you were probably not able to list all seven characteristics of lecture notes correctly.

When you prepare for tests, decide you will study information in your notes and textbooks even though it is easy for you to understand. It is extremely discouraging to lose points on tests by failing to learn information that could have been learned easily.

15.5   Decide what you will not study

The most efficient students are the ones who have a knack for deciding what they *should* and *should not* study. For example, in most mathematics courses students are expected to learn how to solve mathematical problems of specific types, but some math textbooks contain technical information that is not directly related to explaining how to solve mathematical problems. In instances such as these, students must sometimes learn to read the textbook by skipping over the information that is not directly related to helping them understand how to solve mathematical problems.

One of my students studied a textbook for a statistics course that included an algebraic proof for each statistical formula. He felt completely lost in the course because although he was able to compute all the statistical problems correctly, he could not understand the algebraic proofs for the formulas. I advised him to ask his teacher whether he was required to learn the algebraic proofs, and she assured him that he was not. This news was a great comfort to him; it put his mind to rest, and he did very well in his statistics course.

The suggestions in Chapter 14 will often help you decide what you should not learn in a textbook. The following paragraph from a sociology textbook contains many interesting facts that students would not study if they use the methods that are described in Chapter 14.

Cultural Variation

The set of norms and values that exist in the United States is unique to our society. The same is true of the culture of every other society. Each culture is distinctive and contains elements, or combinations of elements, found nowhere else. Americans eat oysters but not snails. The French eat snails but not locusts. The Zulus eat locusts but not fish. The Jews eat fish but not pork. The Hindus eat pork but not beef. The Russians eat beef but not snakes. The Chinese eat snakes but not people. The Jalé of New Guinea find people delicious. We spend our lives accumulating private possessions; the BaMbuti of the Congo forests spend their lives sharing their goods; the Kwakiutl of the Pacific Northwest periodically gave them away or even destroyed them at great ceremonies. Our norms have traditionally valued premarital chastity; the norms of the Mentawei of Indonesia require women to become pregnant before they can be considered eligible for marriage; the norms of the Keraki of New Guinea require premarital homosexuality in every male. Women in traditional Arab societies must cover the entire body and even the face; American women may expose their faces but must keep their breasts and the entire pelvic region concealed; women in many parts of Africa may expose their breasts and buttocks but not the genital region; women in Tierra del Fuego may not expose their backs; and Tasaday women in the Philippines proceed about their daily lives stark naked. The range of cultural variation is so immense that there is probably no specific norm that appears in every human society. How can we account for this variation?

This paragraph is an introduction to a six-page explanation of five *methods* sociologists and anthropologists use to study cultural variation. Those who use the suggestions in Chapter 14 when they skim, read, and underline the passage would decide to underline and study the explanations of the five methods. They would apprehend that the introductory paragraph serves the function of interesting them in the topic of cultural variation and, as a result, they would spend no time learning what foods are preferred by various cultures or what parts of the body may and may not be exposed in various cultures.

By focusing your study to learn the types of information explained in Chapter 14, you will often be able to decide easily what information in a section of a chapter you will study.

15.6   Study everything for the first test

When I was a college freshman, a sophomore gave me the following advice that served me well through many years as an undergraduate and graduate student in college: *"Learn absolutely everything for the first test a teacher gives and when the test is returned to you study it carefully to understand how you should prepare to take all of the teacher's other tests."* There are at least three reasons that this is good advice:

1. When you study absolutely everything for the first tests each term, you will earn the best grades you can on the tests.
2. When you earn the best grades you can on the first tests, you are not likely to settle for lower grades on other tests.
3. When you study hard at the beginning of a term, you are less likely to fall behind in course work.

Throughout my career as a student and teacher I have observed the unnecessary unhappiness students cause themselves by not studying thoroughly for the first tests in their courses. They earn grades that are lower than they should earn and this causes them to become discouraged and give up or to become frantic about how hard they must work to end the term with grades that are acceptable to them. Either way, they are behind in their course work; being behind, they are uneasy; being uneasy, they do not enjoy school.

Don't let yourself become discouraged or frantic. If you follow the suggestion that my friend gave me when I was a college freshman, you will be less harried when you study, you will know that you are doing the best you can on tests, and you are likely to find greater enjoyment in studying.

Use What You've Learned

1. Use the suggestions in Section 15.1 to prepare for tests in your courses. When a teacher returns a test to you, use the following questions to analyze how you should study for future tests that the teacher will give:

a. What proportion of questions are based on information that is in class notes and also in required reading material?

b. What proportion of questions are based on information that is in required reading material but *not* in class notes?

c. What proportion of questions are based on information that is in class notes but *not* in required reading material.

d. What proportion of questions are based on things the teacher wrote on a chalkboard?

e. What proportion of questions are based on topics the teacher stated you should give special attention to when studying for the test?

2. For each course you are taking, give the name of at least one student who took the same course with your teacher some time in the recent past. Did you ask these people for suggestions on how you should prepare for your teachers' tests? Were they helpful to you?

3. If it was possible for you to examine tests that your teachers gave in the past, was this helpful to you when you studied for their tests?

4. Using the method that is described in Section 15.5, select five paragraphs in a chapter of a textbook you are studying that explain information you have decided you will not study.

16 Make Notes for Studying

The fifth step in preparing for tests and examinations is to make notes for the information that you want to learn.

1. Preview before you read.
2. Skim sections of chapters.
3. Read and underline with a purpose.
4. Decide what you want to study.
5. **Make notes for studying.**
6. Recite information you want to learn.

Notes make it possible to learn the most in the least time. If you have not already done so, preview this chapter by reading the headings and examining the figures that illustrate the types of notes that can be used for studying.

16.1   The importance of notes

If you do not have the habit of making notes for information in your books, you may believe that this is a time-consuming way to study. Also, you may wonder why you should rewrite information that is already written in books. There are three reasons it is important for you to make notes for the things you want to learn in your books.

1. *The simple act of writing information in notes will often help you learn it.* When you make notes, you process information in your mind to state ideas in your own words. In many

instances, you will learn information almost completely as you write it in notes.

2. *Written notes reduce the amount of information you need to learn.* When you make notes, you are forced to decide what you will and will not learn; the notes for a book do not include all the information in the book. Also, good notes condense information by summarizing it in fewer words than are used in books.

3. *Your notes are organized in ways that make it easier for you to learn information.* Textbooks are organized to make information understandable to most college students; they are not written with the intention that you will study directly from them. But the notes you make are organized to make it possible for you to learn information in ways that are most efficient and meaningful to you.

Good notes, studied using methods described in Chapter 17, will help you when you want to learn information thoroughly and quickly.

16.2   Notes on paper or cards

Notes for books may be written on notebook paper or on 3 x 5 index cards. Figure 16a and Figure 16b show notes written on paper and cards to study information about defense mechanisms for a psychology course.

The three cards in Figure 16b are from a series of seven cards that can be used to study the information about defense mechanisms. Notice that the first card in the series lists the six defense mechanisms about which information will be learned; the function of this card is to provide an overview of the entire discussion. Figure 16b does not show the four cards for *displacement, repression, sublimation,* and *identification,* which are also part of the series of seven cards.

The following suggestions will be helpful to you when you make notes on cards:

Figure 16a **Notes for a Psychology Course
Written on Notebook Paper.**

<u>Defense Mechanisms</u>

Learned reactions for dealing with painful, frustrating, or anxiety-producing problems.

<u>Rationalization</u> -- Giving reasonable reasons for unreasonable or unacceptable behavior to see oneself in a favorable light. (EX) Child with poor report card claims "The teacher doesn't like me."

<u>Reaction-Formation</u> -- Acting in a way that is the opposite of the way one unconsciously feels. (EX) A daughter takes excellent care of her sick mother but unconsciously hates her mother (although this thought would cause the daughter anxiety if she were aware of it).

<u>Displacement</u> -- Replacing the original object of a drive with a substitute object that is more acceptable to the ego. (EX) A man is angry at his boss (the original object) but shows anger toward his wife (substitute object).

<u>Repression</u> -- Unconsciously forgetting something. (EX) John forgets a dental appointment because he has to have painful treatment for his gums.

<u>Sublimation</u> -- Instinctual drives channeled into socially acceptable forms of behavior. (EX) Sexual impulses may be redirected toward creative achievement in art, literature, or music; aggressive impulses may be directed toward a military career.

<u>Identification</u> -- Unconsciously incorporating qualities of another person into one's personality to keep from acknowledging unacceptable thoughts or feelings of inadequacy. (EX) Bob copies mannerisms of a teacher he views as strong and masculine to cover up his own feelings of weakness.

1. *Write the topics of information on the blank sides of cards and number each card.* Notice in Figure 16b that *defense mechanisms, rationalization,* and *reaction formation* are written boldly on the blank sides of the cards and that the cards are numbered *17, 18,* and *19.* The three cards are from a set of forty-five cards prepared to study for a psychology test; the numbers make it possible to put the cards in correct order easily if they should become disorganized (see also Section 17.2). Since only topics and numbers are written on the blank sides of cards, they may be written boldly.

2. *Write the information to be learned about topics on the lined sides of cards, upside-down in relation to the information on the fronts of cards.* This procedure makes the cards easier to use, because the information on the back is in the proper position for reading when the cards are turned.

Also, if you want the red lines on index cards to be at the top when you flip cards over, the red lines must be at the bottom of cards when you write topics and numbers on their blank sides.

16.3   The advantages of cards

Most students make notes on paper rather than on cards. Paper is usually readily available, while cards usually are not. Also, the advantages of cards are not widely known among first-year college students.

1. *Cards increase the likelihood that information will be learned rather than read.* Examine Figure 16a to observe that it is difficult to read the names of defense mechanisms without also reading some of the explanations about them. On the other hand, when the name of a defense mechanism is read from a card of the type illustrated in Figure 16b, it is impossible to read any information about the defense mechanism until the card is turned over. This tends to ensure that information will be learned by trying to recall it (Chapter 17).

2. *Cards make it easy to separate information that has been*

Figure 16b Notes for a Psychology Course Written on 3 x 5 Index Cards.

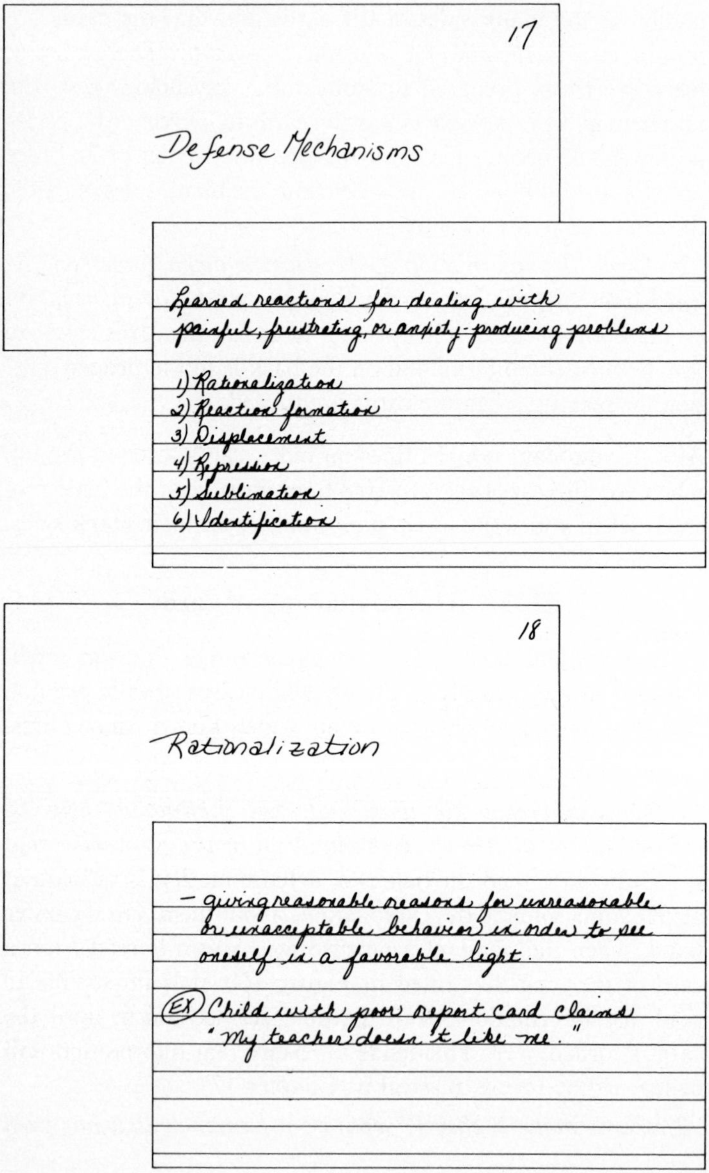

17

Defense Mechanisms

Learned reactions for dealing with
painful, frustrating, or anxiety-producing problems

1) Rationalization
2) Reaction formation
3) Displacement
4) Repression
5) Sublimation
6) Identification

18

Rationalization

- giving reasonable reasons for unreasonable
or unacceptable behavior in order to see
oneself in a favorable light.

EX) Child with poor report card claims
"My teacher doesn't like me."

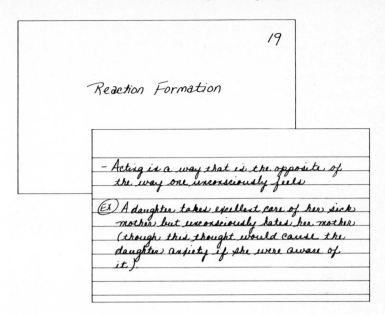

19

Reaction Formation

- Acting in a way that is the opposite of the way one unconsciously feels

(EX) A daughter takes excellent care of her sick mother but unconsciously hates her mother (though this thought would cause the daughter anxiety if she were aware of it.)

learned from information that has not been learned, so that as study progresses, it may be focused easily on learning the things that have not been learned.

3. *Cards make it possible to monitor how much progress is made while studying.* When you separate information you have learned from information you have not learned, you can see exactly how much more you must study. As the stack of cards containing information that you have learned grows thicker and thicker, you will be so encouraged that you will also learn the information on the cards remaining to be studied.

4. *Cards make it possible to integrate textbook notes with class notes easily.* When teachers give information in class that is related to information in books, the information in class notes may be written on the cards made for the books. In this way, all the information about a topic is in one place so it can be studied efficiently at the same time.

5. *Cards are convenient to study during short free periods when it may be difficult to study notes on paper.* Cards may be bound together with a rubber band and studied during spare moments between classes, while walking from one place to another, or while traveling on public transportation. If you travel by bus, for example, you can study from cards while traveling even if you must stand.

Even if you are not convinced that cards have definite advantages, make notes for at least one of your courses on cards. In that way, you will have the experience of using them, which is necessary in order for you to make a wise decision about whether notes on cards are more beneficial to you than notes on paper.

16.4   Guidelines for making notes

After underlining or highlighting a chapter of a book (Chapter 14) and deciding what information you will study in it (Chapter 15), use the following guidelines to write notes on paper or cards:

1. Write titles for notes that describe exactly what you want to learn.
2. List the information about topics in your notes in ways that will help you to learn it.
3. Include examples in your notes.

These three guidelines were used to prepare the notes in Figure 16c. Notice in Figure 16c that the textbook passage has the title "Schizophrenia" but that the notes have the title "Symptoms of Schizophrenia." The title for the notes is a more accurate description of what needs to be learned than is the title for the passage. Also, observe that the symptoms are listed and numbered in the notes so that it is more clear than in the passage that four symptoms must be learned. Finally, examples in the notes make it clear what is meant by each symptom. "May laugh if told his house was destroyed," for example, makes it clear what is meant by "Inappropriate emotional response."

Symptoms of Schizophrenia

1. Inappropriate emotional response. (EX) May laugh if told his house was destroyed
2. Withdrawal (EX) May not move for hours or days at a time. Loses interest.
3. Delusions - Beliefs contrary to reality (EX) Believes thoughts are controlled by God or the Devil
4. Hallucinations - Hearing or seeing things that aren't there. (EX) Voices or people.

Schizophrenia ①

Schizophrenia is the most common of the psychoses. *Inappropriateness of emotional response* is one of the symptoms of schizophrenia. This symptom is observed in the schizophrenic who is sad over what would make most people happy, and happy over what would make most people sad. For example, a schizophrenic man might laugh if told that his home had burned to the ground. A second symptom of schizophrenia is ② *withdrawal.* This is observed in schizophrenics who lose all interest in what is going on around them or assume one physical position for hours or days at a time.

Delusions and hallucinations are also symptoms of schizophrenia. ③ Delusions are beliefs in something that is contrary to fact or reality, such as the belief that one's thoughts are controlled by God or the Devil. ④ Hallucinations are the hearing or seeing of sights or sounds that are not actually present. A schizophrenic may hear voices or see people or objects that do not really exist.

16.5   Descriptive titles for notes

Headings in textbooks will often give you all the help you need to write descriptive titles for notes. The following headings for textbook selections in Chapter 14 may be used as descriptive titles for notes on the information in the selections.

Types of Social Mobility
Maslow's Hierarchy of Human Needs
The Causes of Rapid Population Growth
Effects of Early and Late Maturing

However, some textbook authors do not write titles as descriptive as these. Other writers might have used these headings for the passages:

Social Mobility
Human Needs
Population Growth
Early and Late Maturing

When headings for sections of chapters are not very descriptive of the information they explain, rewrite the titles to make them more descriptive. Following are examples of how a student rewrote headings in a business textbook to make more descriptive titles for her notes:

Heading in business textbook	Descriptive title for notes
News Media	Uses of News Media
Brand Names	Benefits of Brand Names
Small Business	Characteristics of Small Businesses
The Selling Process	Four Steps of the Selling Process
Pricing Strategies	Theories of Pricing Strategies
Oligopolies	Problems with Oligopolies
Buying Behavior	Influences on Buying Behavior

Figure 16d **Notes for Learning a Sequence.**

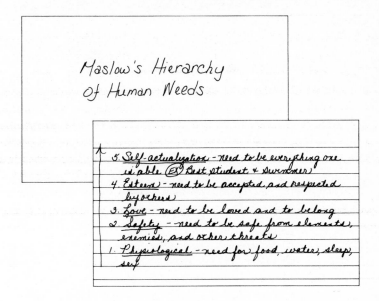

Use words such as *method, types, comparison, benefits, characteristics,* and *sequence* to write descriptive titles for your notes. Descriptive titles will help you remember information correctly and recall it accurately.

16.6   Well-organized information

List information in notes so it will be easy for you to learn. In Section 14.5 there is a textbook passage entitled "Maslow's Hierarchy of Human Needs," which identifies the needs in the following hierarchical sequence: (1) physiological, (2) safety, (3) love, (4) esteem, and (5) self-actualization. Notice, however, that the notes in Figure 16d arrange the needs in the opposite sequence and that an arrow is drawn on the notes to indicate the sequence in which the hierarchy progresses. The notes in Figure 16d emphasize what is very important to learn—the

Figure 16e **Notes for Learning a Comparison.**

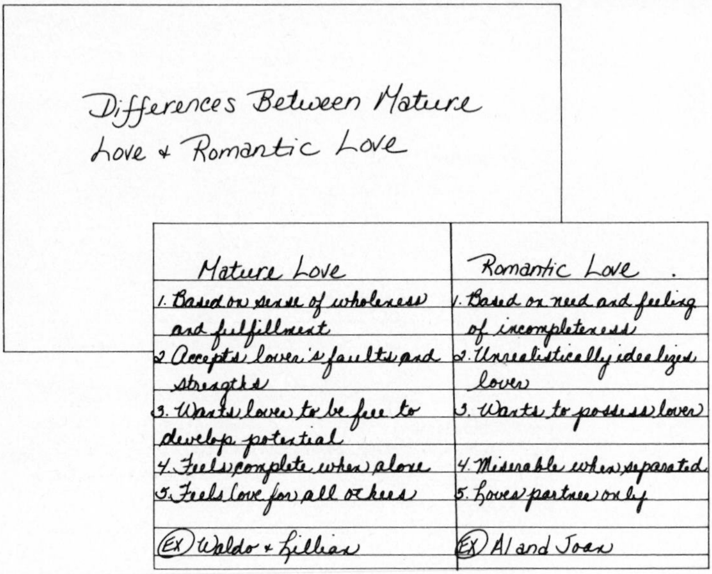

Differences Between Mature
Love & Romantic Love

Mature Love	Romantic Love
1. Based on sense of wholeness and fulfillment	1. Based on need and feeling of incompleteness
2. Accepts lover's faults and strengths	2. Unrealistically idealizes lover
3. Wants lover to be free to develop potential	3. Wants to possess lover
4. Feels complete when alone	4. Miserable when separated
5. Feels love for all others	5. Loves partner only
(Ex) Waldo & Lillian	(Ex) Al and Joan

hierarchical sequence progressing from the lowest level of need to the highest level of need.

Figure 16e shows notes for the passage entitled "Mature Love and Romantic Love," which is in Section 14.8. Notice that the title for the notes and the way in which the information is arranged on the back of the card emphasize the theme of differences between mature love and romantic love that are given in the passage.

Finally, Figure 16f illustrates notes for learning a mathematical formula. You may make notes to learn any type of information that you need to learn for your college course.

16.7 Examples in notes

Examples are included in notes because they aid in understanding the meanings of terms and the explanations of con-

Figure 16f **Notes for Learning a Mathematical Formula.**

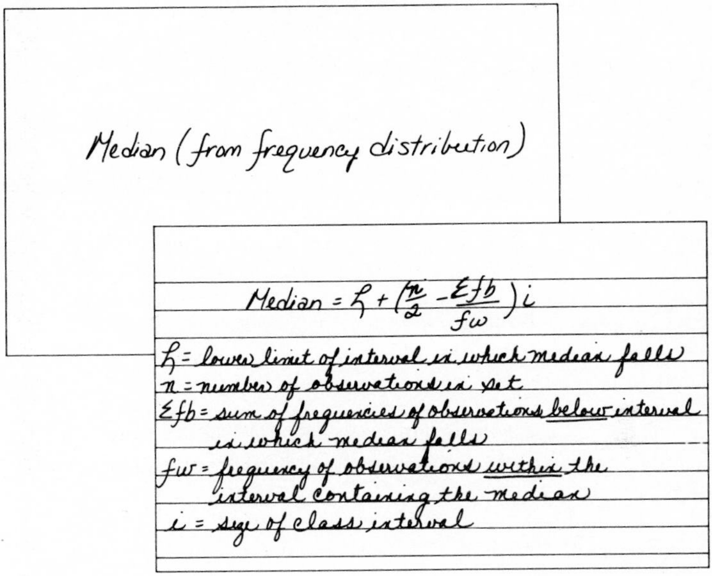

Median (from frequency distribution)

$$Median = \ell + \left(\frac{n}{2} - \frac{\Sigma fb}{fw}\right)i$$

ℓ = lower limit of interval in which median falls
n = number of observations in set
Σfb = sum of frequencies of observations <u>below</u> interval in which median falls
fw = frequency of observations within the interval containing the median
i = size of class interval

cepts. The examples of *self-actualization,* in Figure 16d, are the aspirations of the young man who made the notes; for him self-actualization means to be the best student and swimmer he is able to be. In Figure 16e, the examples are couples who are friends of the young woman who made the notes. She considers Waldo and Lillian to be examples of mature lovers and Al and Joan to be examples of romantic lovers. Thoughts of these couples will help her to recall the differences between the two approaches to love relationships.

If you do not have the habit of using examples to help you in understanding and remembering terms and concepts, you are likely to be pleased when you start using them. Students often report that their ability to remember and recall increases dramatically as a result of studying examples in books and thinking of their own examples (see Section 17.7).

Use What You've Learned

1. Use the suggestions given in this chapter to make notes to study the information in books for all of the courses you are taking.

2. After you have used notes for information in a book to study for a test, explain whether you found notes to have the advantages that are listed in Section 16.1.

3. For at least one of your courses, make notes on 3 x 5 index cards rather than on notebook paper.

4. After you have used notes on cards to study for a test, explain whether you found them to have the advantages that are listed in Section 16.3.

5. Use any of the following passages to practice making notes for studying information in textbooks. Examples of good notes for the passages are in the answer key at the back of the book.

a. "Stages of Pregnancy," Figure 13b, Section 13.2

b. "Types of Families," Section 13.4

c. "Eye Behavior," Section 13.5

d. "The Impact of the Civil War on the South," Figure 14a, Section 14.1

e. "Pretension, Jargon, and Cliché," Section 14.2

f. "Types of Social Mobility," Section 14.3

g. "The Causes of Rapid Population Growth," Section 14.6

h. "Effects of Early and Late Maturing," Section 14.7

i. "The Middle Class," Section 14.8

Recite Information You Want to Learn

Reciting makes it possible to remember and recall information that is needed to answer test questions. It is the sixth and last step in preparing to learn information for tests and examinations.

1. Preview chapters.
2. Skim sections of chapters.
3. Read and underline with a purpose.
4. Decide what you will study.
5. Make notes for studying.
6. **Recite information you want to learn.**

Reciting is the act of repeating information silently or aloud to remember it and to be able to recall it. Most of the information that must be learned for history, business, psychology, and similar courses may be learned by reciting it. For example, if students want to learn the four symptoms of schizophrenia for a psychology course, they would ask themselves, "What are the four symptoms of schizophrenia?" and recite the answer to this question without looking at the answer written in their notes.

When the goal is to learn information, the greatest proportion of study time should be devoted to reciting the information. Students who learn most efficiently are the ones who are very skillful at deciding what is important to learn, at making good notes for studying, and who spend most of their study time for a course reciting the information that they want to learn.

One reason it is important for you to recite is that reciting will give you practice doing what you will do when you take tests and examinations. When you recite, you give answers to your questions; when you take tests, you give answers to your teachers' questions.

17.1   Recite rather than memorize

The five steps for reciting are usually most effective when they are used to recite information that is summarized and well organized in notes.

1. Read the descriptive title of the information you want to learn.
2. Turn the title into a question, and use the question to stimulate recall of the information you want to learn.
3. Give the answer to your question silently or aloud without reading the answer written in your notes.
4. Read your notes to make certain that you recited the answer to your question correctly and completely. If you did not, reread the information that needs to be learned and, immediately after you reread it, attempt to recite it.
5. Repeat this procedure at later times until the information can be recalled easily.

These steps will be illustrated using the information in Figure 17a.

A student needed to learn the information in Figure 17a for her business course. She recited it by reading the title, "Ways Property Can Be Acquired," and by then turning the title into the following question to stimulate her recall of the information she wanted to learn: *What are some ways property can be acquired?* After several attempts she recited the information in the following way:

> Inheritance, legacy, and accession. I get property by *inheritance* when laws specify that I am a relative who must get property if there is no will or that I cannot be excluded from

Figure 17a **Notes for Reciting Information for a Business Course.**

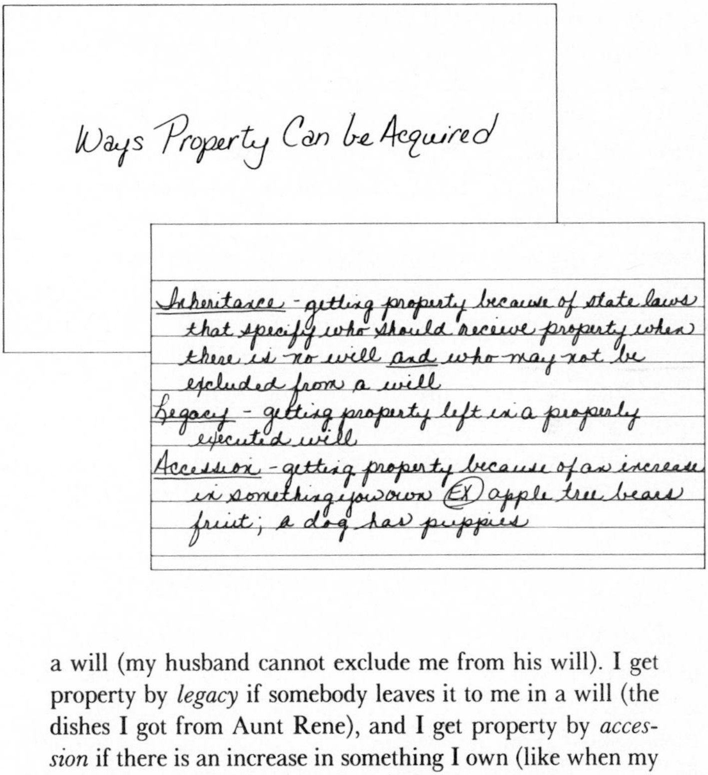

Ways Property Can be Acquired

Inheritance - getting property because of state laws that specify who should receive property when there is no will and who may not be excluded from a will
Legacy - getting property left in a properly executed will
Accession - getting property because of an increase in something you own (EX) apple tree bears fruit; a dog has puppies

a will (my husband cannot exclude me from his will). I get property by *legacy* if somebody leaves it to me in a will (the dishes I got from Aunt Rene), and I get property by *accession* if there is an increase in something I own (like when my avocado seed became a plant and Tiger had kittens).

Compare the student's recitation to her notes in Figure 17a to observe that they are different in several respects. First, she began her recitation by stating three ways property may be acquired; this organized her thoughts about the major aspects of the topic. Second, the explanations she gave while reciting do not duplicate the explanations in the notes word for word. Third, when she recited, she gave an example for each way property may be acquired, but the only examples in the notes are for *accession*. When reciting, she related the information to

her experiences by giving personal examples where there are
no examples in the notes and by giving examples for *accession*
that are different from the examples in the notes.

Most information should not be learned by memorizing it
word for word; it needs to be understood. The student who
recited the information in Figure 17a showed that she understood the information and, when she took a test, she answered
a question about the information correctly.

If you want to be able to recall information when you answer
test questions, spend the greatest portion of your study time
reciting. This is the secret of most students who consistently do
well on college tests and examinations. They are skillful at
deciding what they should learn and in organizing information
so that it is easy to recite; this makes it possible for them to
spend most of their study time reciting. When they take tests,
the information they need to answer questions is stored in their
memories in well-organized ways so that it can be recalled and
used to select or write correct answers to questions.

17.2   Provide for sufficient review

Studies of memory have found that we tend to forget thirty
to forty percent of what we learn within twenty-four hours after
we learn it, and that we remember best the information that we
review most. You must expect that during the time you study
for a test some of the information you learn will be forgotten
within one day after you learn it and that you must review
information frequently if you want to make certain that you
remember it.

For example, if you decide to learn the information on eighty
cards for a midterm test, after you recite the first time you may
select from the eighty cards twenty cards that you have
"learned." If you separate those twenty cards from the set of
eighty and review them the following day, you are likely to find
that you cannot recite all of the information on four, five, six or
more of the twenty cards. If you should have an experience of
this kind, do not worry. If you forget information you learn,

this is only an indication that you are human—we forget much of what we learn and we remember best what we review most.

Notes on cards are ideally suited to the limitations of the human mind. For each course, maintain a deck of cards that is "learned" and a deck of cards that is "unlearned." Then, each time you recite:

1. Begin by reviewing the deck that has been "learned." If you have forgotten any information on a card, put it back where it belongs in the "unlearned" deck. (This is the major reason that it is suggested in Section 16.2 that cards should be numbered.)

2. Then, recite the "unlearned" cards, attempting to move as many of them as possible into the "learned" deck.

Continue in this way until you can accurately recite all the information on cards twenty-four hours after all of the cards are in the "learned" deck. If all information is learned several days or weeks before a test, review the cards frequently to keep the information fresh in your mind and to learn it as thoroughly as possible.

If you have difficulty remembering information you need to answer test questions, you probably do *not* use this method when you study. Students who recall almost all of the information they need to answer questions use this method, or one very similar to it.

17.3   Prepare class notes for reciting

When notes for books are made on cards, information in class notes may be integrated with information in books for more efficient learning. If class notes contain information that is related to information on cards made for books, the information in the class notes may be written on the cards for the books. When there is not enough space to write information in class notes on textbook note cards, additional cards may be made for class notes and placed next to cards that contain related information from books. This procedure is highly recommended because it is much more efficient to recite all information about a topic at one time rather than to recite it in bits and pieces from textbook notes and class notes at different times.

If you wish to recite information directly from class notes, use a highlight pen to mark the topics about which you want to learn and use the words you highlight to stimulate recall. For example, if "Ways Property Can Be Acquired" is a topic in class notes for a business course, highlight these words and use them to stimulate recall of information about the topic. When class notes do not have descriptive titles, use the suggestions given in Section 16.5 to write more descriptive titles for them. These may be written in the margin of notes if necessary. Then, highlight the descriptive titles and use them to stimulate recall of the information in class notes.

17.4   Write to aid learning

Writing is used to learn many of the skills that are taught in colleges, such as the skills that are needed for solving mathematical problems and for translating a foreign language into English. Writing may also be used to learn information of the type that is usually recited silently or aloud. If you have difficulty learning information by reciting it, try writing it on paper. Some students report that writing provides them with the additional reinforcement they need to learn and remember certain types of information.

17.5   Use mnemonic acronyms

It is difficult, perhaps impossible, to find college graduates who did well in school but who did not use mnemonic (ni-mon'ik) devices. **Mnemonic** means "to help the memory," and one type of mnemonic device is the mnemonic acronym. An **acronym** is a word made from the initial letters of other words. The word *homes,* for example, is a mnemonic acronym that may be used to remember the names of the Great Lakes: *H*uron, *O*ntario, *M*ichigan, *E*rie, and *S*uperior. When the

Great Lakes are arranged in this sequence, the initial letters of the names of the lakes spell *homes.*

Mnemonic acronyms do not need to be real words; they may be nonsense words. The nonsense acronym *WHID,* for example, may be used to recall the four symptoms of schizophrenia listed on the card in Figure 16c. Since the symptoms of schizophrenia do not need to be learned in any particular order, they may be rearranged to use the acronym for easier learning:

W̲ithdrawal

H̲allucinations

I̲nappropriate emotional response

D̲elusions

W recalls "Withdrawl," *H* recalls "Hallucinations," *I* recalls "Inappropriate (emotional response)," and *D* recalls "Delusions."

Sometimes it is difficult or impossible to create an acronym using the first letters of key words. For example, no acronym can be made using the initial letters of the three types of social mobility that are explained in a textbook excerpt in Section 14.3.

H̲orizontal mobility

V̲ertical mobility

I̲ntergenerational mobility

In instances such as these, an acronym can sometimes be made by using an additional letter enclosed in parentheses. For example, the acronym *HIV (e)* may be used to learn the three types of social mobility. *H* recalls "Horizontal," *I* recalls "Intergenerational," *V* recalls "Vertical," and the *e* in parentheses is a visual clue that there are three, not four, types of social mobility to learn.

Mnemonic acronyms aid in recalling the numbers of items in lists and key words for each item. When the sequence of information is important, they can also often help in recalling the sequence. For example, psychology, sociology, and health education textbooks often explain the emotional stages through which people pass when they learn they are about to die. The stages are:

<u>D</u>enial
<u>A</u>nger
<u>B</u>argaining
<u>D</u>epression
<u>A</u>cceptance

It is important to learn the stages in this sequence, and the nonsense acronym *DABDA* may be used for this purpose. *D* recalls "Denial," *A* recalls "Anger," *B* recalls "Bargaining," and so on.

In some instances key words in major points may be used to create mnemonic acronyms. Following are the three reasons it is important to make notes for studying that are given in Section 16.1. The italicized words in the reasons have initial letters that spell *ROW,* and this acronym may be used to recall the three reasons:

1. The simple act of *writing* information in notes will often help you to learn it.
2. Written notes *reduce* the amount of information you need to learn.
3. Your notes are *organized* in ways that make it easier for you to learn information.

Lists of this type do not need to be learned in any particular order. Thus, using the acronym *ROW, R* recalls "reduce," *O* recalls "organized," and *W* recalls "writing." These key words, in turn, recall each reason for the importance of notes. *Reduce,* for example, recalls that one reason notes are important for studying is that they reduce the amount of information that needs to be learned.

If you have never used mnemonic acronyms to help you learn, the idea of them may seem silly to you. However, they are used by almost all of the most successful students; they are particularly popular among students who study medicine, law, architecture, and other similarly demanding subjects. They can also be helpful to you. Make mnemonic acronyms to learn information that is difficult for you to learn when you recite it silently or aloud to yourself.

17.6   Use mnemonic sentences

A *mnemonic sentence* is a sentence in which the initial letters of the words in the sentence are the same as the initial letters of words that need to be recalled. Following is a well-known mnemonic sentence for remembering the sequence of the planets in our solar system, starting with the planet nearest the sun and going to the planet most distant from the sun.

My	Very	Earthy	Mother	Just	Served	Us	Nine	Pizzas.
e	e	a	a	u	a	r	e	l
r	n	r	r	p	t	a	p	u
c	u	t	s	i	u	n	t	t
u	s	h		t	r	u	u	o
r				e	n	s	n	
y				r			e	

This sentence makes it possible to learn quickly the information needed to answer questions such as the following: Which planet is closest to the sun? Which planets are on either side of the earth? Which planets are on either side of Saturn, and which of them is farthest from the sun?

Mnemonic sentences are useful when it is difficult or impossible to make a mnemonic acronym. For example, the first letters of the planets in sequence beginning nearest the sun are *MVEMJSUNP*. It is much easier to learn "My very earthy mother just served us nine pizzas" than it is to learn *MVEMJSUNP*.

A student had difficulty making a mnemonic acronym to learn about five types of societies for his sociology course.

Hunting
Pastoral
Horticultural
Agricultural
Industrial

He had two problems in creating an acceptable acronym. First he could not create a word using the initial letters of the names of the five types of societies, and second he wanted to learn the types of societies in the order in which they are presented: they are arranged in a sequence that begins with the most primitive and concludes with the most advanced type of society. The initial letters of the words, *HPHAI,* may be used to construct many different mnemonic sentences. After exploring several possibilities, the student decided to use the following mnemonic sentence to recall the five types of societies in the appropriate sequence.

Harry pleases himself and Ingrid.

This sentence is a true statement about friends of his; he found it easy to recall. The *H* in "Harry" recalled "Hunting," the *P* in "pleases" recalled "Pastoral," the *H* in "himself" recalled "Horticultural," and so on.

Memory experts claim that mnemonic devices are easier to remember when they are funny, fanciful, or ridiculous. According to this theory, it is easier to remember "Your mother wears Army boots" than it is to remember "Your mother will air blankets." Since the theory seems reasonable, you may find it helpful to be as silly as you please when you write mnemonic sentences.

17.7   Use visualizations

A **visualization** is anything that can be pictured in the mind to recall information. Memory improvement courses often stress the value of using visualizations to enhance memory.

The card that summarizes information about mature and

romantic love in Figure 16e includes two examples of visualizations. The student who made the card selected her friends Lillian and Waldo as examples of mature lovers and her friends Al and Joan as examples of romantic lovers. The couples are people whom the student could visualize in her mind, and when she visualized each couple this helped her recall the characteristics of the two types of lovers.

Most examples can be visualized; that is why they are so helpful in understanding and remembering methods, terms, and concepts. In Section 17.5 it is shown that the mnemonic acronym HIV(e) may be used to recall the types of social mobility, but visualizations are more helpful to some students than acronyms. For example, one young man devised the following visualizations from his own experiences to learn the three types of social mobility.

1. For *horizontal mobility,* in which a person goes from one status to another similar status, he visualized himself when he changed his job from pumping gas to parking cars.
2. For *vertical mobility,* in which one moves from one status to a higher or lower status, he visualized himself when he changed his job from parking cars to being a management trainee for an electronics firm.
3. For *intergenerational mobility,* in which the status of family members change from one generation to another, he visualized his grandfather who was a laborer and his father who owned and managed a hardware store.

The student could visualize these events and people; they helped him understand, remember, and recall the three types of social mobility.

Visualizations may also be used to learn sequences. For example, a visualization may be conceived to learn the hierarchy of human needs that are explained in a passage in Section 14.5:

1. Physiological needs (food, water, sex)
2. Safety needs (security from danger)

3. Love needs (love, affection, contact)
4. Esteem needs (acceptance and respect)
5. Self-actualization needs (attainment of what one is able)

Following is a visualization that was made to learn about the needs in the correct hierarchical sequence.

> I am a child at home seated at the dinner table with my family and a school friend—the door to the room is closed. There is food and drink on the table (psychological needs). I feel secure with my father and mother there (safety needs), and loved by them and my friend (love needs). My father tells me he is proud of the good job I did washing the car (esteem needs). I look at the closed door; I see it opening and myself walking through it to leave my family, to be on my own, and to become the person that I am capable of becoming (self-actualization needs).

Well-thought-out visualizations are powerful tools for understanding, remembering, and recalling many types of information.

Use What You've Learned

1. Which of the methods explained in Section 17.3 will you use to recite information in your class notes?

2. Write five mnemonic acronyms that you will use to learn information for courses you are taking.

3. Write two mnemonic sentences that you will use to learn information for courses you are taking.

4. Explain how you will use visualizations to recall information for two topics for courses you are taking.

PART FOUR

How to Take Tests and Examinations

Basic Test-taking
Strategies

Students who consistently do well on college tests use effective study procedures, but they also use good test-taking methods. This chapter explains eight strategies you may use to do your best when you take tests for your college courses.

1. Reduce your test anxiety.
2. Skim tests and plan test-taking time.
3. Read the directions and follow them.
4. Answer the easiest questions first.
5. Usually answer all of the questions.
6. Check your answers carefully.
7. Ignore other test-takers.
8. Learn from your incorrect answers.

These methods will help you answer more questions correctly whenever you take college tests. Chapter 19 through Chapter 23 give specific suggestions for selecting and giving correct answers to multiple-choice, true-false, matching, sentence completion, and essay questions.

18.1 Reduce your test anxiety

Anxiety is the uneasiness or apprehension you experience because of fear or worry for something that might happen in the future. **Test anxiety** is uneasiness or apprehension experienced because of the need to prepare for or take a test. Physical symptoms of test anxiety include excessive sweating, discomfort in the stomach, headaches, rapid heartbeat, and shortness of breath.

Some students have such intense anxiety for tests that they cannot concentrate when they study, or, if they can study, their minds go completely blank when they take tests. Sometimes students' minds go blank during tests because they misinterpret the excitement they feel; they think perhaps it is abnormal to be excited and this causes them to worry about themselves. Actually, excitement for tests is normal and even beneficial, in the same way that excitement helps athletes do their best during athletic competition.

However, in most instances, test anxiety is probably the result of pressure to maintain good grades for reasons such as the following:

1. To receive scholarship assistance
2. To be accepted into a specific academic program
3. To receive approval from parents or other significant persons
4. To maintain good academic standing
5. To maintain a self-image of excellence

There is no doubt that grades are important (Section 2.1), but some students and their parents place unrealistic importance on them. If you feel that you fail a test when you receive a grade lower than A, you may be creating unnecessary unhappiness for yourself by insisting that you be perfect or do better than your best (see Section 8.8).

Since anxiety results from fear, test anxiety can usually be avoided by using the methods that are described in Chapter 11 through Chapter 17 to prepare thoroughly for tests. If you are well prepared to take a test, you will not have much to fear. Also, knowing and using good test-taking procedures usually helps to reduce test anxiety. Anxiety directs thoughts *inward* to think about discomfort; but good test-taking methods direct thoughts *outward* to think about answering test questions correctly. If you use the methods that are explained in this chapter and Chapter 19 through Chapter 23 when you take tests, you will be so busy in the worthwhile pursuit of answering questions correctly that your mind will be less likely to engage in futile thoughts of any fear you have for taking tests.

Sleep and eat well before tests. If you are well rested and nourished, you will be in better physical condition to cope satisfactorily with any nervousness you experience during tests.

You may also find that the following exercise will help you to relax when you are anxious:

1. Without actually smiling, relax your face and feel yourself smiling on the inside.
2. Take a very deep breath—a breath so deep that you imagine it reaches to the soles of your feet.
3. Then, still smiling inside, let your breath out very slowly.

If you have never done an exercise such as this one, it may seem foolish to you. However, it is not foolish; it is very relaxing and composing. The next time you are anxious or uncomfortable, do this exercise; you are likely to find that it helps you feel better.

In summary, these are the suggestions for coping with test anxiety:

1. Use the methods that are explained in Chapter 11 through Chapter 17 to prepare for tests.
2. Use the methods that are explained in this chapter and in Chapter 19 through Chapter 23 when you take tests.
3. Do not insist that you be perfect or do better than your best (Section 8.8).
4. Be well rested and well nourished when you take tests.
5. Use the breathing exercise that is explained in this section to relieve nervous tension during tests.

If you cannot conquer excessive test anxiety by using these methods, seek the help of a counselor. At many colleges and universities, counselors provide assistance for students who experience acute and disabling test anxiety.

18.2   **Skim tests and plan test-taking time**

Before you answer any questions on a test, skim it to learn how many questions you must answer and how many points are given for each correct answer.

For example, when skimming a test, you may find that you need to answer a total of 30 questions: 15 multiple-choice questions, 10 true-false questions, and 5 short-answer questions. If it is not stated on the test how many points you will receive for each correct answer, ask your teacher what the point values are. *You must know the point value for answers to plan your test-taking time wisely.* If the answers to 30 questions have equal value, each correct answer will have a value of 3.33 points (3.33 × 30 = 99.99). In this case, you should plan to spend approximately equal time answering each question; if you have sixty minutes to answer questions, you should plan to spend approximately two minutes answering each of the 30 questions. On the other hand, if the answers to 5 short-answer questions have a value of 10 points each and the other 25 questions have a value of 2 points each, you should plan to spend approximately half of your time answering the short-answer questions. In this case, the 5 short-answer questions will account for half of the test score (5 × 10 = 50) and the other 25 questions will account for the other half of the score (25 × 2 = 50).

When you skim a test, you will sometimes discover that you must *not* answer all of the questions. This is most likely to be the case when you answer essay questions (Chapter 23). Figure 18a illustrates an essay test that might be given during a fifty-minute meeting of a history course. Notice that four questions are listed in Figure 18a but that students are required to answer only two of them. It is extremely important that students *not* answer more than two questions; those who answer more than two questions are likely to be severely penalized. First, if students write four answers during the time they are expected to write two answers, the four answers they write are not likely to be as complete as the two answers they were supposed to have written. Second, if students write four answers when they

Figure 18a **An Essay Test for an American History Course.**

American History: **Test 1**

Answer any two of the following questions. Specify which answer you want to count for a maximum of 60 points of your grade and which answer you want to count for a maximum of 40 points of your grade.   You have fifty minutes to answer the questions.

1.   What impact did the abundance of land in America have on the attitudes and values of the colonists?

2.   Why was the New World more attractive to lower- and middle-class people than to aristocrats?

3.   What was the role and status of women and children in the American colonies?

4.   Explain why the Great Awakening was a revolt against formalism.

---

are supposed to write only two, teachers usually grade only the first two answers. If the third or fourth answer is better than one of the first two answers, students will not receive credit for the better answer.

Also notice in Figure 18a that students must specify which answer they want to count for 60 points and which answer they want to count for 40 points of their grade. Since 50 minutes are allowed for answering the questions, approximately 40 percent of the time (20 minutes) should be spent answering the 40-point question and approximately 60 percent of the time (30 minutes) should be spent answering the 60-point question.

18.3   Read the directions and follow them

If you take a multiple-choice test, you can usually predict that you should select the correct answers to the questions. Also, if you take an essay test, you can usually anticipate that you must give fairly long written answers to questions. However, always read test directions carefully and follow them exactly.

One teacher writes the following direction on all of his multiple-choice tests:

> Show your answers on the answer sheet by clearly printing capital letter A, B, C, or D.

At the beginning of each test the teacher draws this direction to the attention of his students and writes capital letters *A, B, C,* and *D* on the chalkboard so there will be no confusion about how answers must be shown. When he grades tests, he deducts 10 points from students' test scores when they write answers using something other than printed capital letters *A, B, C,* and *D.*

Also, a test direction may be different from what you expect. For example, if a test contains true-false questions, you may expect that you should answer *T* if a statement is true or *F* if a statement is false. However, these may not be the directions.

Some teachers use the following directions for true-false questions:

> Circle T if a statement is true or F if a statement is false. Also, if a statement is false, underline the word or words in the statement that make it false and write the word(s) that makes the statement true.

Following is an example of how the directions are followed correctly:

T   (F)   A store that has a very narrow product mix but depth in lines it does carry is called a <u>department store</u>. *specialty store*

If teachers give explanations after they distribute a test, listen very carefully to everything they say. Students who arrive late to tests often miss the explanations that teachers give and, as a result, lose points that they should not lose. If you must be late to a class, do not be late on the day of a test.

Always read directions carefully and follow them exactly. Failure to read and follow test directions is a major cause of test grades that are lower than they should be. It is extremely discouraging to lose points on tests for failure to read the directions.

18.4   Answer the easiest questions first

When you take a college test your objective should be to answer as many questions correctly as you can in the time that is available. You increase your chance of achieving this goal if you answer the easiest questions first. There are four reasons that this is true.

1. *You are likely to answer correctly all the questions you can answer correctly.* If you answer the easiest questions first, you will answer all of the questions you are most likely to answer

correctly in case time runs out before you are able to answer all the questions.

2. *You will build up your test-taking confidence and perhaps avoid undue test anxiety.* If you dwell on one or two difficult questions during the first few minutes while you are taking a test, you may worry whether you will do well on the test and thus create anxiety that may prevent you from doing your best. On the other hand, if you answer the easiest questions first, you may build up your confidence that you will also be able to answer some of the more difficult questions correctly as well.

3. *You may think of the answers to some of the difficult questions.* You have no doubt had the experience of not being able to answer a question at the moment it was asked but of then remembering the answer later. This often happens while taking tests. If you cannot think of the answer to a question immediately, do not worry. During the time it takes you to answer other questions you will often think of answers to questions that you could not answer the first time you read them.

4. *You may find an answer to a difficult question.* Sometimes the questions on a test are interrelated so that one question suggests the correct answer to another question. As you answer the questions on a test, look for information that will help you give or select an answer to a question that you were unable to answer the first time you read it.

If you do not have the habit of answering the easiest questions first, you are likely to find that your test scores are higher when you use this strategy.

When you answer multiple-choice, true-false, and similar types of questions, read a question twice. If you are unable to answer it after the second reading, move on to the next question. Continue in this way until you have read each question and answered as many as you can after the first or second reading. Then, reread each unanswered question twice again and answer as many of them as you can after the third or fourth reading. If you are unable to answer a question after you have read it four times, move on to the next unanswered question.

Proceed through the test in this way as many times as are necessary for you to select an answer for each question.

Also answer the easiest questions first when you take essay tests. For example, if you have sixty minutes to answer four essay questions which have a value of twenty-five points each, you should plan to spend about fifteen minutes answering each question. But, if you can write answers to the two easiest questions in twenty minutes, you will have forty minutes to write the answers to the two more difficult questions.

Also answer the easiest questions first when you solve problems for mathematics, science, accounting, and similar courses. Skim through the problems on a test to find the ones that you believe you can solve most quickly. If you have ten problems to solve in fifty minutes, you should plan to spend an average of five minutes on each of the ten problems. However, if you can solve five of the easiest problems in an average of three minutes each, you will have solved half of the problems in fifteen minutes. This will leave you thirty-five minutes, or an average of seven minutes each, to solve the five more difficult problems.

18.5   Usually answer all the questions

You should answer all the questions on a college test unless you have specific instructions not to answer all of them. For example, if you take an essay test with directions of the type that are illustrated in Figure 18a, you should *not* answer all the questions. Also, it may not be wise to answer all the questions on a test if you know that you will be severely penalized for guessing incorrect answers. There are a few teachers who deduct extra points for incorrect answers to multiple-choice, true-false, and similar types of questions. If you ever have such a teacher, he or she will make it clear to you that you should not guess.

However, the grades for most college tests are computed by counting the number of correct answers; credit is given for correct answers no matter what method was used to select correct answers. Therefore, when you do not know the answer to a question, you should select or give an answer even if you have to guess.

There are two reasons that you should give an answer for all multiple-choice, true-false, and matching questions. First, other students who take the tests you take know that they may increase their test scores by guessing at answers, and they guess at answers they do not know. Since your test score will be compared to their test scores, you deserve to have the same advantage that they have when they guess. Second, if you gain any points by guessing at answers, these points may offset any points you lose that you should not lose. When you answer a multiple-choice, true-false, or matching question, there is always a chance that you will make an error and give an incorrect answer to a question that you should have answered correctly. If this happens, you will lose points that you should not lose. If you gain points by guessing correct answers, the points you gain will offset any points you lose that you should not lose.

Additional information about guessing at answers to questions is given in Section 19.13 and Section 20.8.

18.6   Check your answers carefully

One careless error on a test can make a great deal of difference when the grade is computed. If there are forty questions on a test and you answer thirty-one of them correctly, your grade is C+, but if you answer thirty-two of them correctly, your grade is B−. It is worth your time to proofread your answers to be certain you do not lose points for carelessness.

When you answer essay questions, plan your test-taking time so that you will have a few minutes to proofread your answers and to correct what you wrote (Section 23.7). Also, when you solve mathematical problems for a test, reserve time to check answers for careless mistakes.

However, when you check your answers to multiple-choice, true-false, and matching questions, take care before you change any answer that you have written. Studies have found that some students have a tendency to change correct answers to incorrect answers. Therefore, once you have written answers for these types of questions do not change them unless you are certain they are incorrect. When tests with multiple-choice, true-false, or matching questions are returned to you, examine any answers you changed when you took the test. You will soon learn whether you have the tendency to change correct answers to incorrect answers; if you do, you know that you must be extra careful about changing answers to questions once you have written them.

18.7   Ignore other test-takers

When you take a test, think only of answering as many questions correctly as you can. Select a comfortable seat where you can answer questions completely free of distractions from other students.

Do not try to impress other students by being the first to finish a test. Instead, impress yourself by following the suggestions in this chapter and in Chapter 19 through Chapter 23 to answer as many questions correctly as you can.

If some students finish before you do, ignore them. Do not worry whether they have answered more questions correctly than you will. Some of the people who finish tests first do receive high test grades, but also some students complete tests quickly because they do not know the answers to many questions. Others who finish tests quickly do satisfactorily, but they would have done better if they had taken the time to check their answers carefully (Section 18.6). Therefore, don't worry about any other students when you take a test; ignore them all and concentrate on doing the best you can do.

Also, if any classmate ever asks to see your answers during a test, do not show them. It is not your problem when other students are poorly prepared to take tests; don't make it your problem. Most colleges have severe penalties for students who cheat while taking tests; those who allow others to see their answers are just as guilty of cheating as those who copy answers. If other students can see your answers when you take tests, your teachers will be justified in assuming that you intend them to see and copy your answers. Avoid being accused of cheating; never let others see your answers while you are taking tests.

18.8   Learn from your incorrect answers

The best opportunity you have to improve your test-taking ability is to learn from the questions that you answered incorrectly. Test-taking is a skill, and skills are learned by making mistakes and learning from mistakes. When teachers return tests and review the answers to questions, study your incorrect answers to understand *why* you answered them incorrectly.

When you analyze tests, you may find that you devoted too much attention to learning information in a textbook and not enough time to learning information in class notes. Or, you may find that you did not make good use of the strategies that are explained in this chapter and in Chapter 19 through Chapter 23. At the ends of each of these chapters, there are suggestions for specific ways to analyze the tests you take.

Also, when test questions are reviewed in class, avoid arguing with teachers about the correct answers to questions. If you disagree with the ways tests are graded, it is usually best to discuss this with teachers in private rather than in classes. Giving tests is an important part of teachers' work; when you criticize their test questions, you criticize the ways in which they do their work. When you criticize people in front of others, you may anticipate that you will annoy or embarrass them. Annoyed or embarrassed teachers are not likely to give your complaints the thoughtful consideration that might benefit you.

Therefore, discuss your disagreements about test questions with teachers in private. Talk with them after class or schedule conferences with them. If you explain your disagreements calmly, you will find that most teachers will try to understand whether they asked poorly worded questions or graded your answers incorrectly. Most of them will adjust your test scores when it is justified or try to help you understand why your answers were incorrect.

On the other hand, there are some teachers who will not be understanding or helpful when you disagree with their test questions or the ways they graded your tests. When you discuss your honest disagreements with such teachers and they leave you with a feeling of intense dissatisfaction, it is probably a waste of your time to discuss their tests with them.

Use What You've Learned

1. Are you excessively nervous or excited when you take tests? If so, discuss this problem with a counselor; some colleges provide help for students who have too much test anxiety.

2. Before you answer any questions on tests, skim them to determine how many questions you must answer and how many points you will receive for each correct answer. Use this information to plan your test-taking time. When tests are returned, decide whether this strategy helped you to do your best on them.

3. Describe a direction for a test you have taken in college that you consider to be unusual but that was very important to answer test questions correctly.

4. When you take tests, use the suggestions in Section 18.4 to answer the easiest questions first. When tests are returned, decide whether this strategy helped you to do your best on them.

5. When a test with multiple-choice, true-false, or matching questions is reviewed, examine the answers that you changed while taking the test. Did you change correct answers to incorrect answers? If so, should you be extra cautious about changing answers to test questions once you have written them?

6. Do you ever become nervous when other students finish tests before you do? If so, use the suggestions in Section 18.7 to overcome this unproductive attitude.

7. When tests are reviewed, study your incorrect answers to understand *why* you answered them incorrectly. Use what you learn to answer more questions correctly the next time you take a test.

Multiple-Choice Questions

There are several reasons that multiple-choice questions are popular among college teachers.

1. They can be used to test all aspects of students' knowledge and their ability to reason with information they have learned.
2. If students have difficulty expressing their thoughts in writing, poor writing ability will not lower their grades on multiple-choice tests.
3. When answers are recorded on answer sheets, multiple-choice questions are easy to grade.

Also, textbook publishers often provide teachers with a book that contains hundreds of multiple-choice questions from which they may select questions for their tests.

It is very likely that you will answer many multiple-choice questions on college tests. This chapter explains how to select correct answers to this type of question.

19.1 Characteristics of multiple-choice questions

Multiple-choice questions are usually either incomplete statements followed by possible ways the statements may be completed or they are questions followed by possible answers. The following question is an incomplete statement followed by ways the statement may be completed.

1. Unless vegetarian diets are well prepared, they
   are likely to be deficient in

   a. calcium and vitamin C.
   b. protein and vitamin C.
   c. protein and riboflavin.
   d. phosphorous and calcium.

This example is a question followed by possible answers to it.

2. Which of the following is the most common cause of
   death among Americans?

   a. stroke
   b. hypertension
   c. cancer of the lungs
   d. coronary heart disease

The first part of a multiple-choice question is called the
stem, and the choices that are given for answers are called
options. Both of these questions have four options: *a, b, c,* and
d. Also, they both illustrate two important characteristics of
multiple-choice questions: (1) they should be clearly stated and
(2) there should be only one correct answer. The correct answer
to the first question is option *c,* and the correct answer to the
second question is option *d*.

19.2   Basic strategy for multiple-choice questions

When multiple-choice questions are properly written, one
option is the correct answer and the other options are **distractors.** The theory is that correct answers should be selected only
by students who know correct answers and other students
should be "distracted" and select one of the other options—one
of the distractors. Therefore, *the strategy to use when answering a multiple-choice question is to decide which options are
distractors and to select as the correct answer the option that is
not a distractor.*

One way to identify distractors is to analyze a multiple-choice question as though it is a series of true-false questions. The following question may be analyzed in this way.

1. Oxygen is produced through a process called

    a. heliotaxis.
    b. eutrophication.
    c. photosynthesis.
    d. oxygenization.

This question, like most multiple-choice questions, is actually a series of true-false questions, only one of which is "true."

    a. Oxygen is produced through a process called heliotaxis. (F)
    b. Oxygen is produced through a process called eutrophication. (F)
    c. Oxygen is produced through a process called photosynthesis. (T)
    d. Oxygen is produced through a process called oxygenization. (F)

When you answer multiple-choice questions, cross out each option that you decide is a distractor. For example,

1. Oxygen is produced through a process called

    a. ~~heliotaxis.~~
    b. eutrophication.
    c. photosynthesis.
    d. ~~oxygenization.~~

In this example, a student has decided that oxygen is not produced through a process called *heliotaxis* or *oxygenization*. She has decided the correct answer must be either *eutrophication* or *photosynthesis,* and eventually she will decide that one of these options is a distractor and cross it out too. She will select as the correct answer, the option she has decided is not a distractor. The correct answer is option *c.*

19.3   Select the answers you learned

The questions on college tests are almost always based on information that is printed in course reading material or that is stated during class lectures or discussions. Keep this in mind and you will avoid making unnecessary errors when you answer multiple-choice questions.

For example, students in a psychology course learn that correlation coefficients are either positive or negative. But some of them are confused when they are called upon to answer the following question:

1. The correlation between the number of sun-
   bathers on a beach and the number of pairs of sun
   glasses present is usually

   a. positive.
   b. negative.
   c. bifurcated.
   d. parallel.

The correct answer is *positive,* but some students are confused by the option *bifurcated* and select it. They are usually insecure individuals who believe that if they don't know an answer then it must be the right answer. This is an example of an extremely poor test-taking strategy. Since test questions are almost always based on information presented in a course, it is irrational to select an answer *because* it is not known. The only time an unfamiliar term or phrase should be selected as the correct answer to a question is when it has been determined that all of the other options are distractors. For example,

2. Jeans are

   a. worn on the head.
   b. worn on the shoulders.
   c. worn on the feet.
   d. bifurcated.

You know that jeans are not worn on the head, shoulders, or feet; therefore, you are forced to conclude that they are *bifurcated*. To bifurcate is to divide into two parts or branches; the legs of jeans are in two parts—one for each leg. Skirts, on the other hand, are not bifurcated.

Also, you may sometimes be able to select correct answers to questions by drawing upon knowledge other than knowledge you acquired in a course. For example, if you know the meaning of *dichotomous* you should be able to select the correct answer to the following question even if you have not studied the college course in which it is sometimes asked.

3. Which of the following questionnaire items is a dichotomous question?

   a. Do you find the subject of test-taking to be interesting?   Yes _____   No _____
   b. What is your opinion of the value of learning test-taking skills?
   c. How do you rate your test-taking skills? Good _____ Fair _____ Poor _____
   d. How many hours will you study today?   1 2 3 4 5 6 7 8

If you know that *dichotomous* refers to a "two-part division," you should have selected option *a* as the correct answer to the first question.

Answer test questions by drawing upon the information you read in required course reading material and hear in class lectures and discussions. But also be ready to draw upon your accumulated knowledge and common sense when you answer questions.

19.4   Underline *not, except, incorrect,* and *false*

Many multiple-choice questions are answered incorrectly because students fail to observe the words *not, except, incorrect,* and *false*. When professional test writers use these words in the stems of multiple-choice questions, they print them in italic type or underscore them. Unfortunately, many teachers do not italicize or underscore these words when they use them in multiple-choice questions. Underline these words where they appear in the stems of the following questions:

1. When trying to learn a long vocabulary list for a Spanish course, it is not recommended that one use

   a. part learning.
   b. immediate feedback.
   c. spaced practice.
   d. massed practice.

2. The Platonic system of thought included all of the following beliefs except the belief in

   a. democracy.
   b. the rule of the philosopher king.
   c. the rule of the just tyrant.
   d. forms as approximations of ideals.

3. With regard to selecting an occupation in the United States, which of the following statements is incorrect?

   a. There are too many different occupations.
   b. People want better jobs than their parents had.
   c. It is difficult to evaluate people's differences.
   d. There is great emphasis on the freedom to choose.

4. Which of the following is a false statement about the function of the packaging in which a product is sold?

   a. It provides protection for the product it contains
   b. It justifies disguising the quality of a product.
   c. It often provides some convenience for buyers.
   d. It informs buyers about characteristics of a product.

Beginning with the first question, you should have underlined in the stems the words *not, except, incorrect,* and *false.* The correct answers to the questions are (1) *d,* (2) *a,* (3) *c,* and (4) *b.*

It is difficult to understand why some teachers do not underscore these words in multiple-choice questions, but some of them do not. It is absolutely essential for you to find *not, except, incorrect,* and *false* in stems because if you do not find them you may select incorrect answers. For example, students in a psychology course will probably select incorrect answers to the first question if they overlook the word *not* in the stem; three of the options are correct if the word *not* is omitted from the stem. Similarly, students in a history course will probably select incorrect answers to the second question if they overlook the word *except* in the stem; three of the options are correct if the word *except* is omitted from the stem.

19.5   Don't be confused by examples

Sometimes multiple-choice questions have an example in the stem or a series of examples for options. The following question that might appear on a test for a business or advertising course has an example in the stem.

1. Charles Martin wants to have a sales promotion that will attract customers and also benefit them in proportion to the amount of money they spend at his hardware store.   Which of the following sales promotion methods will best serve Mr. Martin's objectives?

   a. money refunds
   b. free samples
   c. trading stamps
   d. retailer coupons

Some students are unnecessarily confused by questions such as this one. They worry, for example, who Charles Martin is and what it was they were supposed to have learned about hardware stores. The question, though, is not about Charles Martin or hardware stores, it is about sales promotion methods. It could have been written this way:

2. Which of the following sales promotion methods
   may be used to attract customers to a store and
   also benefit customers in proportion to the
   amount of money they spend at the store?

   a. money refunds
   b. free samples
   c. trading stamps
   d. retailer coupons

Option *c* is the correct answer to both questions. Do not be distracted by the examples in the stems of multiple-choice questions. Instead, try to imagine how the stem would be worded if it did not include an example.

19.6   Don't be confused by sequences

Multiple-choice questions about sequences also often cause unnecessary difficulty for some students. The following question might appear on a test for a psychology, sociology, or health education course.

1. Which of the following is the correct sequence for
   the psychosexual stages of development that
   Freud identified?

   a. oral, anal, phallic, genital
   b. anal, phallic, oral, genital
   c. oral, anal, genital, phallic
   d. anal, oral, genital, phallic

Questions in this format should not confuse you if you use the suggestions in Section 14.5 to find and study sequences in textbooks. Students who study sequences will know that the oral stage comes first and that options *b* and *d* are, therefore, distractors. They will draw lines through these two options and examine options *a* and *c* to decide which of them lists the sequence they studied. The correct answer is option *a*.

If you learn sequences when you study, this type of multiple-choice question will not be difficult for you to answer.

19.7   Absolute statements may be incorrect answers

Absolute statements exclude all possibilities except the one they state. For example,

<u>All</u> children love chocolate.

There is <u>no</u> student who enjoys taking tests.

If there is one child who does not love chocolate or one student who enjoys taking tests, these statements are false. Absolute statements often include words such as *all, every, always, invariably, best, no, none, never,* and *worst.* These and similar words in the options of multiple-choice questions are clues that the options *may be* distractors. Underline the words in the options for the following question that make them absolute statements.

1. When people receive a great deal of information at one time, they select to become aware of

    a. only one piece of information.
    b. a small amount of the information.
    c. all of the information.
    d. only the information that is familiar.

In options *a* and *d* you should have underlined *only,* and in option *c* you should have underlined *all. Only* and *all* suggest that these three statements are probably false. The correct answer is option *b*.

Now, underline the words in the options for the following question that make them absolute statements.

2. In medieval times, women of the nobility

   a. always married men younger than themselves.
   b. invariably became members of religious orders.
   c. pursued only domestic responsibilities.
   d. managed the household when their husbands were absent.

In options *a, b,* and *c,* you should have underlined *always, invariably,* and *only.* These words suggest that the three options are *probably* incorrect answers. The correct answer is option *d.*

On the other hand, words such as *many, most, usually, generally, frequently, often, seldom,* and *some* tend to appear in correct answers. For example,

<u>Many</u> children love chocolate.

Students <u>generally</u> do not enjoy taking tests.

These statements are probably true.

When you have difficulty selecting the correct answer to a multiple-choice question, you will sometimes find help by remembering that statements are probably incorrect when they include words such as *all* or *never* and that they are probably correct when they include words such as *some* or *seldom.*

19.8   Insults or jokes may be incorrect answers

Insulting or ridiculous statements in options for multiple-choice questions are seldom correct answers. For instance,

1. When children have extremely low intelligence, educators refer to them as

   a. idiots.
   b. morons.
   c. imbeciles.
   d. totally dependent.

It is insulting to refer to anybody as an idiot, moron, or imbecile. The correct answer to the question is option *d*.

Insults are practically never the correct answers to multiple-choice questions and neither are ridiculous or ludicrous statements. For example,

2. The real reason that American colonists objected
   to the Tea Tax was that they opposed

   a. taxation with representation.
   b. the competition of smuggled tea.
   c. Britain's monopoly of tea sales.
   d. a man by the name of Lipton.

You may be disturbed by silly options, such as the one in option *d*. When you are taking a test, you may not be in the mood for a dumb joke such as this. However, the silly statement is a clue that the correct answer is either option *a, b,* or *c;* it is option *c*.

When options for multiple-choice questions are insulting or ridiculous statements, assume that they are *probably* distractors and that the correct answer is *probably* one of the other options.

19.9   High or low numbers may be incorrect answers

Some multiple-choice questions have options that are a series of numbers. For example,

1. The number of words per minute in a radio
   advertisement should not exceed

   a. 100.
   b. 150.
   c. 200.
   d. 250.

When you must guess at correct answers to questions of this type, you are likely to increase your chance of selecting the correct answer if you eliminate the lowest and highest numbers and select from between the other options. The correct answer is option *b*.

When you guess at the answers to questions in this format, read the options carefully. The numbers may not be listed in an increasing or decreasing sequence. For example,

2. Approximately what proportion of a population is included in the distance between one standard deviation below the mean and one standard deviation above the mean?

    a. two-thirds
    b. three-quarters
    c. one-quarter
    d. one-half

If you must guess at the answer to this question, the highest number is three-quarters (option *b*) and the lowest number is one-quarter (option *c*). You should eliminate them and make your choice from between option *a* and option *d*. The correct answer is option *a*.

Of course, you should always answer test questions using information you have learned (Section 19.3). However, studies of multiple-choice questions have found that when options are a series of numbers, chances are that the correct answer is *not* the highest or lowest number in the series.

19.10   More complete statements may be correct answers

When one option for a multiple-choice question is a more complete statement than the others, it may be the correct answer. For example,

1. Syntax refers to the arrangement of words into

  a. phrases.
  b. clauses.
  c. sentences.
  d. phrases, clauses, and sentences.

Option *d* includes everything stated in options *a, b,* and *c;* it is the correct answer.

Select the more complete statement as the correct answer to the following question:

2. The standard deviation for weight is likely to be larger for a group of

  a. females who are ballet dancers.
  b. adults in the general population.
  c. males who are football line backers.
  d. male and female jockeys.

Option *b* includes the persons identified in options *a, c,* and *d,* and all other adults as well; it is the correct answer to the question.

Please notice that an answer does not need to be longer than other answers to be more inclusive and complete.

19.11   *All of the above* may be the correct answer

There is a definite *tendency* for the option *all of the above* to be the correct answer to multiple-choice questions. *All of the above* often serves the same function as a more complete answer. Compare the following questions.

1. Partners in a marriage are likely to be similar in

  a. height and weight.
  b. hair and skin color.
  c. general health.
  d. all of the above.

2. Partners in a marriage are likely to be similar in

    a. height and weight.
    b. hair and skin color.
    c. general health.
    d. size, coloring, and health.

Option *d* is the correct answer to both questions.

Also, when you know that two options are correct and a third option is *all of the above,* you know that *all of the above* is the correct answer. For example,

3. Napoleon was admired by French

    a. peasants.
    b. soldiers.
    c. business people.
    d. all of the above

If you know that Napoleon was admired by French peasants and soldiers, then you must select *all of the above* as the answer to this question even if you do not know that he was admired by French business people. The reason for this is that there must be only one correct answer to a multiple-choice question. If you answer *a,* you do not include soldiers; if you answer *b,* you do not include peasants. To include both peasants and soldiers, you must select option *d.*

Studies of multiple-choice questions have consistently reaffirmed that it is good advice to give serious consideration to whether *all of the above* is the correct answer to a question whenever it is one of the options.

19.12   One of two similar-looking answers may be correct

When two options for a multiple-choice question are similar looking, the correct answer is likely to be one of the two similar-looking options. For example,

1. The loss of all sensation in your hand would most
   likely result from

   a. aphasia.
   b. hallucinations.
   c. damage to afferent spinal nerves.
   d. damage to efferent spinal nerves.

Options *c* and *d* are very similar looking; the correct answer is
option *c*.

Experienced question writers usually write multiple-choice
questions so that test-takers will not be able to use this clue to
correct answers. For example,

2. The loss of all sensation in your hand would most
   likely result from damage to

   a. afferent spinal nerves.
   b. efferent spinal nerves.
   c. afferent cranial nerves.
   d. efferent cranial nerves.

Written this way, the clue of two similar-looking answers cannot be used. The correct answer is option *a*.

When two options for a multiple-choice question are similar
looking, seriously consider whether one of them is the correct
answer.

19.13   All questions should be answered

Unless you are told that you will be severely penalized for
incorrect answers, always select an answer for every multiple-
choice question even if you must guess at some answers (see
Section 18.5). When you guess at an answer to a multiple-
choice question with four options (*a*, *b*, *c*, and *d*), you have a
25 percent chance of guessing the correct answer. When you

guess at an answer to a multiple-choice question that has five options (*a, b, c, d,* and *e*), you have a 20 percent chance of guessing the correct answer. As a result,

1. If you guess at the answers to twelve multiple-choice questions that have four options, by chance you will guess three correct answers (.25 × 12 = 3).
2. If you guess at the answers to twelve multiple-choice questions that have five options, by chance you will guess two correct answers (.20 × 12 = 2.4).

Of course, in any instance of guessing you may guess more or fewer correct answers than are predicted by chance.

Some of the suggestions in this chapter will help you increase your chances of guessing correct answers when you are forced to guess. In addition, it may benefit you to know that when multiple-choice tests are properly prepared, each option will be a correct answer an approximately equal number of times. For example, if a test has forty questions and the options are *a, b, c,* and *d, a* will be the correct answer about ten times, *b* will be the correct answer about ten times, and so on. Therefore, when you can assume that a multiple-choice test is properly prepared, you may have an advantage by guessing that the correct answers to unanswered questions are the option you have used least often to answer other questions. For example, if you have used mostly *a, b,* and *c* to answer questions and must guess at the answers to some questions, you may have an advantage if you guess that the correct answers to unanswered questions are option *d.*

On the other hand, when multiple-choice tests are improperly prepared, one option may be the correct answer much more frequently than other options. A teacher may favor option *c* for correct answers, reasoning that *a* is too soon, *d* is too late, and students will guess that correct answers are probably option *b.* Therefore, when multiple-choice test questions are reviewed, count the number of times various options are correct answers.

Use what you learn when you must guess at the answers to questions on future tests teachers give.

However, do not generalize what you learn from one teacher to another. For example, if one of your teachers tends to place correct answers at option *b,* do not use this to predict that one of your other teachers has the same habit. Analyze each teacher's tests separately.

Use What You've Learned

1. When you answer multiple-choice questions, find correct answers by crossing out all the distractors. When tests are reviewed, decide whether this strategy helped you answer questions correctly.

2. When you answer multiple-choice questions, underline the words *not, except, incorrect,* and *false* when they appear in stems. When tests are reviewed, decide whether this helped you answer questions correctly.

3. When you answer multiple-choice questions, keep in mind that words such as *always, never, all,* and *none* tend to be in distractors and that words such as *sometimes, seldom,* and *many* tend to be in correct answers. When tests are reviewed, decide whether this helped you answer questions correctly.

4. When you answer multiple-choice questions, keep all of the following in mind:

a. insults and jokes may be distractors.
b. the high and low numbers in a series may be distractors.
c. more complete statements may be correct answers.
d. *all of the above* may be a correct answer.
e. one of two similar-looking answers may be a correct answer.
When tests are reviewed, decide if any of these thoughts helped you select correct answers.

5. When you answer multiple-choice questions, make marks on your answer sheets so you'll know which answers you guessed at. When tests are reviewed, evaluate how successful you were at guessing correct answers. If you are not very successful, examine the questions you guessed at to determine if any suggestions in this chapter could have helped you guess more correct answers.

6. When a teacher reviews multiple-choice questions, estimate whether each option is the correct answer approximately an equal number of times or if one option (such as *c*) is the correct answer more often than other options. Use what you learn if you must guess at the correct answers to questions on the next test that the teacher gives.

True-False
Questions

I t is easy to write true-false questions and it is easy to grade the answers to them. As a result, true-false questions appear on many college tests. This chapter explains how to decide whether true-false statements are true or false.

20.1   Characteristics of true-false questions

True-false questions are statements that test-takers must decide are either true or false. They are well suited for testing whether students know straightforward factual information such as the following fact students learn in accounting courses.

T   F   A company suffers a loss when expenses exceed revenues.

In accounting, there is no argument whether this statement is true or false; it is true. When a company's expenses (money spent) exceeds its revenues (money received), the company suffers a loss.

Unfortunately, some instructors use true-false questions to test knowledge and understanding for which they are not well suited. For example, the following question was asked on a test for a marketing course.

T   F   Data were collected about people's attitudes toward a particular product. The

```
data were used to test a hypothesis about the
product, and then they were stored. If these
data are used at a later time in another
research study, they will be considered
primary data.
```

This statement is confusing; students who have the information to answer it correctly may be so confused that they will answer it incorrectly. It would be better for students if the marketing instructor asked them to write an answer to the following question:

```
What is primary data?
```

Unfortunately, it is easier to score the answer to the true-false question than to score the written answer to this question. As a result, some teachers use true-false questions in instances when some other type of question might give students better opportunities to reveal what they know.

20.2   Basic strategy for true-false questions

An effective strategy for answering a true-false question is to assume that it is a true statement unless you can determine that it is false. This strategy will focus your attention on a specific task and help you arrive at accurate decisions efficiently. Also, there is a *slight tendency* for true-false tests to include more true statements than false statements. The reason for this seems to be that it is easier to write true statements than it is to write false statements that appear to be true.

As with all test questions, true-false questions should be answered using information that is learned for courses. However, the ways in which true-false questions are worded often provide hints whether they are true or false statements. These hints are discussed in the remaining sections of this chapter.

20.3   All parts of a statement must be true

For a true-false statement to be true, all parts of the statement must be true. As a result, the more facts that are included in a statement, the more likely it is to be false. A statement does not need to be long to contain several parts. For example,

T   F   `Disposable income is used to spend, save,`
                 `and pay taxes.`

For this statement to be true, disposable income must be used for (1) spending, (2) saving, and (3) paying taxes. It is used for spending and saving, but it is *not* used for paying taxes. The statement is false.

However, the fact that a true-false statement includes several parts does not guarantee that it is false. One of the following statements is true but the other is false.

T   F   `The three major issues of the consumer`
                 `movement are working conditions,`
                 `information disclosure, and environmental`
                 `protection.`

T   F   `The three main issues of the consumer`
                 `movement are product performance safety,`
                 `information disclosure, and environmental`
                 `protection.`

The first statement is false, but the second statement is true.

The words underscored in the following true-false questions make them false statements.

T   F   `Abraham Maslow `<u>`discovered the human needs`</u>
                 `and arranged them in a hierarchical`
                 `sequence.`

T   F   `Solon, `<u>`Hesiod`</u>`, and Cleisthenes were`
                 `Athenian leaders.`

When you answer true-false questions, keep in mind that if any part of a statement is false, the statement is false.

20.4   Absolute statements may be false

Absolute statements exclude all possibilities except the one they state. They often include words such as *all, every, only, no, never, none, always, invariably,* and *best.* For example,

`All` `college students like hamburgers.`

`College teachers are` `never` `six feet five inches tall.`

If there is one college student who does not like hamburgers or one college teacher who is six feet five inches tall, these statements are false.

On the other hand, words such as *many, most, some, a few, generally, frequently, usually, often, sometimes, ordinarily,* and *seldom* tend to be found in true statements. For example,

`Many` `college students like hamburgers.`

`College teachers are` `seldom` `six feet five inches tall.`

It is true that many college students like hamburgers and that college teachers are seldom six feet five inches tall.

Each of the following statements contains a word that suggests whether it is true or false. Underline the word in each statement that is a clue to its truthfulness or falseness and then circle *T* if you believe a statement is true or *F* if you believe a statement is false.

T   F   1. `Firms always adopt and use new technology.`
T   F   2. `Firms frequently adopt and use new technology.`

T   F   3. When one group of a society receives satisfaction, this may cause dissatisfaction for another group.

T   F   4. When one group of a society receives satisfaction, this invariably causes dissatisfaction for another group.

T   F   5. Identification and imitation refer to similar processes.

T   F   6. Identification and imitation refer to exactly the same process.

Following are the words that should be underlined, and the answers to the questions: (1) *always, F;* (2) *frequently, T;* (3) *may, T;* (4) *invariably, F;* (5) *similar, T;* and (6) *exactly the same, F.*

Of course, absolute statements may be true. For example, the following statement is true.

T   F   When measuring liquid, one liter is <u>always</u> equal to one cubic decimeter.

When you answer true-false questions, keep in mind statements that include words such as *all* and *none* are likely to be false, and statements that include words such as *many* and *few* are likely to be true.

20.5   Statements of reasons may be false

When true-false questions state reasons, they tend to be false. For example, the following statement is false.

T   F   The reason the government protects consumers is that consumer lobbyists fought for this protection.

This statement is false because the government protects consumers as a result of the efforts of *many* groups and individuals (who were, or are, not necessarily lobbyists). Though we tend to think of the consumer movement as a new force in our society, it has been very strong since the 1880s and it was not started by lobbyists.

True-false questions that state reasons tend to be false because they usually do not state *all* the reasons, or causes, for an event. The following statement is true.

T   F   One reason the government protects
             consumers is that consumer lobbyists fought
             for this protection.

The word *one* makes the statement true. See Section 25.5 for a full explanation of the problems associated with stating reasons, or causes.

A true-false question does not need to include the word *reason* to state a reason; *because, therefore, so, consequently, was the cause,* and *as a result* are some of the other words and phrases that may be used to state reasons. For instance,

T   F   Consumer lobbyists fought for consumer
             protection; therefore, the government now
             protects consumers.

Therefore is used to state a reason in this sentence.

Of course, a true-false question that gives a reason may be a true statement. For instance,

T   F   Retailers use the markup pricing method
             because it is convenient and easy to use.

This statement is true, as are many true-false statements that include reasons. However, statements of reasons do *tend* to be incomplete or inaccurate, and false. The discussion in Section 25.5 will give you insight into why this is true.

20.6   Be alert for *not* and other negatives

Words such as *not* and *cannot* and negative prefixes such as the *in-* in *infrequently* can completely change the meaning of a statement. Compare the following two questions.

T   F   One's buying power depends partly on the state of the economy.

T   F   One's buying power does not depend partly on the state of the economy.

The questions are identical except for the word *not;* the first is true, but the second is false.

Half of the following questions include a negative, such as *not* or a negative prefix, such as the prefix *il-* in *illegal.* Underline the negatives and circle *T* if you believe a statement is true or circle *F* if you believe a statement is false.

T   F   1. Alcohol is not a stimulant.
T   F   2. Alcohol is a stimulant.

T   F   3. Those who have strong self-awareness are likely to cope inefficiently with anxiety.
T   F   4. Those who have strong self-awareness are likely to cope efficiently with anxiety.

T   F   5. Vitamins give us energy.
T   F   6. Vitamins do not give us energy.

T   F   7. Most saturated fats are of animal origin.
T   F   8. Most unsaturated fats are of animal origin.

Following are the answers to the questions and the words or prefixes that should be underlined: (1) *not, T;* (2) *F;* (3) *in-, F;* (4) *T;* (5) *F;* (6) *not, T;* (7) *T;* and (8) *un-, F.*

Be alert for negatives when you answer true-false questions; they usually change the meanings of statements completely.

20.7 Explain your answer, if necessary

If you are uncertain whether a teacher intends a statement to be true or false, write an explanation so your teacher will know why you selected the answer you did. For example,

T (F) Disposable income is used to purchase necessities such as food, clothing, and shelter. *It is also used for luxuries and savings.*

This statement is true, but the written explanation makes it clear why the student decided it is false.

20.8 All questions should be answered

Unless you are told that you will be severely penalized for incorrect answers, always answer true-false questions even if you must guess at some answers. When you guess at the answer to a true-false question, you have a 50 percent chance of guessing the correct answer (it is either true or it is false). Thus, if you guess at the answers to eight true-false questions, by chance you will guess four correct answers (.50 × 8 = 4). Of course, by chance you may select fewer than four or more than four correct answers when you guess at eight answers.

Some of the suggestions in this chapter will help you increase your chances of guessing correct answers when you are forced to guess. In addition, it may benefit you to know that when true-false tests are properly prepared approximately half of the statements are true and approximately half of them are false. Thus, if you can assume that a true-false test is properly prepared, you may have an advantage by guessing that the correct answers to unanswered questions are the answer you used less often to answer other questions. For example, if you use mostly *false* to answer questions you know and must guess at the answers to some questions, you may have an advantage if you guess that the correct answers are *true*.

On the other hand, when true-false tests are improperly prepared, there are likely to be more true statements than false statements. The reason for this is that some teachers find it easier to write true statements than to write false statements that appear to be true. When you can assume that a true-false test is improperly prepared, you may have an advantage by guessing that more statements are true than false.

When a test with true-false questions is reviewed, study it to determine how many times *true* and *false* were correct answers. Use what you learn when you must guess at answers to true-false questions on the next test that the teacher gives. However, do not generalize what you learn from one teacher to another. For example, if one of your teachers includes more true statements than false statements, do not use this to predict that one of your other teachers has the same habit. Analyze each teacher's tests separately.

Use What You've Learned

1. When you answer true-false questions, assume that statements are true unless you can determine that they are false. When tests are reviewed, decide if this helped you answer some questions correctly.

2. When you answer true-false questions, keep in mind that
a. if any part of a statement is false, the statement is false.
b. statements of reasons tend to be false.
c. words such as *always* and *never* tend to be in false statements.
d. words such as *usually* and *seldom* tend to be in true statements.
When tests are reviewed, decide if these thoughts helped you answer some questions correctly.

3. When you answer true-false questions, underline *not, cannot,* and negative prefixes (such as *un-, non-, dis-, in-, im-, il-,* and *ir-*). When tests are reviewed, decide if your attention to negatives helped you answer some questions correctly.

4. When you answer true-false questions, make marks on your answer sheets so you will know which answers you guessed at. When tests are reviewed, evaluate how successful you were at guessing correct answers. If you were not very successful, examine the questions you guessed at to determine if any suggestions in this chapter could have helped you guess more correct answers.

5. When a teacher reviews true-false questions, estimate whether statements are true about half of the time or whether there are more true statements or more false statements. Use what you learn when you must guess at correct answers the next time you take a test the teacher gives.

Matching Questions

Matching questions appear on college tests less frequently than do multiple-choice and true-false
questions. But when teachers like matching questions, they tend
to include at least one of them on each test they give. This
chapter explains how to select correct answers to matching
questions.

21.1 Characteristics of matching questions

Matching questions present two lists of items and require
test-takers to associate items in one list with items in the other
list. When they are properly prepared, the items in a column
are all similar. For example, one column might be all terms and
the other might be all definitions, or one column might be all
dates and the other might be all historical events.

Figure 21a illustrates a properly prepared matching question
for a literature course in which one column lists the names of
authors and the other column lists the titles of short stories. If
you do not know who the authors of the short stories are,
chances are that you will not make more than one correct match
by guessing at the answers to the question in Figure 21a. If you
wish to try your luck at matching, answer the question in Figure 21a before you read the answers for it. It is extremely difficult to guess the correct answers to properly prepared matching questions.

Figure 21a **A Matching Question for a
Literature Course.**

Matching

Match the short story titles in the second column with the authors in the first column.   Use each
item in the second column one time only.

_____	1. Singer	a. "Bartleby, the Scrivener"
_____	2. Paley	b. "The Tree of Knowledge"
_____	3. Melville	c. "The Secret Sharer"
_____	4. Oates	d. "A Hunger Artist"
_____	5. Cheever	e. "Tanhum"
_____	6. James	f. "The Country Husband"
_____	7. Allen	g. "Train Whistle Guitar"
_____	8. Kafka	h. "A Conversation with My Father"
_____	9. Conrad	i. "The Kugelmass Episode"
_____	10. Murray	j. "The Lady with the Red Dog"
		k. "Mrs. Yardley's Quilting"

Answers: (1) e, (2) h, (3) a, (4) j, (5) f, (6) b,
(7) i, (8) d, (9) c, and (10) g.

21.2   Strategy for matching questions

The correct procedure for answering matching questions is to use the items in one column as the starting point from which to make all matches and to cross out items as you match them.

In Figure 21a either column may be used as a starting point for making matches. It is equally logical to match authors to the short stories as it is to match short stories to the authors. Whichever column is used as the starting point for making matches, after Singer has been matched with the short story he wrote ("Tanhum"), both Singer and "Tanhum" should be crossed out (and the letter *e* added beside number 1) before attempting to match Paley with the short story she wrote.

However, when items in one column are much longer statements than the items in the other column, use the column with the longer statements as the starting point for making all matches. For example, in Figure 21b the second column contains definitions that are much longer than the terms listed in the first column. It would be confusing and inefficient to read and reread the definitions in the second column. Therefore, one should attempt to match "computes expected claims and calculates cost of insurance premiums" with "actuary" before attempting to match "acts on behalf of another" with "agent." As items are matched, they should be crossed out.

It is extremely important to make as many correct matches as possible before guessing at any matches. If one error is made in matching, the chance that additional errors will also be made is greatly increased. The mathematics of the effects of guessing at answers to matching questions is too complicated to explain here, but the more correct matches you make the more likely you will be to match remaining pairs correctly by guessing. For example, if there are eight items in each of two columns and you are able to make six correct matches before guessing at the last two matches, you will either guess the last two matches correctly or you will guess them both incorrectly.

Figure 21b **A Matching Question for a**
Business Course.

<u>Matching</u>

Match the definitions in the second column with
the terms in the first column.   Use each item in the
second column one time only.

_____	1. grantor	a. computes expected claims and calculates cost of insurance premiums
_____	2. conciliator	
_____	3. maker	b. acts on behalf of another
_____	4. beneficiary	c. receives proceeds of an insurance policy
_____	5. entrepreneur	d. helps labor and management resolve disputes
_____	6. actuary	
_____	7. agent	e. agrees to pay a supplier a certain sum on a certain date
_____	8. drawee	f. takes risks in starting a business
		g. transfers interest in real property to another
		h. agrees to pay a certain sum on a certain date
		i. protects the rights of bondholders

Answers: (1) g, (2) d, (3) h, (4) c, (5) f, (6) a,
(7) b, and (8) e.

21.3 Logical clues in matching questions

Figure 21a and Figure 21b are examples of properly written matching questions; the items in each list in the questions are similar. In Figure 21a one column lists authors and the other column lists short stories; In Figure 21b one column lists terms and the other column lists definitions. Only those who have the necessary knowledge will be able to match the items correctly. Of course, you do not need to have taken a literature course in college to know that Herman Melville wrote "Bartleby, the Scrivener," and you do not need to have taken a business course to know that a beneficiary is one who receives the proceeds of an insurance policy. But for those who lack these kinds of knowledge, there are no hints in the questions as to what the correct answers are.

When matching questions are improperly written, various types of information are mixed together in lists. The mixture of information may provide clues that can be used to make matches. Figure 21c is an improperly prepared matching question for a psychology course. Different types of information are mixed in the lists and this provides logical clues that may be used to guess at answers. For example, the first item in the first column is "located in the ear." It is not logical that "trust," "James B. Watson," "convergent thinking," or most of the other items in the second list are located in the ear. Use logical clues to match as many of the pairs as you can in Figure 21c. After you have matched as many items as you can, read the following explanations of logical clues that might help in making matches.

1. The ear is part of the body and organs are located in the body (c).
2. The suffix *-ist* indicates that *behaviorist* refers to a person, and James B. Watson is a person (d).
3. It makes sense that children must learn to trust (f).
4. Tests measure abilities or learning (i).

Figure 21c **A Matching Question That Gives Logical Clues to Answers.**

<u>Matching</u>

Match the items in the second column with the items in the first column.   Use each item in the second column one time only.

_____	1. located in the ear	a.	James-Lange theory
		b.	parapraxis
_____	2. behaviorist	c.	organ of Corti
		d.	James B. Watson
_____	3. childhood crisis	e.	convergent thinking
		f.	trust
_____	4. measures capacity to learn	g.	frequency distribution
_____	5. tally of scores	h.	ideographic study
		i.	aptitude test
_____	6. study of an individual		
_____	7. feelings are the result of emotional behavior		
_____	8. leading to one answer		

---

5. A tally is used to keep records of amounts and frequency refers to amounts (g).

6. The word *study* appears in only one item in the second list (h).

7. This statement sounds more like a theory than any other statement in the list (a).

8. Thinking (e) leads to answers, and there is no logical reason to match this item with *parapraxis* (b).

It is not likely you will answer a matching question on a college test that has as many logical clues as the one in Figure 21c. However, when you do not know the answers to matching questions, your only alternatives are to use logical clues or to guess. Since the odds are very much against you when you guess at matching questions, sound reasoning is likely to be the better choice.

Use What You've Learned

1. When you answer matching questions, select the items in one column as the starting point from which to make matches and cross out items as you match them. When tests are reviewed, decide if this helped you make correct matches.

2. When the statements in one column are much longer than the statements in the other column, use the column with the long statements as the starting point from which to make matches.

3. After you have made as many correct matches as you can, use logical clues to help you make additional matches. When tests are reviewed, decide if you were as logical as possible when you guessed at answers.

4. When you answer matching questions for a specific teacher, make a note of what types of items you were asked to match. When you prepare for the next test the teacher gives, study so that you will be able to match similar types of items.

22 Sentence Completion Questions

Sentence completion questions are easy to write. They are usually devised by lifting sentences directly from a book and eliminating words from them. However, since students often have difficulty writing answers for them, most teachers avoid including these types of questions on tests. In case you must answer sentence completion questions for any of your teachers, this chapter explains the procedures to use.

22.1 Characteristics of sentence completion questions

Sentence completion questions are statements that have deleted portions that test-takers must supply. When they are properly written it is clear exactly what type of answer is required. For example,

1. The emperor _____ divided the Roman Empire into two parts.

2. The year _____ is used as the base for measuring the consumer price index.

Even if you do not know the correct answers to these questions, you can tell by reading them what *types* of answers they require: (1) the name of an emperor and (2) a year. The answers are *Diocletian* and *1967*.

Unfortunately, teachers sometimes write sentence completion

questions so that it is unclear what *types* of answers are required for them. Compare the following questions to the first two questions:

1. The _____ divided the Roman Empire into two parts.

2. _____ is used as the base for measuring the consumer price index.

Written in these ways it is not completely clear what types of answers are required. Since it is not indicated in the first question that the name of an emperor is wanted, perhaps the teacher intends students to identify the governmental need that inspired the division of the Roman Empire into two parts. Since the second question does not indicate that a year is required, perhaps the teacher intends *100* to be the answer; this is the base that was established for the dollar when the consumer price index was introduced (in 1967).

Most teachers avoid asking sentence completion questions because the answers to them are often the cause for arguments when tests are reviewed. When students give reasonable answers to poorly worded completion questions, teachers often find themselves defending an answer they marked correct as "better" than logical answers that they marked incorrect. Unfortunately, there is little for you to gain by arguing with teachers who give this kind of explanation for how they grade answers to sentence completion questions.

22.2   Strategy for sentence completion questions

The only strategy for answering most sentence completion questions is to determine what *type* of answer is required and to give that type of answer. Even when questions are not written with complete clarity it is usually possible to figure out what type of answer is wanted. For example,

```
Constantine made _____ the capital
of the Eastern Roman Empire.
```

This question could be written as follows to make it clear exactly what type of answer is required.

```
Constantine made the city of _____
the capital of the Eastern Roman Empire.
```

However, the word *capital* in the first version of the question is a good clue that the name of a city is wanted; a capital is ordinarily a city. Constantine made Byzantium the capital.

When you are stymied in your attempt to decide what type of answer is required for a question, consider asking your teacher for clarification. Prepare your question carefully so that your teacher will know you are making an earnest effort to write an appropriate answer. For example, don't point to a question and ask a teacher "What do you mean?" or "What kind of an answer do you want?" Rather, decide what the logical alternatives are and use them to formulate your question. For instance,

```
The Boer War was fought in _____.
```

If you are uncertain what type of answer is required for this question, you might ask a history teacher: "Do you want me to give the place where the war was fought or the time when it was fought?" The teacher should realize that the question is ambiguous and give you the direction you need.

22.3   Clues to correct answers

There are only two clues to correct answers to sentence completion questions, but they are so well known that most teachers avoid them both.

The word *an* just before a write-on line can sometimes suggest a correct answer. For example,

```
Fear is an _____ motive for making a
purchase.
```

The word *an* just before the write-on line limits the answers to words that begin with vowel sounds such as *a, e, i, o,* and *u.* Those who have studied motives for buying know that they are of two basic types: emotional and rational. The correct answer to the question is *emotional.* However, few instructors provide this clue. The *an* clue is usually eliminated by writing *a(an), a(n),* or *a/an* instead of *an.*

The length of write-on lines can also sometimes be a clue to the required answer, or more than one line may provide a clue. For example,

```
_____ _____ is the
defense mechanism by which people act in a way that is
the opposite of the way that they unconsciously feel.
```

Those who have learned about defense mechanisms know that the only two-word defense mechanism is *reaction formation,* which is the correct answer to the question. Again, few instructors provide this type of clue to answers. Sentence completion questions usually have write-on lines of exactly the same length so that line length will not give hints to correct answers.

22.4   Guessing at answers

One reason teachers like sentence completion questions is that it is almost impossible to guess correct answers for them. However, when you do not know the answer to a completion question, you should make the best guess you can, unless your best guess is an answer you are certain is incorrect. For example,

```
"What Lips My Lips Have Kissed" was written by
_____ .
```

If you are studying American literature and do not remember that "What Lips My Lips Have Kissed" is a poem written by Edna St. Vincent Millay, you should guess the name of an author—you may guess Edna St. Vincent Millay. However, if the best answer you can think of is *a woman, a man, somebody,* or *an American,* it may be better not to write any answer at all. These types of answers are so obviously incorrect that they aren't even worth a try.

Use What You've Learned

1. When you answer sentence completion questions for a teacher, notice what *types* of answers are required by most of the questions (people's names, terms, and so on). When you study for the teacher's next test, prepare to answer sentence completion questions about the same types of information.

2. When you answer a sentence completion question, try to determine what *type* of answer is required and write that type of answer.

3. If a teacher writes the word *an* before write-on lines or uses write-on lines of various lengths, determine if these are clues to correct answers (see Section 22.3).

4. When the answers to sentence completion questions are reviewed, observe whether students argue with teachers about the correct answers to them. If they do, what advice do you have for the teacher?

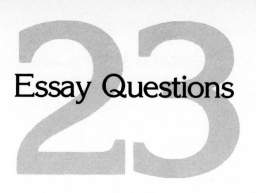

Essay Questions

Questions that require written answers a paragraph or more in length are called **essay questions**. Many students consider them to be the most difficult type of test question.

If you have poor writing skills, writing essay answers and all other tasks that require writing will cause you difficulty. On the other hand, if you have reasonably good writing ability, essay tests should not be especially difficult for you if you use the methods explained in Chapter 11 through Chapter 17 when you prepare for essay tests, and the suggestions in this chapter when you take them. *Also, Chapter 25 and Chapter 26 give explanations that are useful for writing answers to essay questions.*

23.1 Characteristics of essay tests

Figure 23a is an example of an essay test that might be given during a sixty-minute class meeting of an introductory psychology course. Notice that five questions are listed in the test but that students must answer only three of them (see Section 18.5). Figure 23b is an example of a good answer to the fifth question on the psychology test. The answer is a summary of information studied using the methods that are described in Chapter 11 through Chapter 17.

The grades for essay questions are derived from the judgment of the teachers who grade them; they give the grades for answers that, in their opinions, are merited. When grading the answer in Figure 23b, a psychology teacher will have some expectations about what should be included in the answer. For

Figure 23a **An Essay Test for a Psychology Course.**

Psychology 101:   Test 2

Write your answers to the following questions in the booklet that you have been provided.   Answer any two of the 25-point questions and one of the 50-point questions.   You have 60 minutes to write your answers.

Answer Two (25 points each)

1. Define brainstorming, and give an example of it.

2. Compare and contrast aptitude and achievement tests.

3. Justify the following statement: A test must be both valid and reliable.

Answer One (50 points)

4. Trace the sequence in which language is acquired by human infants.

5. Briefly explain the four broad bases of mental retardation.

Figure 23b An Answer to the Fifth Question in Figure 23a.

> The four important factors in mental retardation are (1) inheritance, (2) illness and disease, (3) emotional factors, and (4) cultural deprivation.
>
> Low mental functioning can be *inherited*. Microcephalic people are born with unusually small brains, for example. Also, Down's syndrome (mongolism) is inherited as a result of an extra chromosome.
>
> *Illness or disease* can also cause mental retardation. Malnutrition, infection, or loss of oxygen to the brain can cause brain damage. An underactive thyroid gland may cause cretinism, so that a person doesn't grow properly and has a very low I.Q. There are medical treatments for some of these causes of inferior mental functioning.
>
> *Emotional problems* are a common cause of people's inability to achieve their full intellectual capacity. Sometimes, too, people are so disturbed that they are unable to read or to solve simple math problems.
>
> *Cultural deprivation* also often results in inferior intellectual performance. Children need parents or other models who help them to develop language and other learning skills. An enriched environment can sometimes help to overcome these deprivations so that mental functioning improves.

example, he or she would probably expect students to state the four broad bases for mental retardation: (1) inheritance, (2) illness or disease, (3) emotional factors, and (4) cultural deprivation. A teacher is likely to give some credit for any answer that includes all of these major points and whatever additional credit answers receive will probably depend on how a teacher reacts to comments students make about the major points.

Usually when students write answers to essay questions, they see the questions for the first time during a test session and answer the questions from memory in bluebooks. **Bluebooks** are small booklets that contain lined paper. They got their name from the fact that at one time their covers were always blue, but today the covers of bluebooks may also be yellow, pink, green, or some other color.

Some teachers give take-home or open-book tests. A **take-home test** may be test questions that students actually answer "at home." Or, students may be given a list of possible test questions to study "at home." The students would then answer some of the questions from memory during a test session. It may seem that take-home tests give students an advantage, but they usually do not. The questions on take-home tests are ordinarily much more difficult than the questions on tests students see for the first time during a test session. Also, teachers tend to grade answers to take-home test questions strictly.

Open-book tests are tests during which students may refer to their textbooks, and sometimes their notes, as they write the answers to test questions. The term *open-book test* is misleading; it suggests that students may copy the answers to test questions from their books. However, open-book tests seldom include questions for which answers can be copied. Whatever benefits students receive by being able to refer to their books is directly related to how thoroughly they studied. Since there is a limited amount of time to answer open-book test questions, students who have studied most thoroughly benefit most when they refer to their books or notes. Prepare for open-book tests just as you would for any other type of test.

23.2   Understand the direction words

Direction words are the words in essay questions that inform students what types of answers they are to write. Direction words are italicized in the following essay questions:

Define brainstorming, and give an example of it.

Justify the following statement: A test must be both valid and reliable.

Explain the four broad bases of mental retardation.

The following discussions explain the meanings of some of

the direction words that appear frequently in essay test questions.

Discuss, describe, and explain. *Discuss, describe,* and *explain* appear very frequently in essay questions and they are often used as though their meanings are identical.

> *Discuss* the characteristics of a good test.
>
> *Describe* the characteristics of a good test.
>
> *Explain* the characteristics of a good test.

All three of these statements have essentially the same meaning: *Write as much as you can* about the characteristics of a good test. When *discuss, describe,* or *explain* appear in essay questions, they are likely to mean "write as much as you can in the time that you have."

Describe can also mean to "write about a subject so that it can be visualized." This meaning seldom gives difficulty. For example,

> *Describe* a meal that is nutritionally well balanced.

It is impossible to write an answer to this question without naming foods that can be visualized.

However, *explain* may mean to "give reasons." For example, when you explain to an employer why you are late to work, you give reasons for being late. *Explain* means "give reasons" in the following essay question:

> *Explain* this: James I was the "wisest fool in Christendom."

Answers to this question must give the reasons James I of England was said to be the "wisest fool in Christendom." When *explain* appears in an essay question, consider whether it means "give reasons."

Compare and contrast. *Compare* is one of the most frequently misinterpreted of the direction words. If you state a comparison between two things, you state how they are similar *and,* if they have any differences, you also state how they are different. For example,

> *Compare* Chomsky's view and Skinner's view of language development.

Many students believe that *compare* means to state similarities only. But if they state only how Chomsky's view and Skinner's view are similar, they will write very incomplete answers to the question. There are more differences than similarities between the two views.

On the other hand, a *contrast* between two things emphasizes their differences.

> *Contrast* the impressionistic and postimpressionistic schools of painting.

This question requires students to emphasize the differences between the two schools of painting. The two schools could be compared, but, if they are contrasted, the answers to the question will be shorter.

Some instructors know that students misinterpret the meaning of *compare* and so they include both *compare* and *contrast* as direction words in questions for which they want students to make comparisons.

> *Compare* and *contrast* Chomsky's view and Skinner's view of language development.

When questions are worded in this way, it is more clear that both differences and similarities must be stated. (Section 25.4 explains two methods that may be used to write about comparisons.)

Criticize, evaluate, and justify.   *Criticize, evaluate,* and *justify* are discussed together because similar thought processes are used to answer questions that contain these direction words. All three words direct you to draw a conclusion about the merits of something. If you *criticize* or *evaluate* something, you consider its positive and negative aspects and come to a conclusion about its merits. For example, if you criticize or evaluate a movie you saw, you would consider the things you liked and did not like about the movie and come to a conclusion whether you would recommend that others should spend their time and money to see it.

If you *justify* something, you emphasize why it is appropriate and right and come to the conclusion that it is appropriate and right. If there are negative aspects, you may consider them, but you come to the conclusion that whatever you justify is good and right. For example, if you justify why you voted for a particular political candidate, you emphasize the good things about the candidate for whom you voted and come to the conclusion that it was appropriate and right that you voted the way you did.

The following questions are identical except for the direction words in them.

> *Criticize* the death sentence.
> *Evaluate* the death sentence.
> *Justify* the death sentence.

The answers to all three of these questions should include the arguments for and against the death sentence. However, students who *criticize* or *evaluate* the death sentence must decide whether the arguments for or against it are more convincing. Those who *justify* the death sentence must come to the conclusion that, at least in some instances, it is correct, appropriate, and right to sentence people to death. (Section 25.7 gives suggestions for writing evaluations and criticisms.)

Diagram and illustrate.   *Diagram* and *illustrate* may both mean to "make a drawing and label it." The following questions might appear on a test for a criminology course.

> *Diagram* a bullet passing through a plate glass window.
> *Illustrate* what happens when a bullet passes through a plate glass window.

Figure 23c **A Diagram or Illustration for
an Essay Answer.**

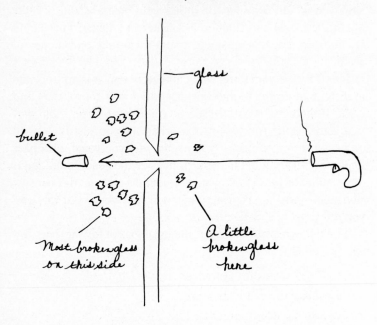

A bullet passing through glass

Both of these questions require a drawing of the type that is illustrated in Figure 23c. However, *illustrate* may also mean to "include a written example." This is its meaning in the following question:

> *Illustrate* how visual aids may be used to communicate ideas while giving a speech.

In this question *illustrate* means to give a fairly long written example. Test-takers need to select a hypothetical speech topic and explain how visual aids may be used to communicate ideas about the topic. For example, if the hypothetical speech topic is "How to Take Better Snapshots of Family Groups," the answer might explain how members of the audience may be used to demonstrate how to group people for more interesting snapshots. This illustrates a visual aid; the audience members are the visual aid for the speech.

Enumerate, list, outline, and summarize.   *Enumerate, list,* and *outline* may all mean to "present and number items so the points stand out clearly." This is the meaning of these direction words in the following essay questions:

> *Enumerate* the psychosexual stages that Freud identified.
>
> *List* the psychosexual stages that Freud identified.
>
> *Outline* the psychosexual stages that Freud identified.

The correct answer to all of these questions is a numbered list of the psychosexual stages and a description of each stage.

Summarize means to "state in a few words." But some teachers use *summarize* and *outline* in essay questions as though their meanings are identical.

> *Summarize* the psychosexual stages that Freud identified.
>
> *Outline* the psychosexual stages that Freud identified.

Summarize does not specify that the psychosexual stages should be listed and numbered, but it is appropriate to list and number the stages when summarizing them.

Since there is a great deal of information about some subjects, *summarize* and *outline* do not necessarily indicate that a short answer is required. For example,

> *Summarize* the major changes in the power of the Presidency of the United States, beginning with George Washington and continuing up to the present time.

Entire books have been written on this subject. If you summarize or outline the changes in the power of the Presidency, you will not write a short answer. (Information about how to write outlines is given in Section 24.4, and methods for writing summaries are explained in Section 25.3 and Section 28.4.)

Relate and trace.   *Relate* means to "show the connection or relationship that exists between two things." For example,

> *Relate* cigarette smoking to heart disease.

This question requires statements of whatever connection or relationship there is between cigarette smoking and heart disease. Complete answers will include statistics about the greater incidence of heart disease among smokers as compared to nonsmokers.

Trace usually means to "report a series of events in a logical or chronological sequence." For example,

> *Trace* the evolution of the English legal system in the period of Henry II and John.

Correct answers to this question will state, in chronological order, the major changes in the English legal system during the time that Henry II and John were English monarchs.

23.3   Find all parts of questions

A major cause for essay test grades that are lower than they should be is that students fail to find and answer all parts of questions. Most of the examples of essay questions in Section 23.2 have one major part to them. But essay questions frequently have two or more parts that must be answered. Compare the following two questions:

> Relate cigarette smoking to heart disease.
>
> Relate cigarette smoking to heart disease and cancer.

The second question has two parts that must be answered; students must explain how cigarette smoking is related to (1) heart disease and (2) cancer. If they answer only one part of the question, they will probably receive only half credit for their answers.

When essay questions are well written, it is usually easy to find how many parts they have. For example,

Describe the political, economic, and religious achievements of Louis XIV.

Explain the chances of survival for those who lived in the eighteenth century, considering infant care, childhood, diet, and medical care.

Correct answers to the first question will discuss three aspects of achievement: (1) political, (2) economic, and (3) religious. Correct answers to the second question will include discussions of (1) infant care, (2) childhood, (3) diet, and (4) medical care during the eighteenth century.

Sometimes teachers include several questions within one essay question, when it would be better for them to ask several questions. For example,

What was the New Deal? What was its aim? Did it succeed? Was it satisfactory to the left? To the right? Explain what you mean.

When an essay question is confusing to you, keep in mind that your teacher probably wants you to write as much as you can about the topic of the question. The teacher who wrote this question about the New Deal really wanted the answers to the following four questions:

1. What were the three major components of the New Deal?
2. What did President Roosevelt hope that the New Deal would accomplish?
3. Did the New Deal achieve the objectives that President Roosevelt hoped it would?
4. Why was the New Deal unsatisfactory to those on the right as well as to those on the left of the political spectrum?

When you do not understand essay questions, you will either need to figure out as best you can what they mean or ask teachers to clarify the meanings of questions for you. It is appropriate for you to assume that teachers want you to understand their test questions.

23.4 Write well-organized and complete answers

After you have used the suggestions that are given in Section 23.2 and Section 23.3 to understand what type of answer is required for a question and how many parts a question has, prepare to write a well-organized and complete answer. A well-organized answer begins with an introduction that summarizes the answer, and the major points in the answer are made to stand out clearly; a complete answer includes all the relevant information that answers the question.

It is very much to your advantage to write answers that are complete and well organized. They must be complete to receive full credit; and if they are well organized, they will be easy for your teachers to read and understand. It is difficult to read and grade answers to essay questions; if you make your teachers' work easier they will appreciate this and they may give you the benefit of the doubt when they grade your answers. For example, if a teacher has difficulty deciding whether you should receive a B+ or an A— for an answer, he or she may give you an A— if you were thoughtful enough to make your answer well organized and easy to read.

23.5 How to write well-organized answers

Well-organized answers are written by planning what the major points will be, by writing clear introductions, and by making the major points stand out clearly.

Plan the major points. In some instances the major points to include in an answer are directly stated in essay questions. For example,

> Describe Maslow's hierarchy of human needs (physiological, safety, love, esteem, and self-actualization).

The five needs are listed in the correct sequence so they may be used as an outline for writing an answer to the question. However, the question could also be worded in the following way:

Describe Maslow's hierarchy of human needs.

To answer this question, students must recall the five human needs in the correct hierarchical sequence. Chapter 11 through Chapter 17 explain how to study so that you will be prepared to plan outlines for essay questions when outlines are not stated for you.

You may find it helpful to make a list of the major points that you want to include in an answer before you actually write the answer. Notes of this type may be made on the back of the page on which test questions are printed or on pages in the back of the bluebook in which answers are written.

Write a clear introduction.   The introduction for an essay answer should be a summary of the answer. Therefore, after you have decided what your major points will be, summarize them in the first sentence of your answer. The introduction for the essay answer in Figure 23d states the five human needs in the sequence in which Maslow arranged them. Also, in Figure 23b, the four bases of mental retardation are summarized in the introduction to the answer.

When you make only one major point in an answer, also state that major point in the introduction. For example, only one major point would be made in the introduction for an answer to this question:

> Explain why you agree or disagree with the following statement: "Regressive taxes, such as the sales tax, should be abolished because they place an undue burden on the poor."

The introduction for the answer to this question should be a summary of the answer. For example: "I agree that since regressive taxes place an undue burden on the poor, they should be abolished" or "Regressive taxes place an undue burden on the poor, but I disagree that they should be abolished." Whichever point of view is taken, it should be clearly stated in the introduction. Other statements in the answer would be reasons

Figure 23d An Answer to the Essay Question: Describe Maslow's Hierarchy of Human Needs.

> Maslow said there are five needs that must be fulfilled in the following sequence: physiological, safety, love, esteem, and self-actualization.
>
> 1. _Physiological needs_ include the needs for water, food, sleep, and sex. These needs must be satisfied before other needs can be fulfilled.
>
> 2. _Safety needs_ are the needs to be secure from danger. For example, if we have safe places to live and know that we will be cared for if we become ill or unemployed, this satisfies some safety needs.
>
> 3. _Love needs_ are the needs to have affectionate relationships with others.
>
> 4. _Esteem needs_ are the needs to approve of oneself and to be accepted and respected by others. For students, some esteem needs may be satisfied when they receive good grades, because good grades are evidence that work is competent and respected. Maslow believed the first three needs must be satisfied before esteem needs can be fulfilled.
>
> 5. _Self-actualization_ needs are the needs to be the most of whatever a person can be. For example, when people are the best students, musicians, or professionals they can be, they satisfy self-actualization needs.

for agreeing or disagreeing that regressive taxes should be abolished.

Make the major points stand out clearly. If the major points in your essay answers stand out clearly, it will be easier for you to check and make certain that you have included all the information that you want to include in them. Also, your answers will be easier to read and grade; this may be a benefit to you (see Section 23.4).

Notice in Figure 23b and Figure 23d that the major points are underlined to make them stand out clearly. In Figure 23d they are also numbered to emphasize the hierarchical sequence in which human needs are satisfied. When students write essay answers in these thoughtful ways, teachers are likely to assume that the answers are good even before they read them.

23.6   How to write complete answers

You are likely to write complete answers to essay questions if you imagine you write them to an uninformed reader and if you write more than you think you need to write.

Write to an uninformed reader.   When essay tests are returned to students and the answers to them are reviewed, students who received low grades for answers often think to themselves, "I knew that, but I didn't include it." When these students are asked why they did not include relevant information in answers, they often say "I didn't think it was important" or "I thought the teacher would realize that I know that." Unfortunately, everything is important in the answers to essay questions and teachers do not know what students know unless they include what they know in answers.

If you tend to write incomplete answers to essay questions, you may find it helpful to forget that you are writing to a teacher and imagine instead that you are writing to a friend or relative to whom you want to explain what you know. The thought that the reader is uninformed about the answers to questions may help you write more complete answers and explain your thoughts more carefully.

This method was used to write the answers in Figure 23b and Figure 23d. The person who wrote them had his teen-age sister in mind; he believed that if he wrote answers his teen-age sister could understand, his teacher would have no difficulty understanding them either.

Write more than you think you need to write. You may also write complete answers to essay questions if you write more than you think you need to write. The students who receive the highest grades for essay answers are the ones who include all relevant information in them. It is almost always better to include too many facts and details in an essay answer than it is to include too few. Whenever you are uncertain whether to include a piece of information in an answer, include it.

Also, include examples whenever they help to make it clear that you understand course subject matter. Notice in Figure 23d that examples are included for some of the human needs; the examples make it completely clear that the student understands esteem needs and self-actualization needs. Textbook writers use examples to make terms and concepts easy to understand, and you may also use examples to explain information in your essay answers.

Sometimes teachers lead students astray by emphasizing that they want short answers. What they usually mean is that they do not want to read long-winded answers filled with irrelevant comments; they want to read statements that answer questions. If teachers really want short answers to questions they will give an instruction such as this one: "I will give a grade of F to any answer that is longer than 150 words." Unless a teacher tells you that you will be severely penalized for writing everything that is relevant to an answer, include all relevant information in your answers.

Also, some essay tests are printed on sheets of paper with each question followed by a space in which to write answers. When a space on a test in this format is not large enough for you to write a complete answer, continue your answer on the back of the page. For example, if there is not enough space for you to write your complete answer to a third question, write as much as you can in the space provided and the word *over* in parentheses. Then, on the other side of the page write *3* and complete your answer.

23.7   Proofread your answers

Teachers know that students cannot do their best writing when they write answers to essay questions under the pressure of time limitations. However, the answers to questions should be as well written as possible. Therefore, plan your test-taking time so that you will have a few minutes at the ends of test sessions to proofread your answers and to correct what you wrote. When you proofread, check especially for incomplete thoughts and for places where you can add additional information or examples. Any improvements you can make to your answers while proofreading will benefit you when they are graded.

23.8   What to do if time runs out

When you take essay tests, it is extremely important to plan carefully how you will use your test-taking time (see Section 18.2). But, no matter how well you plan, there are likely to be instances when you will not have time to write the most complete answers you can to essay questions. Your problem will be that if you write no answer your teacher will assume that you do not know the answer and if you write a very short answer your teacher will assume that it is the best answer you can write. In the first case you will receive no credit and in the second case you will probably not receive as much credit as you should.

One solution to this problem is to write a complete outline of the answer that you would have written if you had time. If you do this, show your outline to the teacher and request additional time to write the complete answer. Another solution is to request time to answer some other question in place of the one that you did not have time to answer. A reasonable teacher will respond favorably to one of these requests or offer some other solution to the problem. Teachers are unreasonable and unfair when they allow students less time than they need to answer test questions.

Use What You've Learned

1. If you have ever answered questions for a take-home or open-book test, did you find the questions especially difficult?

2. Learn the meanings of the direction words that are given in Section 23.2. When you answer essay questions, decide whether this helped you write good answers.

3. When you write answers to essay questions,

a. plan the major points for answers.
b. write introductions that summarize answers.
c. make the major points stand out clearly.
d. write to an uninformed reader.
e. write more than you think you need to write.

When tests are reviewed, decide if these strategies helped you write good answers.

4. When you take essay tests, reserve time to proofread your answers before you give them to teachers.

5. Use the suggestions in Chapter 25 and Chapter 26 to write better answers to essay questions.

PART FIVE

How to Prepare Papers and Reports

Write Papers
a Step at a Time

You may be required to write a paper five, ten, fifteen, or more pages long for almost any course you take in college. This chapter explains how you may write the best papers you can, one step at a time, and have them ready when they are due.

1. Understand the assignment.
2. Prepare a schedule.
3. Select a topic.
4. Collect information and prepare an outline.
5. Organize your information.
6. State the central theme.
7. Draft the body of the paper.
8. Write an introduction and a conclusion.
9. Revise and rewrite the draft.
10. Put the paper in final form.

These ten steps may be used to write almost any type of paper that you may be required to write for college credit.

Chapter 25 through Chapter 28 give suggestions that will help you solve problems you may encounter as you use the steps that are outlined in this chapter.

1. You may have difficulty deciding how to develop or discuss a topic (see Chapter 25).
2. You may need ideas about the kinds of evidence you can use to support statements or conclusions in papers (see Chapter 26).

3. You may want to know how you can find information for papers quickly in a library (see Chapter 27).

4. You may need to know how to present and document information in a research paper (see Chapter 28).

Information in this part of the handbook should also be helpful to you when you answer essay questions (Chapter 23).

24.1   Understand the assignment

The requirements for written assignments may be explained in a course syllabus or some other paper a teacher distributes, or they may be explained orally in class. Learn the answers to these questions for each written assignment.

1. *When is the paper due?* Record the date in the place where you keep records of assignments (see Section 4.3), and prepare a schedule that allows for time to complete the four stages of the writing process described in Section 24.2. You are responsible for having papers ready when they are due even if teachers do not remind you when they are due; your grade may be lowered if you turn in a paper late (see Section 4.5).

2. *How many pages long must the paper be?* The length of a paper will usually help you decide how much time you must schedule for writing (Section 24.2). Write papers of the length your teachers request; they may be slightly shorter or longer than specified, but they should not be much shorter or longer than requested. For example, if you are assigned to write a five-page paper you may write a paper one-half page shorter or longer, but it would probably not be wise to write a four-page or a seven-page paper.

3. *What type of information must I use to write the paper?* Papers must often include references to information in books or in magazines, newspapers, and other periodicals. However, you may be asked to write papers based on what you learned or observed when you visited a museum, business, hospital, school, governmental agency, or other institution. Or, you may write

reports based on interviews you conduct (Section 26.4), scientific experimentation you do, or observations you make of people's behavior. Schedule the time that is necessary for you to collect the information you need to write papers (Section 24.2).

4. *In what format must the paper be presented?* If you receive specific instructions about what headings to use in a paper, the amount of space to leave for margins, or any other detail about the format for a paper, be certain to follow the directions exactly. Your grade may be lowered if you do not follow them. When you write a research paper, use the format described in Chapter 28, unless a teacher specifies that you must use some other format.

5. *What are acceptable topics for the paper?* Teachers may assign you to write on any course topic that interests you, they may provide a list of topics from which you may select, or they may request you to write about one specific topic. Make certain to learn exactly what are acceptable topics for papers.

It is essential for you to know the answers to all five of these questions before you begin work on a paper. When you are uncertain about the requirements for papers, schedule appointments with your teachers to discuss your uncertainties and to receive the clarification you need.

24.2   Prepare a schedule

When professional writers have deadlines to meet, they prepare schedules to guide them so they will have their projects ready when they are due. If professional writers need schedules, chances are that you do too. Plan to write papers in four basic stages.

1. Prepare so that writing may begin.
2. Write a draft of the paper.
3. Revise and rewrite the draft.
4. Put the paper in final form.

The first stage includes the first six steps in the writing process: understand the assignment, prepare a schedule, select a topic, collect information and prepare an outline, organize your information, and state the central theme (Section 24.1 through Section 24.6).

To decide how many days or weeks you should schedule for writing a paper, you will need to consider how many hours you have available each week that you may devote to writing and, of course, how quickly and easily you write. The nature of an assignment will also determine how much time is needed for writing. For example, if an instructor for a business course asks you to find and summarize a newspaper or magazine article on any business topic you select, the first stage of the writing process may take only an hour or two. On the other hand, if the assignment is to write a twenty-page research paper on a subject of your choice for a history course, it may take you a few days to decide on a topic and several weeks to collect the information you need to write the paper.

When papers account for a substantial proportion of a course grade, it is wise to begin work on them as soon as they are announced. If you put off writing a paper, you may need to devote many hours to writing at the time you want to prepare for midterm or final examinations. Therefore, prepare schedules for major papers so that your work on them will be spread over as many weeks as possible. For example, a student learned on September 17 that he had eight weeks to write a ten-page term paper. He set up the following schedule to make certain he would complete the paper on time.

	Deadline	Number of weeks
1. Prepare so writing may begin.	October 8	3
2. Write a draft of the paper.	October 22	2
3. Revise and rewrite the draft.	November 5	2
4. Put the paper in final form.	November 12	1

Notice that the student set aside the most weeks to prepare for writing the paper. He used good planning because careful preparation made it easier for him to complete the other three stages of the writing process.

24.3   Select a topic

The first and crucial step in preparing to write a paper is to select a good topic. A topic for a paper should have these characteristics:

1. It should be narrow enough so that you will learn a good deal about a specific aspect of a topic.
2. It should be broad enough so that sufficient information is available for you to use when you write about it.

The following topics are listed in sequence with the broadest topic first and the narrowest topic last:

> Human Behavior
> States of Consciousness
> Sleeping and Dreaming
> Dream Theories
> Freud's Theory of Dreams

The last topic in this list is narrow enough so that students who write a paper about it will learn a great deal about a specific aspect of a topic. It is also broad enough so that sufficient information should be available in a college or university library to write a paper about it. Information about Freud's theory of dreams may be found in many books and periodicals in most college libraries.

Use the following procedures when you have freedom to write a paper about any topic that is related to the subject matter for a course:

1. Examine the table of contents and index of your course textbook and make a list of the topics that interest you most;

record the page numbers on which the topics are discussed in the book.

2. Read about each topic in the textbook, and select two or three that you find most interesting.

3. Visit a library to learn how many articles and books are available for the topics (Section 27.1 through Section 27.3).

4. Use what you learn in a library to select a topic that is interesting to you and for which sufficient information is available for you to write a paper.

By using this method, a student of psychology read his textbook and selected *hypnotism* and *dreams* as two topics of special interest to him. When he visited the library he found several recent journal and magazine articles explaining how hypnotism was used to brainwash political prisoners. This aspect of the topic fascinated him, and so he wrote a paper explaining how hypnotism is used for brainwashing.

If you select a topic, but have difficulty deciding exactly how you will discuss it, ask yourself the following questions about the topic:

1. Is there something I can define?

2. Is there a method I can explain?

3. Is there information I can summarize?

4. Are there things I can compare?

5. Are there causes I can discuss?

6. Is there something I can analyze?

7. Is there something I can evaluate?

8. Is there something about which I can persuade others?

For example, in preparing to write about *drug abuse* for her health education course, a student asked these questions and gave the following answers:

1. *Is there something I can define?* I can define what an addiction is.

2. *Is there a method I can explain?* I can explain a method for curing people of drug addiction.

3. *Is there information I can summarize?* I can summarize the experiences of a drug addict reported in an autobiography.

4. *Are there things I can compare?* I can compare what drugs have been most widely used in this country at various times in history.

5. *Are there causes I can discuss?* I can discuss what causes some people to become drug addicts.

6. *Is there something I can analyze?* I can analyze what seem to be the difficulties in controlling widespread drug use.

7. *Is there something I can evaluate?* I can evaluate the effectiveness of various methods for treating drug addiction.

8. *Is there something about which I can persuade others?* I can persuade others that they would be better off if they did not use drugs.

There are many other answers to these eight questions when they are asked about drug abuse, but these answers were sufficient for the student to narrow the topic for her paper. She decided to use the answers to the second and seventh questions, and wrote an evaluation of two methods used for treating addiction to alcohol.

Chapter 25 gives full explanations of these eight ways to develop and discuss topics; refer to Chapter 25 when you select topics as well as when you write about them.

It is important that topics for papers are interesting to you because if they are interesting you will learn things you want to learn and, as a result, you will enjoy writing papers more. However, there are some types of topics that are wise to avoid:

1. *Controversial issues.* Avoid writing papers about controversial issues unless you have been assigned to write about them. If you write about topics such as premarital intercourse, abortion, life after death, and capital punishment, you run the risk of expressing opinions with which your teachers disagree

strongly (see Section 25.8). Teachers are human; some of them may give you low grades when you state beliefs that are very different from the ones they hold.

2. *Your emotional responses.* Avoid writing papers that include information about your emotional responses unless you have been assigned to explain your feelings. Do not, for example, state in a paper what you like or do not like, unless you have been asked to make such statements. Papers written for college credit are usually supposed to be about a specific course topic, not about what students feel or what they like and do not like (see Section 25.7).

3. *Scientific and technical subjects.* Do not write papers about specialized aspects of scientific or technical subjects unless you have been assigned to write about them. Ask your teachers for their approval before you start work on these types of papers. When teachers lack the scientific and technical knowledge required to understand your papers, they cannot grade them appropriately.

Chapter 25 includes explanations of what should be avoided when discussing causes, presenting analyses, making evaluations, and persuading others to change (Section 25.5 through Section 25.8).

24.4   Collect information and prepare an outline

After you have used the suggestions in Section 24.3 and Chapter 25 to decide how you will develop and discuss a topic, you need to collect information that you can use to write a paper. It is likely that you will need to read books and articles in a library (Chapter 27). But you may also collect information by conducting interviews (Section 26.4); by attending an event, such as a concert; by visiting a museum, business, governmental agency, or other institution; or by doing scientific experimentation.

Figure 24a Notes on Information for Writing a Paper.

Cross-reference
to outline for
paper

Cross-reference
to bibliographic
note (see Section
28.1)

Information for
paper

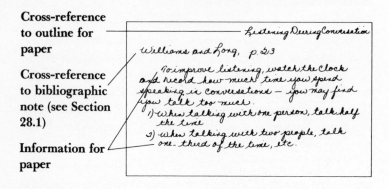

Whatever method you use to collect information, make notes of the type that are illustrated in Figure 24a; procedures for making notes on information for papers are explained in Section 28.2. You need to collect at least some of the information for a paper before you prepare an outline of how you will organize a paper; you need to know what information is available in order to plan the content of a paper. When you know what types of information are available, you can write an outline to guide you as you collect additional information and write the draft of the paper.

Outlines are well-organized summaries of the major points in a paper. For example,

Reasons for Giving Tests

I. To compute final course grades
II. To plan instruction
III. To evaluate students' progress
IV. To evaluate the effectiveness of instruction

Notice that the outline begins with a title and that the major points are labeled with Roman numerals. Also, observe that the major points are not stated in complete sentences; they are stated in phrases. This is an example of a *topic outline.*

Outlines may also be written using complete sentences, as in the following example:

Reasons for Giving Tests

I. Test grades may be used to compute final course grades.
II. First-of-term test scores may be used to plan instruction.
    A. A teacher of writing may give an essay test to determine what special writing instruction students need.
    B. A teacher of intermediate algebra may give a test of beginning algebra to determine how much algebra review students need.
III. First-of-term test scores may be compared to end-of-term test scores to evaluate how much progress students made as a result of instruction.
IV. Test scores may be used by instructors to evaluate whether their teaching methods are effective.

This is an example of a *sentence outline.* Notice that details are listed under the second major point and that they are labeled with capital letters.

When you prepare outlines for your own purposes, you do not need to use Roman numerals and capital letters, and you may write some statements as phrases and some statements as sentences. However, *if you submit an outline to a teacher, use these procedures:*

1. Write a title that summarizes the information in the outline.
2. Write the major points and details so that they are all phrases *or* all sentences; do not mix phrases and sentences.
3. Include at least two major points in the outline (I and II).
4. If you include details under a major point, include at least two (A and B).

Also, make certain that major points and details are logically related to one another. For example,

Causes of Rapid Population Growth
in Developing Countries

   I. The ratio of births to deaths is increasing.
  II. Populations were very large before growth increased.
 III. The very poor value large families.
 IV. Religious beliefs encourage large families.

The major points in this outline are all logically related because they are all causes of rapid population growth.

In addition, when details are included under the major points in an outline, they must be logically related to the major points under which they are listed. For example,

IV. Religious beliefs encourage large families.
   A. Arabs believe it is a blessing from Allah to have many children.
   B. Islam believes birth control methods should not be used.
   C. The Judeo-Christian tradition believes that people should "be fruitful and multiply."
   D. Roman Catholics believe contraceptives should not be used.

The details are all logically related to the major point because they are all religious beliefs that encourage people to have large families.

The major points in the outline about rapid population growth are all causes, but papers usually include various types of information. When they do, the information must be arranged logically. For instance,

Stuttering: Causes and Treatments

   I. What is stuttering?
  II. Why do people stutter?
 III. What are the methods for treating stuttering?

This outline is logically arranged. It is logical to begin the paper with an explanation of what stuttering is. It is also logical to explain the causes of stuttering before explaining methods for treatment; the reasons people stutter influence the ways in which they are helped to stop stuttering.

Another logical arrangement for a paper that includes more than one type of information is illustrated in the following outline:

The Problems of Product Packaging

   I. Benefits of packaging
  II. Problems of packaging
III. Solutions to the problems of packaging

This outline was prepared for a paper in which the writer explained that, while packaging has obvious benefits, there are serious problems associated with it (it wastes natural resources and it is expensive to dispose of). He then stated the solutions that have been offered to deal with the problems. The development was logical. He began with a comparison of the benefits and problems, and he stated the problems before he stated the solutions to them because an understanding of the problems is essential to understanding their solutions.

24.5   Organize your information

Use your outline for a paper as a guide to collect the information you need and take notes of the type that are illustrated in Figure 24a (see Section 28.2). Then, group together the notes that belong together. For example, the following outline for a paper is in four major parts, so notes must be organized into four groups.

Remedies for Poor Listening

    I. Poor listening habits
   II. Good listening habits
 III. Listening during conversations
 IV. Listening during formal presentations

After the notes for this outline are organized into four major groups, the notes for each group must be further organized. For example, if there are five poor listening habits that will be discussed in the paper, then the notes that pertain to each poor listening habit must be grouped together.

When you have your information organized the way you want it, state the central theme for a paper.

24.6   State the central theme

The first crucial step in writing a paper is to select a good topic; the second is to write a good central theme. A **central theme** is a sentence that states exactly what information will be discussed or what conclusion will be drawn in a paper.

When the purpose of a paper is to present information about a highly structured subject, the central theme is simply a sentence that summarizes the information in the paper. For example,

> There are five steps in the selling process.
>
> There are four major causes of birth defects.

These central themes make it clear exactly how the discussions will be limited. The first paper will explain five sequential steps in the selling process and the second paper will discuss four causes of birth defects.

Central themes for informative papers about highly structured subject matter are usually easy to write. However, you may encounter difficulty in writing central themes for papers in which you draw conclusions; they must state *exactly* what conclusion you will draw. Following are central themes of this type:

> Generic drugs are equal to brand name drugs in all respects except cost.
>
> The audience for Broadway productions has little interest in classical or serious drama.

The United States has inadequate defense against nuclear attack.

Notice that the conclusions are clearly stated in each of these central themes. For example, the first central theme makes it clear that the writer will conclude that generic drugs are equal to brand name drugs in all respects except cost (generic drugs are less expensive). Also notice that the central themes are complete sentences. "Generic drugs and brand name drugs" may be a good title for a paper, but it is not a central theme.

In addition, central themes do not include phrases such as *in my opinion* or *I think*. For example, "I think television is degrading to the intelligence of viewers" is not a proper central theme for a serious paper, but the following sentence is: "Popular television programs do not depict life crises in ways that help viewers deal constructively with the crises in their lives." The first theme provides writers with opportunities to discuss themselves, but the second theme provides them with opportunities to write something of value about a specific aspect of the topic *television*. Serious papers written for college credit are usually not supposed to be about students' emotional responses; they are usually supposed to present information or draw a conclusion about a specific aspect of a topic (see Section 24.3 and Section 25.7).

Your central themes should summarize exactly what information you will discuss in a paper or exactly what conclusions you will draw. When you write a central theme, ask this question about it:

Does this sentence summarize exactly what information I will include in my paper or state exactly what conclusion I will draw?

If the answer is no, rewrite the central theme until the answer to this question is yes.

When you are uncertain of the merits of central themes, ask your instructors to evaluate them for you. It is essential that you have good central themes to guide you when you write drafts of papers. If you do not, you may find that you will need to do a great deal of unnecessary rewriting.

24.7   Draft the body of the paper

A draft is written by referring to an outline, well-organized notes, and a central theme (Section 24.4 through Section 24.6). Chapter 25 and Chapter 26 also give suggestions that should be helpful to you when you write the draft of a paper.

Do *not* begin by writing an introduction; it is a waste of time to write an introduction to a paper that has not been written. Instead, begin by writing the draft of the first major section of a paper. For instance, if the first major section is about five poor listening habits, begin by writing about one of the poor habits.

Be prepared to use a great deal of paper. If you type, double or triple space; if you write, skip one or two lines between each line you write. The blank space will give you room to write corrections and revisions in the way that is illustrated in Figure 24b. Also, *write information about each aspect of a topic on one sheet of paper, even if the information does not fill a sheet.* For example, if you write about five poor listening habits, write the information about each habit on a separate sheet of paper. This procedure will save you time when you revise and rewrite because you will be able to change the organization of a paper easily or to integrate additional information exactly where you want to include it in a draft (see Section 24.9).

When you write, use the sentence patterns and words that you ordinarily use. You will, of course, need to use any specialized terminology that is essential for discussing the topic of a paper; but do not use obscure words and long, convoluted sentences because you believe that this is the way you are expected to write in college. Write the way you write when you do your best writing; do not try to write in any other way. If you write in a way that you are unaccustomed to writing, your papers will be stilted, pretentious, and unappealing.

Use the skills you learned or are learning in a writing course.

Figure 24b Revised Draft for a Research Paper.

In a recent interview, Lyman K. Steil, ~~an~~ *a nationally known* authority on communications, stated that poor listening complicates relations among ~~epople~~ *people*, and sometimes even has fatal ~~results~~ *consequences*:

> The sinking of the <u>Titanic</u>, Pearl Harbor, ~~the Jamestown, Guyana, incident~~ and some recent airplane disasters are classic examples of a breakdown in communication and in judgment. A message was sent and listening broke down.[1]

Fortunately, good listening habits can be learned ~~in the same way good writing habits can be learned.~~ This paper explores the characteristics of poor listening and the remedies for it.

Poor Listening Habits

~~Students~~ *Studies* have found that within two days after listening to a ~~10~~ *ten*-minute presentation, ~~the~~ average listener ~~can~~ remember only about one-fourth of what was said. *and* ~~P~~oor listeners, ~~of course~~, remember even less.[2] ~~If you ever speak in front of a group, you~~ *Any speaker* can quickly identify the poor listeners in an audience.

If you are uncertain about mechanics of writing, such as punctuation and capitalization, you may own a textbook for a writing course that explains the things about which you are uncertain. If you do not own an English handbook, you may purchase one in a bookstore.

Be certain to study Chapter 25 and Chapter 26; they give suggestions that are likely to be helpful to you when you write drafts of papers.

24.8   Write an introduction and conclusion

After you have completed the draft for the body of a paper, write an introduction and conclusion. This section gives some suggestions that may be helpful to you at this stage of the writing process.

Introductions.   The introduction to a paper should be interesting and it should include a statement of the central theme. The following suggestions may give you ideas for introductions:

1. *Ask a thought-provoking question.* "What should parents do if their teenage child comes home drunk?"

2. *State a serious problem.* "Thousands of bridges in the United States are in such poor repair that they pose a serious threat to human life."

3. *State an opinion.* "The prestige of the United States is suffering because we do not provide adequate care for the aging, infirm, and poor."

4. *Begin with a quotation.* "An expert is one who knows more and more about less and less."—Nicholas Murray Butler.

5. *Begin with an interesting or unusual fact.* "The vision of a fifty-year-old man, blind from birth, was restored by the use of microsurgery."

6. *Make a prediction.* "If immediate changes are not made in the social security system, there will be no money for benefits by the year 2000."

7. *Give a definition.* "*Charisma* is an attractive quality a person may have that captures the imagination of others and causes them to be unswervingly devoted to the person who possesses it."

The examples are all sentences, but introductions are usually at least one paragraph long. All the examples could have been written as paragraphs. For instance,

```
What role do parents play in teaching their
children to be responsible users of alcoholic
beverages?  Should parents drink excessively in
front of their children?  Should they offer a young
son or daughter a glass of wine to toast birthdays,
anniversaries, and other occasions?  What should
parents do if their teenage child comes home drunk?
The evidence is that the ways parents answer these
questions plays an important part in determining
whether their children will become responsible
users of alcoholic beverages.
```

The last sentence is the central theme.

The purpose of an introduction is to engage the interest of readers and to establish rapport with them. Therefore, avoid the following types of introductions:

1. *Apologies.* Don't make statements such as "I'm not an expert, but. . . ."
2. *Complaints.* Don't make statements such as "I found the book extremely difficult to understand, but. . . ."
3. *Obviousness.* Don't state something that everybody knows, such as "*Gone With the Wind* is a famous motion picture."

4. *Long-windedness.* Don't bore your readers with rambling, long-winded introductions; grab their attention and move on to your discussion.

The reason you do not want to apologize in a paper is that it is unnecessarily belittling to you; do not belittle yourself to your readers. The reason you do not want to complain is that nobody likes a complainer; you want to establish good rapport with your audience.

Conclusions.   Good papers do not stop, they end with a satisfying conclusion. Good conclusions can ordinarily be written by doing one of the following:

1. Restate the central theme.
2. Restate the major points in the paper.
3. State an opinion or belief and explain how the information in the paper supports it.

When you write papers for English, music, history, and other humanities courses, it may be appropriate to end them with quotations, stories, humor, irony, or suggestions about the broader implications of the information in papers.

24.9   Revise and rewrite the draft

After you have written the draft of the introduction, body, and conclusion for a paper, follow these procedures:

1. Underline one sentence in each paragraph that states the major point made in it.
2. If there is no sentence to underline in a paragraph, eliminate the paragraph or rewrite it to include a sentence you can underline.
3. Read all the underlined sentences to decide if they summarize all the major points you want to include in the paper. If they do not, write additional paragraphs and insert them where you want them in the draft.

4. Rearrange the pages of the draft if this will improve the organization of the paper.

5. Read the entire paper aloud, and make a tape recording of what you read.

6. Listen to the recording to decide if what you hear will be completely understandable to a person who is completely uninformed about the information in the paper.

7. If you are dissatisfied with what you hear in any way, make changes by revising, adding, or deleting material from the paper.

8. Proofread the revised draft to make certain that it is free of all writing errors. You may need to refer to an English textbook you own, or you may need to purchase an English handbook in a bookstore.

Repeat these procedures until you are satisfied that your draft is ready to be written or typed in final form. Figure 24b illustrates revisions made for part of a draft.

24.10   Put the paper in final form

After you have revised a draft, wait at least one day before you prepare the final paper. The passing of time will help you be more objective about your paper when you reread it before you write or type it in final form. Last minute changes you make with an open mind toward your writing can make the difference between a good paper and an excellent one.

When teachers give instructions for the format in which papers should be presented, follow them exactly. For instance, teachers might state the width of margins so there will be room for them to write comments. Also, when you write research papers, use the format explained in Chapter 28 unless you have been told to use some other format.

If you have not already done so, decide on a title for the paper. Titles for serious college papers should describe the information included in them, and, as a result, they often include words that are in central themes. For example, "Classical and Serious Drama on Broadway" might be the title for a paper that has the following central theme: "The audience for Broadway productions has little interest in classical or serious drama."

After you have written or typed a paper, carefully proofread it to make certain that it is free of all errors. Some teachers become extremely disturbed when they find even one misspelled word in an otherwise perfect paper; you do not want to annoy teachers when they read your papers to decide what grades you should receive for them.

Also, don't be annoyed when teachers correct your writing errors. Instead, use their comments to eliminate errors from your writing. If you can learn to write error-free prose, it will serve you well no matter what occupation or profession you pursue. When you assume a responsible job, you will be at an advantage if you can write well; you will always have an advantage when you possess an important ability that some of your coworkers do not have.

Use What You've Learned

1. If you have papers to write this term, use the suggestions in Section 24.1 to understand exactly how to complete the assignments. Use the suggestions in Section 24.2 to prepare schedules to write the papers and have them ready when they are due.

2. Use the suggestions in Section 24.3 to select a topic that is discussed in this handbook about which you could write an eight-page paper. State the topic and how many books and articles you found in a library that you could use as sources of information to write a paper about the topic.

3. Prepare an outline and state a central theme for writing about the topic you selected when you did the preceding activity.

Develop the Topics for Papers

Papers are written about topics; most topics can be developed, or discussed, in many different ways. For example, the topic *kindness* may be developed by defining what kindness is, by explaining a method for being kind, by comparing it to unkindness, by discussing what causes some people to be kind, and in many other ways.

This chapter gives information that you can use to think creatively about how you may discuss the topics for your papers. It also explains specific strategies you may use when you write papers. You may

1. state a definition.
2. explain a method.
3. summarize information.
4. make a comparison.
5. discuss causes.
6. present an analysis.
7. evaluate something.
8. persuade others to change.

As you read this chapter, keep in mind that a topic may be developed in one way or in two, three, or more ways. For example, an entire paper may be written about inflation by discussing only its causes. But a paper about inflation may also be written by defining what it is, discussing its causes, and analyzing what might be done to control it.

This chapter explains basic methods for organizing and presenting information in papers. Chapter 26 gives suggestions about the types of evidence you can use to support statements and conclusions in your papers.

25.1   State a definition

When the topic for a paper is a term or concept, give a definition of it. For example, if the topic is *work,* begin the paper with a definition of what work is. Also, an explanation of what something is may be sufficient subject matter for an entire paper. For example, so much has been written about what work is that an explanation of the nature of work could easily be used to write a long paper.

Terms and concepts may be defined by giving synonyms, statements of meaning, or examples that disclose their characteristics.

Synonyms.   A **synonym** is a word that has the same meaning or nearly the same meaning as another word; in English, synonyms are usually similar in meaning rather than identical in meaning. For example, synonyms for *work* include *employment, occupation, calling, labor, pursuit,* and *business.* None of these synonyms for *work* has exactly the same meaning as *work.* Find synonyms by consulting standard desk dictionaries (Section 9.5), dictionaries of synonyms, and thesauruses. Standard desk dictionaries present discussions of synonyms such as the following:

> **Synonyms:** *work, labor, toil, drudgery, travail.* These nouns refer to the exertion of physical or mental faculties in order to accomplish something, contrasted with play or recreation. *Work* is the most widely applicable; it alone can refer not only to the effort of persons but also to the activity of machines and of the forces of nature. *Labor* is largely restricted to human effort, especially physical and manual. *Toil* is principally applicable to strenuous and fatiguing labor; *drudgery,* to dull, wearisome, monotonous, and sometimes demeaning labor; and *travail,* to work involving great effort and pain or suffering.

Webster's Dictionary of Synonyms also discusses synonyms; it includes many more discussions of synonyms than do standard desk dictionaries, and the discussions are longer.

Thesauruses also list synonyms, but they usually do not include definitions. For instance, most thesauruses list *labor, toil, drudgery, travail, employment, occupation,* and other words as synonyms for *work,* but they do not explain the differences among the meanings of these words. One exception to this rule is *Roget's II: The New Thesaurus,* published by Houghton Mifflin Company; it includes definitions. Look for dictionaries of synonyms and thesauruses in the reference section of your library (see Section 27.3).

Statements of meaning.   The meanings of words may be directly stated in papers. For example: "I use *work* to refer to any physical or intellectual effort that is expended to make or do something."

Statements of the meanings of terms and concepts may be found by consulting glossaries, indexes of books, standard desk dictionaries (Section 9.5), and specialized dictionaries and encyclopedias (Section 27.3).

When you write research papers (Chapter 28), it may be advisable to quote the definitions of important terminology that have been written by recognized experts. For example, a research paper for a linguistics course on the topic of English morphology, might include the following quotation:

Eugene Nida, one of the foremost scholars of English

morphology, offered the following definition for

the word morpheme:

> Morphemes are the minimal meaningful units
> which may constitute words, e.g., re-, de-, un-,
> -ish, -ly, -ceive, -mand, tie, boy, and like in
> the combinations receive, demand, untie,
> boyish, and likely. [1]

---

[1] Eugene Nida, Morphology (Ann Arbor: The University of Michigan Press, 1949), p. 1.

A footnote is shown as it would be in a research paper (Section 28.7).

Examples.   An **example** is something selected to show the general characteristics of a person, place, or thing that is identified by a term or concept. For instance, milk, orange juice, and beer are examples of what is meant by the word *beverage*.

The following discussion about psychopaths includes a synonym (*sociopath*), a statement of the meaning of the term, and an example.

The Psychopath

A psychopath is a self-centered, often charming person without care or concern for others, lacking the basic essentials of conscience that restrain us in many of our actions. The psychopath (sometimes referred to as a *sociopath*) believes that he or she is more intelligent than other people (although this is not necessarily the case), socially superior, and free of the social and legal restraints that govern the lives of others in society. The psychopath is likely to be an antisocial personality, since he or she does not feel any compunctions about committing acts that others would not even consider.

When a young man was arrested for setting fire to a house, killing two sleeping children, his mother was brought down to the police station. She asked him how he could do such a thing, and he tried to explain, saying that the owner of the house, who was his employer

had the nerve to fire me when I'm twice as smart as he is, and customers only came to his store because they liked me. This was just his punishment—it had nothing to do with the kids, and I'm really sorry they had to get it too. Anyway, they'll never convict me—I've covered up my tracks too well for these flatfoot idiots to make a case.

He said all this without the slightest trace of remorse, without the slightest concern that two children had died. Instead, he thought only about himself and how he would outwit everyone.

Observe that the example is interesting and that it makes clear the thought processes and behaviors of psychopaths. Use examples to explain terms and concepts in your papers (see Section 26.2).

25.2   Explain a method

Always consider whether you can explain a method that is associated with a topic (Section 14.4). There is a way for doing almost everything that is done, and explanations of methods make excellent subject matter for papers. Research papers (Chapter 28) should usually not be devoted exclusively to the explanation of one method, but they may compare various methods or include an explanation of a method together with other information.

There are many methods to explain for most college subjects. For a psychology course you might explain a method for helping children develop their intellectual abilities; for a business course you might explain a method for finding employment in a specific occupation. What you learn may be helpful to you if you have children or look for a job. What could be better than to write a paper that satisfies a requirement for a course and that *also* helps you learn information that might be useful to you?

Many methods must be done, or are best done, in a specified sequence. For example, you *must* select a topic before you write a paper for college credit, but it is *best* to put on your jeans before you put on your shoes. Use the following suggestions when writing about a method that must be done or is best done in a specific sequence.

1. Identify the steps in the method.
2. Arrange the steps in the sequence in which they must be done or are best done.
3. Explain each step of the sequence so that it can be easily understood or visualized by your readers.

For example, if you write a paper for a business course on the topic of selling, you will find there are steps in the selling process. It would be important to your discussion for the steps to be arranged in the correct sequence.

However, not all methods are done in a sequence; some are combinations of components. For example, Chapter 8 of this handbook explains nine strategies that, taken together, are a method that can be used to improve concentration while studying. However, the strategies that are suggested in Chapter 8 do not need to be done in any specific sequence; indeed, it is not necessary to use all of the suggestions to improve concentration. When a method does not need to be explained in a sequence, consider one of the following ways to present information about it.

1. *Discuss the easiest-to-execute behaviors or strategies first and the more difficult ones later.* For example, if you examine Chapter 8 in this handbook, you will discover that the easiest-to-execute strategies for improving concentration are given toward the beginning of the chapter.

2. *Group behaviors together that logically belong together.* For example, in a paper about table manners, all behaviors associated with polite conversation could be discussed together. Behaviors associated with using knives, forks, and spoons, and other divisions of the topic could also be discussed together.

If you are interested in the ways that things are done, give serious consideration to writing about methods. You will enjoy the task of writing more.

25.3   Summarize information

When you write a paper, consider whether some part of it could be a summary of an article or book you read. However, when you select your own topics for papers, it is usually wise to give papers substance by combining a summary with some other type of information. For example, if you decide to write a paper about a book, your summary of the book might be accompanied by your analysis or evaluation of it (Section 25.6 and Section 25.7).

Any instructor may require you to write a summary of the information in a book or article. Use the following suggestions to write these types of papers.

1. Write an introductory paragraph (Section 24.8) that includes the name of the author, title of the work, and other bibliographic information (see Section 28.1).

2. Use your own words to summarize or paraphrase the information in the book or article (see Section 28.4 and Section 28.5).

3. Use direct quotations sparingly (Section 28.6).

4. Write your summary so that it reflects the emphasis of the author.

It is often fairly easy to decide how to reflect an author's emphasis. For example, if each chapter of a ten-chapter book is very informative, a summary of it would devote about equal attention to each chapter; three or four paragraphs might be written for each chapter. On the other hand, judgment sometimes needs to be exercised to reflect a writer's emphasis accurately. In one eight-chapter book, the first seven chapters are written to prepare readers to accept important conclusions that are stated in the eighth chapter. Since the author's emphasis is in the last chapter, a summary of the book should discuss the last chapter in more detail than is used to discuss the first seven chapters.

If you are required to write a book report or book review, use the suggestions in this section together with those in Section 25.6, Section 25.7, and Section 27.3 ("When you write about a book").

25.4   Make a comparison

Comparisons are explanations of similarities and differences (see Section 14.8). Since almost anything can be compared to something else, always consider whether you want to discuss a topic by making comparisons.

For example, comparisons may be made when discussing the topic *selling;* different writers give different advice about how to sell. Also, methods for selling products vary; the methods for selling underwear and socks are different from the methods for selling automobiles and expensive appliances. Comparisons of these differences could be used to develop a paper about selling.

There are two basic methods for writing about comparisons; the divided method and the alternating method. The divided method is the easiest to use; it was used to write "The Middle Class" in Section 14.8. Following is the skeleton outline for the passage:

The Middle Class

  I. The upper-middle class
 II. The lower-middle class

In this example, the topic, *Middle Class,* is divided and each division is discussed separately. This is what is meant by the divided method.

The passage entitled "Mature Love and Romantic Love" in Section 14.8 was written using the alternating method. Following is the skeleton outline for the passage:

Mature Love and Romantic Love

  I. Basis for the love relationship
      A. Mature love
      B. Romantic love
 II. Attitude toward the lover
      A. Mature love
      B. Romantic love

III. Need to control the lover
   A. Mature love
   B. Romantic love
IV. Sense of completeness in absence of lover
   A. Mature love
   B. Romantic love
 V. Capacity to love those other than the lover
   A. Mature love
   B. Romantic love

The alternating method is more difficult to use than the divided method, but, fortunately, information presented using the alternating method may also be presented using the divided method. The following skeleton outline, which employs the divided method, could be used to compare mature and romantic love.

Mature Love and Romantic Love

 I. Mature love
   A. Basis for the love relationship
   B. Attitude toward the lover
   C. Need to control the lover
   D. Sense of completeness in absence of lover
   E. Capacity to love those other than the lover
II. Romantic love
   A. Basis for the love relationship
   B. Attitude toward the lover
   C. Need to control the lover
   D. Sense of completeness in absence of lover
   E. Capacity to love those other than the lover

Whichever method you use to discuss comparisons, include in your discussions words that make it clear that comparisons are being made. Among the words and phrases that indicate similarity are *like, likewise, similarly, in common,* and *resemblance.* Some of the words and phrases that suggest differences are *but, however, in contrast, on the contrary,* and *on the other hand.*

25.5   Discuss causes

Causes are explanations that help us understand why things are as they are (Section 14.6). Many topics lend themselves to discussions of causes. For example, papers about the facts that many criminals are never punished, that child abuse is widespread, or that the value of the dollar has decreased, present opportunities to discuss causes. Why are many criminals never punished? Why is child abuse widespread? Why has the value of the dollar decreased?

Causes are excellent subject matter for papers, but they pose problems. For example, it is often difficult, or impossible, to determine which of two events is a cause: Is drug use caused, in part, by permissiveness, or is permissiveness caused, in part, by the difficulties in controlling drug use?

Some of the problems in discussing causes can be avoided by using words such as those that are italicized in the following sentences.

> Among the many reasons that people become criminals, there are three causes that *seem to be* most significant:
>
> 1. Research *suggests that one reason* people become criminals is that . . .
> 2. *Another factor* that *appears to* contribute to whether a person will become a criminal is . . .
> 3. There is also *evidence that another cause* of criminal behavior *may be* . . .

If causes are not stated carefully, they may be imprecise and incorrect. For instance,

> Smoking causes cancer.

This statement may appear to be true, but it is imprecise and, therefore, it is incorrect. The following statement is precise and correct:

> Smoking is *one cause* of *some forms* of cancer.

The italicized words make the statement precise and correct. It is incorrect to say that smoking causes cancer because there are other causes of cancer and because it is not a cause of all forms of cancer.

To state accurately that one event causes another, the event identified as the cause must be able, *all by itself,* to produce the specified result. For example,

> A nuclear bomb exploded on a house will cause the house to be destroyed.

An exploded nuclear bomb is able, all by itself, to produce the result stated in the sentence. However, most causes are not sufficient, *all by themselves,* to produce a specified result. For example,

> An unhappy and disturbed childhood causes people to become criminals.

This is incorrect because an unhappy and disturbed childhood is not sufficient, all by itself, to cause a person to pursue a life of crime. One proof of this is that many honest, hard-working citizens had childhoods more unhappy and disturbed than some criminals.

An additional error in discussing causes is to state that one event is the cause of another simply because it came before the other event. For example, a man got fat because he ate much more food than he needed to eat. His mother speculated that his overeating was caused by the sharp increase in his salary; just before he started overeating he changed jobs and his salary increased from $25,000 to $35,000 a year. His mother's reasoning was faulty; her son could have gotten fat when he earned $25,000 a year. His overeating may have been caused by stress on the new job, disappointment in love, or some other factor. Do not jump to the conclusion that one event is the cause of another simply because it came before the other event.

When you discuss causes, state them carefully using the methods that are explained in this section. Also, keep in mind:

1. There are usually several causes for an event.
2. It is often difficult to understand what the causes for an event are.
3. Do not state that one event is the cause of another event unless you can present convincing evidence that it is.

Discussions of causes are excellent subject matter for papers when these guidelines are observed.

25.6   Present an analysis

As **analysis** is a discussion that uses specific categories to organize observations about a topic. For example, when you analyze a piece of clothing in a store to decide whether you will purchase it, you may use the following categories to make your observations: cost of purchase and upkeep, compatibility with other items in your wardrobe, attractiveness, durability, and serviceability.

You make analyses in your everyday life and you may decide or be required to write analyses for some of your college courses. Following are a few examples of what students are required to analyze when they write papers for college credit:

1. A work of art, such as a painting, sculpture, or photograph
2. A literary work, such as a novel, short story, play, or poem
3. An artistic performance, such as a musical, dance, or dramatic performance
4. An institution, such as a hospital, school, philanthropic organization, consumer agency, or business
5. A method, such as a method for teaching, providing health care, or constructing a bridge
6. An athletic performance, such as a performance by a runner, gymnast, or tennis player

Almost anything can be analyzed, and categories have been established for analyzing almost everything.

Use the following procedures when you write analyses:

1. Decide what categories you will use to organize your observations.
2. Make your observations.
3. Take notes about what you observe.

If a teacher gives you an assignment to write an analysis, the categories to use are likely to be written in your course textbook or in notes you took during class lectures. When the categories are not stated in a course textbook or class notes, you will almost always find them by studying books in a library.

For instance, if you are assigned to write an analysis of a short story, play, or novel for an English course, you will almost certainly find the categories for making observations listed in your course textbook or in your class notes. You may find that these types of literature may be analyzed by considering an author's point of view, characters, plot, theme, dramatic conflict, mood, tone, and other characteristics. Three or four of these categories may be selected to write an analysis of a piece of literature. For instance,

  I. Author's point of view
 II. Theme
III. Dramatic conflict

Also, one category may be used to write an analysis. For example, an analysis may be written by considering only the important characters in a novel and the interactions among them.

Good analyses are written by first understanding the conventional ways subjects are discussed. The ways judges of track meets discuss the performance of pole vaulters are the categories to use when analyzing the performance of pole vaulters; the ways music scholars discuss operas are the categories to use when analyzing an opera; and so on.

Some topics may be analyzed by making comparisons; theories, methods, and processes are often analyzed in this way. For instance, a "new" method for teaching writing may be analyzed by comparing it to "old" methods for teaching writing; it may be found that the "new" method is nothing more than a variation on one or two of the "old" methods. Other topics may be analyzed by studying their effects (see Section 14.7). For example, a public policy, such as a policy to reduce pollution standards, may be analyzed by studying whether the effects of the policy are beneficial or detrimental.

It would be wise to use analysis whenever you can. There is no better way to learn about a topic than to analyze it, and the primary reason you are required to write papers is so that you will learn. Analyses are often accompanied by evaluations (Section 25.7).

25.7   Evaluate something

When you **evaluate** something, you consider its positive and negative aspects and come to a conclusion about its merits. For example, when you go to a party, you may ponder afterwards what was good and what wasn't so good about the party and arrive at a conclusion about its overall merits. If you do, your conclusion is your evaluation of the party.

It is likely that you will be required to write analyses or criticisms for some of your college courses. Also, since thoughtful evaluations are appealing to most college instructors, it would be a good idea to include evaluations in papers whenever it is appropriate to do so.

Good evaluations, or criticisms, are usually based on analyses. Use the following procedures to write evaluations:

1. Decide what categories you will use to organize your observations (Section 25.6).
2. Make the necessary observations.
3. Take notes about the positive and negative aspects about each category for which you make observations.
4. Draw a conclusion about the overall merits of what you evaluate.

Also consider the following suggestions when you write evaluations or criticisms:

1. *Write about both good things and bad things.* The words *evaluate* and *criticize* are sometimes misinterpreted to mean "make only negative statements." However, as you probably know from reading reviews of motion pictures, criticisms do not need to be all positive or all negative. Since very little is completely perfect or imperfect, an evaluation that can find nothing good or bad to say has probably overlooked something. The most perfectly performed ballet may have a minor flaw—one scene may be too dimly lit, for example. The most unsatisfactory novel may include one interesting passage or one intriguing character. Evaluations should discuss pros and cons, advantages and disadvantages, strengths and weaknesses—what is good as well as what is not good. Of course, if there is very little to object to or very little to approve of, you should make this completely clear in an evaluation.

2. *Write about your topic, not about yourself.* Unless you know you must explain your emotional responses, do not discuss them. If you like something, make this clear by your favorable comments; don't say "I like it." The evaluations you write for college credit will seldom be evaluations of what you like and do not like. In evaluating a scene in a play, one student wrote: "It lacked dramatic interest because there was no basis for conflict between the mother and the daughter." In discussing the same scene, another student wrote: "The scene between the mother and daughter was so boring that I almost went to sleep." The first student wrote about the play, but the second student wrote about himself.

3. *Do not evaluate irrelevancies.* Always stick to the topic of your paper. For example, if you evaluate a painting that you saw in a museum, evaluate the painting and nothing else. When you write about a painting, it is irrelevant if a guard was kind to you or if another museum visitor was rude to you when you visited the museum. If you evaluate the experience of visiting a museum, then by all means discuss the guards, other visitors,

lighting, the cafeteria, and whatever else is relevant to your experience. But all these things are irrelevant when your purpose is to evaluate a painting.

4. *Evaluate things for what they are, without considering the intentions behind them.* The fact that something is exactly as it was intended to be, or that it was prompted by good intentions, is irrelevant to an evaluation of it. For example, if you evaluate a building and determine that it is inappropriate and displeasing, you do not need to be concerned about whether the building is exactly as the architect intended it to be. Evaluate the building; you are not required to defend or explain the architect's intentions. Similarly, if you evaluate a service provided to elderly people as careless, inept, and otherwise unsatisfactory, you do not need to be concerned about whether the people who provide the service have good intentions. If you know that the providers of the service mean well, you might mention it, but this is irrelevant in deciding whether the service is careless, inept, and otherwise unsatisfactory.

The suggestions in this section should be helpful to you also when you write evaluations or criticisms for essay tests (Section 23.2).

25.8   Persuade others to change

A final suggestion for developing topics is to persuade readers to accept an opinion, belief, or point of view that they do not hold. For example, you may write a paper in which you attempt to persuade others that solar energy should be used instead of oil, gas, or coal; that public schools are doing an excellent job of educating young people; that library users should pay a fee for the service; of some other issue.

Reflect on your strong convictions, and you may be guided to a good topic for a paper. However, it is wise to avoid trying to persuade others to accept your views about controversial issues such as abortion, premarital sex, homosexuality, gun control, and life after death (see Section 24.3).

Consider the following suggestions when you write papers in which you attempt to persuade others that they should give up what they believe and adopt what you believe.

1. *Do not offend your readers.* The purpose of persuasion is to convince people they should change their minds; if you offend them, they will resent you and resist your argument. Your readers are as devoted to their beliefs as you are to yours; do not suggest that they are stupid, wrong, or immoral to believe as they do. Almost everybody resents being classified in one of these ways. Also, take care not to make any statement that might offend readers because they are members of a particular ethnic, religious, or political group.

2. *Present both sides of the argument.* A one-sided argument reinforces the opinions that readers already hold; if readers disagree with your argument, they will disagree more unless you present their side of the issue as well as yours. Therefore, understand both sides of the issue and present the side with which you disagree in such a way that your readers will perceive that you respect the intellectual, religious, philosophical, and other motivations that cause them to believe differently than you do.

3. *Do not present only two alternatives if there are more than two.* Many issues can be discussed from two basic perspectives. For example, you may argue for or against continuing in the arms race with Russia. This is appropriate. What needs to be avoided is false alternatives. It would be inappropriate, for instance, to argue that our military strength must be superior to Russia's *or* we must be pleased when Russia devastates us in a nuclear attack. Perhaps we need equal rather than superior military strength, and, if Russia should attack us, we do not need to be pleased about it.

4. *Use many sources of evidence to support your belief.* The more evidence you provide for a belief, opinion, or point of view, the more convincing your argument will be. The information you present should be so complete and convincing that

your readers will feel they have erred in judgment to believe differently than you believe.

5. *Explain to readers how they will benefit by embracing your belief.* If your readers can understand how they will benefit by believing as you do, they will have good reason to give up what they believe and to accept what you believe. On the other hand, if your readers can see no benefit in believing as you do, they will have no good reason to change their beliefs.

6. *Do not introduce irrelevancies.* All the evidence you introduce must support your argument. For example, if you argue that women should not be permitted to work as firefighters, discuss why you believe they are incapable of fighting fires. Do not introduce irrelevancies such as the fact that women are sometimes shown preferential treatment by men when they are taken out on dates. What men and women do when they are on dates has nothing to do with the work of fighting fires.

7. *Do not attack people when you argue about issues.* Attacks on people are a special type of irrelevancy to avoid in all arguments. For example, if you argue that concern for consumer safety is unjustified because it contributes unduly to inflation, present the facts that you believe support this argument, but do not make a personal attack on any consumer advocate. Do not, for example, describe a consumer advocate as stupid, immoral, greasy-looking, loudmouthed, publicity-seeking, or in any other unkind manner. Attacks on people are irrelevant to issues and, of course, offensive.

Beliefs, opinions, and points of view are often held more for emotional reasons than for intellectual ones. As a result, an emotional appeal is often effective in getting people to change their beliefs. However, it takes great skill to write an emotional appeal that will elicit a *desired* emotional response. If you lack this skill, you may write an appeal that elicits from your readers a response you do not want—you may hope they will cry, but instead they may laugh or become angry.

Despite the challenges inherent in writing persuasive arguments, consider them seriously when you write papers. You may find that it is satisfying to write when the topic is one about which you have strong convictions.

Use What You've Learned

1. Write a one-page definition of a term or concept; include synonyms, a statement of meaning, and at least one example (Section 25.1).

2. Write a one-page explanation of a method that is important to a subject that you are studying (Section 25.2).

3. Write a one-page summary of a newspaper or magazine article that discusses a topic that is relevant to a subject you are studying (Section 25.3, Section 28.4 through Section 28.6).

4. Use the divided method and alternating method to prepare two outlines that could be used to write about comparisons (Section 25.4).

5. Prepare an outline with four major points and a central theme for a paper that discusses causes (Section 24.4, Section 24.6, and Section 25.5).

6. Use the information in Chapter 8 of this handbook to write a two-page analysis of the methods you use to concentrate when you study (Section 25.6).

7. Use the information in Chapter 5 of this handbook to write a two-page evaluation of the lecture note-taking methods used by one of your friends (Section 25.7). Collect information by examining your friend's class notes and by interviewing him or her (Section 26.4).

8. Write a two-page paper in which you persuade others to accept an opinion, belief, or point of view you hold (Section 25.8).

Support Statements and Conclusions

The statements you make and the conclusions you draw in papers must be supported by convincing evidence. The suggestions in this chapter will help you think creatively about the types of supporting evidence you may include in the papers you write for college credit. You may

1. state facts.
2. give examples.
3. share your experiences.
4. discuss your interviews.
5. cite a quotation.
6. present a drawing.
7. give statistics.

When you write papers, use various types of evidence to support statements you make and conclusions you draw.

26.1 State facts

A **fact** is any statement that represents reality the way it really is. Statements and conclusions in papers should be supported by good, up-to-date factual information.

For instance, if you write a paper about the American novelist Theodore Dreiser and want to support the statement that his writing was shocking to his contemporaries, you might include the following fact:

On April 17, 1981, <u>The New York Times</u> reported
on the front page that the manuscript for Dreiser's
first novel included material that was so sexually
explicit that 36,000 words were deleted from it
before it was published in 1900.   The full text of
<u>Sister Carrie</u> was not printed until 1981.

Facts for papers may also be statements of the beliefs, **opinions,** and points of view of others. For instance, following is one of my opinions.

> I believe that all college students should be given full academic credit for taking a course in which they learn skills of the type that are explained in this handbook, but they are not. It is clear to me that I would have been much better off if I had been taught all the things in this book during my first year of college; but some of the skills are ones that I did not learn until I was a graduate student.

It is a fact that I believe this, and it may be treated as a fact about what I believe if it is used in a paper that argues that college credit should be given for learning skills courses. However, when there are contrasting points of view, there is an obligation to present both sides of an argument. For instance, many college educators disagree that academic credit should be given for learning skills courses. If you write a paper about this topic, you have an obligation to present both sides of the issue.

Use the following guidelines when you present facts in papers you write for college courses.

1. Represent them fairly.
2. State where you found them.
3. Make certain they are up to date.

The following discussions explain how to achieve these objectives.

Represent facts fairly. The following quotation appears on page 3 of the Spring 1980 edition of the *Occupational Outlook Quarterly,* which is a publication of the United States Government.

> Employment is expected to increase in almost all occupations through the 1980's if past trends continue and if the assumptions made about the future are accurate. Between 1978 and 1990, total employment will rise from 94.4 to 114.0 million workers, or 21 percent. One way to view this increase is that the expansion of the economy will create nearly 20 million new jobs.

The following statement is a misrepresentation of these facts:

> Between 1978 and 1990, nearly twenty million new jobs will be created for American workers.

Although this is an accurate summary of the information in the third sentence, it does not take into account the information in the first sentence. The following statement represents the facts fairly.

> It has been estimated that between 1978 and 1990, nearly twenty million new jobs will be created for American workers.

It is a fact that an estimate has been made of how many jobs will be created, but it is not a fact that nearly twenty million jobs will be created.

A common way in which facts are misrepresented is to present writers' statements as though they are representative of their points of view when they are not. For instance, if you write a paper in which you attempt to show that a book was negatively criticized by reviewers, you may find a review of the book that is mostly favorable but that includes one negative statement that you can use to support the theme of your paper. It would be unfair to use one negative statement from an otherwise favorable review to support your thesis unless you state that the reviewer's other comments were favorable.

State the sources of facts.   When you write papers, you are obligated to state the sources of your facts so that others can locate them if they want to; when you write research papers, you must document facts with footnotes or endnotes (Chapter 28). You may have noticed in this section that sources are given for the facts about Theodore Dreiser and the number of new jobs that may be created by 1990. The sources are likely to be available in your college or university library; if you refer to them, you will find the facts printed exactly where it says they are. State the sources of the facts you use in your papers.

Use facts that are up to date.   Books and articles written many years ago are reliable sources of information for certain types of facts. For example, if you write a paper about Phoenix, Arizona, you may find a book written a century ago that states Phoenix is located in south-central Arizona, on the Salt River, and that it was founded in 1867. With regard to these facts, a book published one hundred years ago is just as reliable as a book published yesterday. However, if you consult a book written in the late 1970s to present information about the population of Phoenix, you will find its population given to be about 580,000. A book written in the late 1970s is out of date for this information; by 1980 the population of Phoenix was more than 880,000, and, if this trend of growth has continued, the population of Phoenix may be approaching or surpassing 1,000,000 as you read this page.

Always research recent periodicals to make certain your information is up to date and complete. Recent information or thoughts may be published about almost any topic. Theodore Dreiser died in 1945, but he is the subject of an article that was printed on the front page of *The New York Times* in 1981. A year ago, rummaging through a trunk, somebody may have discovered an unpublished manuscript written by Dreiser. Today, the novel and many reviews of it may be in print. When you research topics for papers, you cannot afford to overlook the recent literature.

26.2   Give examples

If you are alert when you read books and articles, you are likely to find excellent examples that you may use in your papers to illustrate statements and conclusions. For instance, if you do research to explain that parents treat boy children and girl children differently, you may find the following intriguing example.

> The consequences of sex can be awesome to contemplate. Physician Estelle Ramey tells the poignant story of a set of identical male twins.* A short while after their birth, they were being routinely circumcised when the penis of one of the children was accidentally destroyed in the operation. After much professional conferring among physicians and psychiatrists, the decision was made to surgically convert the injured young boy into a female. Ramey told of the decidedly different ways these two identical twins were treated and responded to in the years following the operation. The boy, as we would expect, was rough-housed, indulged in noisy play; given mechanical toys, play trucks, cars, and building sets; and in general, tumbled about in good-natured physical activity. The other, in contrast, was dealt with delicately; given dolls, tea sets, and play ovens; admonished not to get dirty; and, in general, restricted more in physical activity. By the time she was 10, the "girl" was baking cookies. Commented Ramey with irony, "She doesn't even have the genes for cookies!" Ramey lamented that no one would even advise *her* to aspire to be President.
>
> *Estelle Ramey, Address before the National Association for Women Deans, Administrators and Counselors, Spring 1973.

This example is appropriate for illustrating the statement that parents treat boy children and girl children differently. Use the methods explained in Section 28.4 and Section 28.5 to summarize or paraphrase examples and other information you find in books and articles.

Your own experiences and the experiences of others are also good sources for examples that you may include in papers (see Section 26.3 and Section 26.4).

26.3   Share your experiences

Your experiences are a rich resource for writing examples to explain statements and conclusions in your papers. You have had thousands of experiences in your lifetime, and, since nobody has had exactly the same experiences you have had, you possess valuable information that is not available to others.

By reflecting on his experiences, one student wrote the following example for a paper about air pollution.

I learned one detrimental effect of air pollution when I took a guided tour of Central Park in the summer of 1980.   In the park there is a monument that stood on the sands of Egypt for thousands of years and that was brought to New York City less than a century ago.   The obelisk is completely covered with writing that was easy to read a hundred years ago.   However, pollutants in the air of the city have accelerated the deterioration of the monument to such an extent that the hieroglyphics are now so worn that they are impossible to read.

This example was drawn from a student's experiences, and you, too, can draw on your experiences when you write papers.

You have lived your life with others, including friends, neighbors, classmates, shopkeepers, teachers, and, perhaps, employers and fellow workers. You have visited other people's homes or apartments, and you have probably stayed overnight in a tent, motel, or hotel. You have been in schools, museums, theaters, stores, libraries, parks, and many other public places. You have visited many neighborhoods and probably other towns, cities, and states, or even foreign countries. You may have an interest for which you collect, create, or repair something or that causes you to participate with others in some religious, political, humanitarian, or athletic activity. You have been exposed to people, places, television, motion pictures, recordings, books, magazines, newspapers, and many other sources of information. You have lived through part of the history of humankind during which you have observed advances in technology; complications with international relations; changes in elected officials; difficulties with the economy; changes in fashion; and the rise and fall of the popularity of television programs, motion picture stars, and recording artists.

You have had many experiences; when they are appropriate for supporting statements or conclusions in papers, share them with your readers. They will make your papers easier to write and more interesting to read.

26.4   Discuss your interviews

Interviews are conversations that are engaged in for the purpose of collecting information. They are excellent sources of facts, opinions, examples, and other types of information that you can use to support the statements you make and the conclusions you draw in papers.

By interviewing neighbors, a student collected information she used to write the following example for a paper about the advantages and disadvantages of married life.

```
Neighbors of mine (I'll call them Ben and Anne),

told me during an interview that before they got

married they were both living comfortably in
```

separate apartments.   They were not rich, but they

had sufficient money for luxuries such as stylish

clothing and meals in restaurants.   Within a year

after they married, Anne had a baby and quit her job;

another child was born not long after the first one.

Anne will not be able to return to work for at least

three years, and, though Ben's salary has increased,

their family income is far less than it was before

Anne quit working.   They are happy they have

children, but they regret that there is no money in

the family budget for stylish clothing and meals in

restaurants.   In fact, they cannot afford many

things they used to consider necessities--such as

meat for dinner every night.

You, too, have classmates, neighbors, friends, and relatives who can provide you with examples and other information for your papers.

Also, members of the faculty and staff of your college or university may be experts on subjects as diverse as nuclear physics and building maintenance, counseling and food service, orchestral conducting and the security of building and grounds. Close at hand you have many persons who are rich resources of information, and they may be willing to share their knowledge, expertise, opinions, or experiences with you.

People do not need to be professionals to have worthwhile information. Volunteers and hobbyists may have inside knowledge or expertise. For example, people who volunteer their services to a political campaign or who have the hobby of restoring old houses are knowledgeable about aspects of politics and house restoration.

Interviews are useful for collecting information about conflicting points of view. For example, if your subject is a service, such as a health, food, or police protection service, interview those who receive the service as well as those who provide it. Those who receive a health service, for example, may have very different things to tell you than the doctors, nurses, administrators, and other people who provide the service. Similarly, if your topic is an event, such as a strike, political campaign, war, or flood, interview those who witnessed the event, those who participated in it, and those who were affected by it. For example, a labor leader who participated in strike negotiations may give you very different information about a strike than a worker who suffered financial hardship because of pay lost due to the strike.

Use the following guidelines when you interview people at their homes, offices, or work places.

1. Prepare questions you may ask.
2. Arrive for the interview on time; if the interviewee is late, make no comment about it.
3. Dress appropriately.
4. Do not chew gum, eat candy, or smoke.
5. Begin the interview by explaining its purpose.
6. If the interviewee asks a question, answer it honestly.
7. Do not tape-record the interview if you have any reason to believe that this will make the interviewee uneasy.
8. Do not interrupt the interviewee while he or she is speaking.
9. If the interviewee wanders off the topic, do not worry; the digression may lead to important information.
10. If something is unclear to you, ask for clarification.

Also, of course, take notes on what the interviewee says.

At the end of the interview, thank the interviewee for taking time to talk with you. Following the interview, write a letter to the interviewee stating your appreciation for the interview and mentioning one or two specific ways in which the interview was helpful to you.

26.5   Cite a quotation

The exact words of historic, literary, and other well-known persons can be used to support or summarize a statement or conclusion in a paper. For instance, the following quotation could be used to support the statement that work should be done in a happy spirit.

> Work is love made visible
> And if you cannot work with love but only
> with distaste, it is better that you should leave
> your work and sit at the gate of the temple and
> take alms of those who work with joy.
> For if you bake bread with indifference, you
> bake a bitter bread that feeds but half man's hunger.
>   *Kahlil Gibran*

You may find quotations of this type when you research a topic by reading books and articles (Section 27.1 and Section 27.2). If you do not, visit the reference section of a library (Section 27.3) and consult the *Dictionary of Quotations* or *The International Thesaurus of Quotations;* the quotations in both of these reference books are arranged so you can find the ones that pertain to topics that interest you. For instance, if you are interested in the topic of *work,* these books are arranged so you can find the quotations that pertain to this topic.

Most of the other books of quotations are arranged so you must know the author of a quotation or important words in a quotation to locate it. Among the best known of the books arranged in this way are *The Oxford Dictionary of Quotations* and *Familiar Quotations.*

Figure 26a **Drawings to Include in a Paper
About Greek Architecture.**

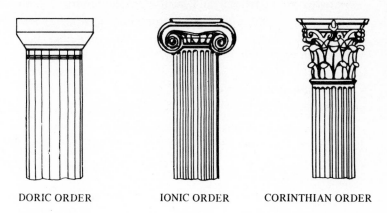

DORIC ORDER   IONIC ORDER   CORINTHIAN ORDER

26.6   Present a drawing

Whenever you write a paper, consider whether information in it can be depicted; in some instances you will find that a writing problem can be solved by including a drawing or other graphic material. For example, if the drawings in Figure 26a were included in a paper about Greek architecture, they would help in explaining the differences among Doric, Ionic, and Corinthian capitals and shafts.

A cartoon that illustrates the central theme of a paper might be appropriate to include in the paper.

Also, maps are helpful for explaining migrations, journeys, battles in wars, escape routes of assassins, and many other topics, including the relationships among places in a town, city, state, or other geographic area.

However, do not include graphic materials in a paper with the intention of distracting your readers from the inadequacy of your research or reasoning. Use them only when they make it easier for you to write an explanation or when they clearly support a statement you make or a conclusion you draw.

26.7　Give statistics

Statistics are numerical data, such as the data in Figure 26b. Some statements and conclusions require that statistics be given. For example, if you state in a paper that muggings have increased in your community, you would need to present statistical data to support this statement. If you conclude that food is a better value today than it was two years ago, you will need to present statistical data to support this conclusion.

Statistics may be presented in graphs or tables (Section 13.6), and most statistics that can be presented in graphs can also be presented in tables; the circle graph and table in Figure 26b present the same statistics.

Statistical data may also be presented in paragraph form in papers. The following paragraph summarizes some of the numerical data in Figure 26b.

The Bureau of Labor Statistics projects that in 1990 approximately 114.1 million persons will be working in the United States and that nearly half of them will be employed in four occupational areas.　It is estimated that in 1990 there will be 22.5 million clerical workers, 16.3 million professional and technical workers, 16.8 million service workers (including private household workers), and 14.5 million craft workers.

Present statistics using the guidelines that are explained in Section 26.1: (1) represent them fairly, (2) state where you found them, and (3) make certain that they are up to date.

If you have difficulty finding statistics, visit the reference section of a library (Section 27.3) and consult *The World Almanac & Book of Facts* or the *Information Please Almanac*. Both of

Figure 26b **A Graph and a Table Presenting Identical Statistical Data.**

PROJECTED DISTRIBUTION OF EMPLOYMENT
BY OCCUPATION IN 1990

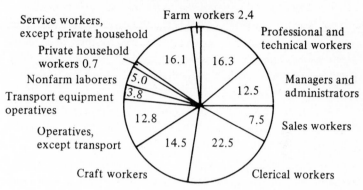

Projected Distribution of Employment by Occupation in 1990

Occupation	Millions of workers
Clerical workers	22.5
Professional and technical workers	16.3
Service workers, except private household	16.1
Craft workers	14.5
Operatives, except transport	12.8
Managers and administrators	12.5
Sales workers	7.5
Nonfarm laborers	5.0
Transport equipment operatives	3.8
Farm workers	2.4
Private household workers	0.7

SOURCE: *Occupational Outlook Handbook,* 1980–81 Edition, U.S. Department of Labor, Bureau of Labor Statistics, Bulletin 2075.

these books give numerical data for government, industry, sports, politics, the arts, personalities, dogs, and just about any other topic you can think of. Also, the *Statistical Abstracts of the United States* is an excellent source for statistics about crime, education, politics, economics, and many other subjects; the title is forbidding, but the statistics are interesting and they are introduced by well-written explanations.

However, *no matter how authoritative statistics are, be cautious when you use them to support statements or conclusions in your papers.* Highly trained statisticians frequently disagree about what a statistic indicates; you may unwittingly use a statistic to support a statement it does not support or to draw a conclusion that cannot be drawn from it.

The following discussions explain some ways to avoid misrepresenting statistics when you write papers.

Use a combination of statistics.   Statements of the following type are extremely difficult to prove:

> The death penalty is a deterrent to crime.
>
> Excessive television watching is a cause of lower academic achievement among high school students.
>
> Lower taxes will benefit the economy.

If you can present only one or two statistics to support statements such as these, it is very likely that your argument is weak. On the other hand, if you use a combination of statistics, your argument is likely to be more convincing, and you may avoid some of the other difficulties that are associated with using statistical evidence.

Do not generalize what a statistic indicates.   The statistics you use must represent the specific people, events, objects, or other items that are the topic of your paper. For example, if your paper is about all college students in the United States, your statistics must represent all college students in the United States. If your statistics are only about a few college students in a few states of the country, do not use them to make statements about all college students unless you can show that they are representative of all college students.

Also, do not generalize that a statistic measures anything other than what it measures. For instance, if you have a statistic that only 45 percent of students who enroll in a particular high school actually graduate from the school, do not use this to generalize that the students at the school have disturbed home lives, that the teachers of the school are ineffective, or that the students do not value education. All of these things may be true, but the statistic does not prove them. If you want to state that the students at the high school do not value education, you must document the statement with statistics or other evidence that will convince your readers what the students' values are.

Present meaningful averages.   Averages can be misleading, primarily because a few very low or very high numbers in a set can distort the average. For example, the average annual income of families in a neighborhood can be unusually high because a few extraordinarily wealthy people live there. If one hundred families live in a community, and ninety-eight of them have average annual incomes of $20,000 but two of them have average annual incomes of $1,000,000, the average annual income for the one hundred families will be $39,600. It is correct to say that the average annual family income is $39,600, but this is not an accurate description of the distribution of wealth in the community. Before you state an average, determine whether it represents information accurately.

Present meaningful percentages.   When you compare percentages, make certain the comparison is fair. For example, a politician argued against increases in welfare payments by stating that during a period in which his constituents' annual incomes increased by only 10 percent, welfare payments increased by 25 percent. This apparent inequity was due to the fact that the bases for comparison were grossly different. Welfare payments increased from $2,400 to $3,000 during the period that the politician's middle-class constituents' incomes increased from $37,000 to $40,700. The welfare recipients were desperately in need of more money while the politician's constituents had above-average family incomes.

Make certain you have all the facts.   An apparently meaningful statistic may be meaningless when all the facts are known. For example, a supplier of food services at a large university requested to increase food prices because December sales were several thousand dollars less than sales during three previous Decembers. However, close inspection of sales figures revealed that daily sales surpassed those of previous Decembers; the difference in sales was accounted for by the fact that the university was open fewer days than it had been in the three previous Decembers.

Use What You've Learned

1. Find four facts in newspaper or magazine articles that support any statement you choose. If you do not want to choose a statement, use the following one: "Millions of people in the world are undernourished and starving." State the sources of your facts (Section 26.1).

2. Write three examples to support any statement you choose. If you do not want to choose a statement, use the following one: "Most worthwhile goals are achieved by working hard." Write examples of the following types:

a. Summarize an example you find in a book or article (Section 26.2 and Section 28.4).

b. Write an example based on your own experiences (Section 26.3).

c. Write an example you learned by conducting an interview (Section 26.4).

3. Examine a book of quotations in the reference section of a library and copy three quotations from the book that are interesting or appealing to you. State the book to which you referred and the names of the authors of the quotations (Section 26.5).

4. Analyze textbooks you are studying to select three possible topics for papers for which it would be easier to write explanations if drawings were included in the papers. State the topics and describe the drawings that would be appropriate to include in the papers (Section 26.6).

5. Examine a book of statistical data in the reference section of a library and copy three statistics from it that are interesting or appealing to you. State the book to which you referred (Section 26.7).

Collect Information in a Library

Information for writing college papers is usually collected by reading books and articles in a library. This chapter explains how to locate library materials quickly and how to evaluate whether books and articles are useful for your purposes.

It is likely that the library at your school offers a service to teach you about its facilities and their proper use. The instruction may be printed in a booklet or a series of leaflets, it may be recorded on a videotape, or it may be presented by a librarian to small groups of students at various times during the school year. Take advantage of whatever instruction is available; you will enjoy your visits to the library more when you know what is there for you and how to find it.

Also, when you do research in a library, keep in mind that there is no better resource than a helpful librarian. Whenever you have a problem, ask a librarian for help. Remember which librarians give you good suggestions and go back to them when you need assistance in the future.

As you read this chapter, also keep in mind that *libraries are not the only sources of information for papers.* You may collect information by interviewing people (Section 26.4); by attending events, such as concerts; and by visiting businesses, museums, governmental agencies, and other institutions. Businesses, churches, consumer organizations, philanthropic foundations, and governmental agencies are also sources for collecting printed materials. Appendixes of textbooks sometimes list these types of sources. For instance, the appendix of a business textbook lists free sources of information about advertising, accounting, insurance, publishing, computer technology, and more than twenty other topics. If you are unable to find sources such as these, an instructor or librarian may be able to give you guidance.

27.1   Read periodicals

Periodicals include newspapers, magazines, and journals. Journals may be thought of as specialized magazines written for specific groups of people such as historians, nurses, teachers, psychologists, artists, chemists, and economists.

It is usually a good idea to begin a search for information about a topic in the periodical section of a library. Periodicals contain the most up-to-date information about topics. Also, the papers you write in college will be closer in length to articles in periodicals than to books and, as a result, the way a topic is discussed in articles is likely to give you some ideas about the way you can discuss the topic in a paper.

Articles in magazines, journals, and newspapers are found by using periodical indexes.

Index to popular magazines.   The *Readers' Guide to Periodical Literature* is an index to the articles that appear in more than one hundred widely read magazines including *Business Week, Consumer Reports, Dance Magazine, Film Quarterly, The New Yorker, Newsweek, Science News, Time,* and *U.S. News & World Report.* Most articles are listed by subject and author; only stories are listed by title.

Figure 27a is an excerpt from the *Readers' Guide.* Notice that the magazine articles listed for the topic *secret service* are grouped under subheadings for Canada, Chile, Iran, Russia, and the United States. Also observe that cross references are indicated by the words *see also.* For example, notice that readers who are interested in secret service in the United States are

Figure 27a **Excerpt from the *Readers' Guide*,
a Periodical Index.**

SECRET service
    See also
    Intelligence service
                    Canada
        See also
        Canada—Royal Canadian Mounted Police
                    Chile
        See also
        Letelier, Orlando, case
                    Iran
        SAVAK: like the CIA. Time 113:32 F 19 '79
        Savak U.S.A. Nation 230:5 Ja 5 '80
                    Russia
        Moscow subway crime; KGB execution of inno-
          cent dissidents in subway bombing case. M.
          Hopkins. il New Leader 62:14-15 O 8 '79
        Paddler is up the creek; abduction of Soviet
          defector V. Cesiunas from West Germany. P.
          Lewis. il Macleans 92:42 O 22 '79
                    United States
        Guarding the candidates a rugged job. il U.S.
          News 87:63 D 10 '79
        Lincoln assassination and its investigation; ad-
          dress, February 12, 1979. W. H. Webster. Vital
          Speeches 45:347-51 Mr 15 '79
            See also
        Intelligence service—United States
        United States—Central Intelligence Agency
        United States—Strategic Services, Office of
SECRET societies
    See also
    Freemasons
    Ku Klux Klan
SECRETARIAT of the United Nations. See
    United Nations—Secretariat
SECRETARIES
    Can the C.E.O. hang on to his secret weapon?
      R. Rowan. il Fortune 99:120-4+ Mr 12 '79
    Church secretary: third person out. E. J. Mall.
      Chr Today 23:34-5 Je 29 '79
    Great secretary shortage to grow incredibly
      worse. H. A. Rubenstein. il USA Today 107:
      42-4 My '79
    Help wanted: a shortage of secretaries. il Time
      114:55 S 3 '79
    How to hire a secretary: work of Thomas J.
      Lorenzen. D. Seligman. Fortune 100:25-6 D
      31 '79
    What do secretaries want—and what are they
      getting—today? E. F. Shimberg. il Glamour
      77:60+ D '79
        See also
    Receptionists

Figure 27b **Notes for a Listing in the**
Readers' Guide.

United States
Guarding the candidates a rugged job. Il U.S.
News 87:63 D 10 '79

"Guarding the candidates, a rugged job "

U.S. News + World Report

Volume 87, page 63

December 10, 1979

referred to three other subject headings in the index; the first is
"Intelligence service—United States."

When you locate an article that you want to examine, make
notes of the following information:

1. The title of the article
2. The name of the magazine
3. The volume number of the magazine, if one is given
4. The pages on which the article is printed
5. The month, day (if one is given), and year the magazine
    was published

Figure 27b illustrates how to make these notes.

Compare the *Readers' Guide* entry and the notes in Figure
27b. The abbreviations used in the entry are clearly explained

on the first pages of each volume of the *Readers' Guide.* By consulting those pages, it was learned that *U.S. News* is the abbreviation for *U.S. News & World Report.* In the sequence *87:63,* the volume number is printed before the colon, and the page number is printed after the colon. Months are abbreviated using one or two letters. For example, *D* indicates *December,* but *Je* is used for *June* and *Jl* is used for *July.* Again, all abbreviations are clearly explained on the first pages of each volume of the *Readers' Guide.*

There are two problems you may encounter when you use the *Readers' Guide* and other indexes to periodical literature.

1. *You may need to consult more than one volume of an index.* Several paperback editions of a periodical index may be published each year. When you look for very recent articles, be certain to examine all of the paperback volumes for the current year. If you want to read articles published during the five years just past, you will need to consult five cumulated indexes—one for each of the five years.

2. *Most libraries do not subscribe to all magazines that are indexed in a periodical index.* For instance, if you want to read an article in a 1982 issue of *Motor Trend,* your library may not subscribe to this magazine. In the periodical reading section of your library, there is a list or file of all the magazines, newspapers, and journals that are part of the collection of the library. This list or file will tell you whether your library owns a periodical and, if so, for which years it owns the publication. If a periodical you want is not available, a librarian may be able to inform you whether it is in the collection of some other library in your community.

When you consult periodical indexes, make notes for many articles so that you will not be discouraged in case some of the articles you want to read are in magazines that your library does not own.

Indexes to specialized periodicals.   There are also indexes for articles that appear in periodicals that publish scholarly articles and articles about specialized subjects. For instance, the *Art Index* lists journal articles about fine arts but also about many other related subjects including architecture, industrial design, interior decoration, photography, film, and landscape design. Other specialized indexes to periodical literature include the following:

> *Applied Science & Technology Index*
> *Biological and Agricultural Index*
> *Business Periodicals Index*
> *Education Index*
> *Engineering Index*
> *General Science Index*
> *Index to Legal Periodicals*
> *Music Index*
> *Social Sciences and Humanities Index*

It is important for you to consult indexes such as these, especially when you write research papers (Chapter 28). For example, if you write a research paper for a business course, you should consult the *Business Periodicals Index*. If you are uncertain which specialized indexes to use when you research a topic, ask a librarian for help.

Index to newspapers.   When you want to find articles in newspapers, consult *The New York Times Index;* it lists all the articles that have appeared in that newspaper since 1851. All issues of *The New York Times,* beginning in 1851, are available on microfilm at most college and university libraries. Also, since news events are printed in most newspapers at about the same time, *The New York Times Index* may be used to locate articles published in other newspapers. For example, if you consult the index for 1981 to find articles about the first soft landing of a spaceship on earth, you will find that articles about this event were published in the paper on April 15. You may then be certain that your local newspaper for April 15, 1981, also published articles about this historic landing of the space-ship Columbia.

27.2 Examine books

A book a library owns is usually located by looking for the author, title, or subject card for the book in a card catalog. Figure 27c shows the author, title, and subject cards for a book. Author cards are useful when you know the author of a book, and title cards are useful when you know the title of a book. But, in most instances when you do research, you will not know the authors or titles of the books you want to examine. In these instances, consult subject cards. You may find, though, that it is sometimes difficult to imagine exactly how subject cards are worded. For example, if you want to read a book that gives short biographies of famous Americans, you may not think to look for the following subject in a card catalog: United States—Biography—Dictionary. Ask a librarian to help you when you have difficulty in locating subjects in a card catalog.

When you find a card for a book that you want to examine, list the following information on a piece of paper:

1. The call number
2. The name of the author
3. The title of the book

The letters and numbers typed in the upper left corners of the cards in Figure 27c are call numbers; they identify where the book is located in a library. The call number in Figure 27c is the Library of Congress call number for *The War Film.* Library of Congress call numbers always begin with a letter (such as *B*) or a combination of letters (such as *PN*). The letters indicate various categories of subject matter. For instance, *B* is the letter that is used for books on the subject of philosophy. However, not all libraries use Library of Congress call numbers; some use Dewey Decimal System call numbers, which begin with numbers instead of letters. For instance, 100–199 is

Figure 27c **Author, Title, and Subject
Cards for a Book.**

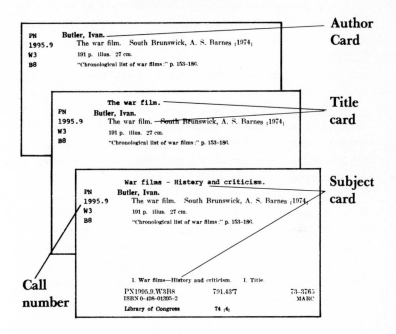

the range of numbers used for books about philosophy when
the Dewey Decimal System is used.

Libraries print leaflets or post signs to guide library users to
the locations of books that have call numbers that begin with
specific letters or numbers.

27.3   Consult reference books

The collection of a library may include specialized encyclopedias, dictionaries, indexes, and other reference books for art,
anthropology, economics, education, history, chemistry, physics,
sociology, sports, and just about any other subject you can think
of. *When you do research in a library, ask a librarian to help*

*you find specialized reference books that pertain to the topics
that interest you.*

This section gives suggestions about reference books that are
useful when you write about any topic, when you write about
a person, or when you write about a book. Suggestions for
locating quotations of famous people are given in Section 26.5,
and some reference sources for statistical data are identified in
Section 26.7.

When you write about any topic.   Articles in general encyclopedias may give you good ideas about how you can narrow
the topic for a paper, and they sometimes include titles of books
or articles that are worthwhile to examine.

The two best-known general encyclopedias are the *Encyclopedia Americana* and the *Encyclopaedia Britannica;* however,
some articles in these encyclopedias are written using technical
language. Therefore, do not overlook *Collier's Encyclopedia,
Merit Students Encyclopedia,* and *World Book Encyclopedia.*
All three of these are easy-to-read, well-written, and authoritative encyclopedias.

When you write about a person.   If your topic is the life or
accomplishments of a well-known American, *The Dictionary
of American Biography* and *Webster's American Biographies*
are good sources for you to consult. Also, the monthly issues of
Current Biography are extremely useful if you are interested
in information about a person who is currently the subject of
news stories. The monthly issues of *Current Biography* have
been cumulated yearly since 1940 in the *Current Biography
Yearbook.* If you are interested in a person who was newswor-
thy ten, fifteen, or twenty years ago, consult the *Current Biography Yearbook* for the year the person was the subject of news
stories.

In addition, there are reference books for biographies about
people who are well-known within specific disciplines, such as
the *Dictionary of American Scholars,* the *Dictionary of Scientific
Biography,* and *American Men and Women of Science.*

Also, and very important, the *Biography Index* lists biographies that appear in periodicals and other sources. It is published four times a year, and there is a cumulated index for each year since 1946. If you are interested in information about the life of a person who died in 1905 or later, the *Readers' Guide* (Section 27.1) for the year of his or her death will lead you to biographical articles in popular magazines. For instance, Helen Keller died in 1968, and you will find articles about her life by consulting the *Biography Index* and the *Readers' Guide* for 1968.

When you write about a book.   If your topic is a book that was published in 1905 or later, consult the *Book Review Digest;* it indexes reviews of fiction and nonfiction and includes excerpts from reviews. Also, the *Book Review Index* lists book reviews that have been published in periodicals since 1965, and *The New York Times Index* lists book reviews that have appeared in that newspaper (see Section 27.1).

27.4   Evaluate books and articles

Use the previewing and skimming skills that are explained in Chapter 12 and Chapter 13 to decide quickly whether books or articles are useful sources of information for your purposes.

Begin your examination of a book by searching for your topic in its index and table of contents. Unfortunately, some excellent books have incomplete indexes and skimpy tables of contents. If you do not find your topic listed in an index, study the table of contents to imagine where it might be discussed in the book. For instance, if your topic is *forgetting* and a table of contents lists a chapter about learning, *forgetting* may be discussed in that chapter.

Use the suggestions given in Chapter 13 to skim sections of books and articles. Especially, read introductory paragraphs, headings, and words printed in special type to decide whether a book or article contains information that you can use when you write a paper.

As you skim, be on the alert for primary sources. **Primary sources** are firsthand sources of information; they are compared with **secondary sources,** which are statements made about primary sources. For example, if you write a paper about the accomplishments of Franklin Roosevelt, a word-for-word copy of a speech he gave would be a primary source, but a newspaper editorial about the speech would be a secondary source. However, whether a source is primary or secondary often depends on the topic of a paper. If you wrote a paper about the opinions of Franklin Roosevelt's contemporaries toward him, a newspaper editorial about a speech he gave would be a primary source for your purposes. Refer to primary sources in your papers whenever possible; they are considered superior to secondary sources because they are original and have not been interpreted by someone else.

When you decide that a book or article is a likely source of information for a paper, continue your evaluation of it by asking the following questions:

1. *Can I understand what it says?* If a book or article is written in such a way that it is extremely difficult for you to understand, it is not a good source for you to use when you write a paper because you may misinterpret it. Find other material that is easier for you to read.

2. *Is the information up to date?* When you write about topics in the news or new developments in a field, all or most of your sources should be from recent newspaper, magazine, or journal articles. However, recent information or thoughts may be published about almost any topic. No matter what your topic, always search for recent newspaper, magazine, or journal articles (see Section 26.1).

3. *Is the material appropriate for my purposes?* Any material is appropriate if it is appropriate for your purposes. For example, if the purpose of a paper is to explain methods that are to teach science to third-grade children, then textbooks that are used to teach science in third-grade classrooms are excellent

primary sources for writing the paper. If the purpose of a paper is to explain the effects of the economy on retired people who are living on fixed incomes, articles in newspapers and magazines are excellent sources for writing the paper (articles written by retired people living on fixed incomes are primary sources). On the other hand, if the purpose of a paper is to explain a theoretical model of how people learn, appropriate sources are scholarly books, articles in learned journals, and monographs published by the professional societies for psychologists. Articles in newspapers and popular magazines are not appropriate sources for explaining a theoretical model of learning.

4. *Is the source appropriate for the level of understanding that I am expected to acquire as a result of preparing the paper?* Sources that are appropriate for papers written at an early stage of studying a subject may not be appropriate for papers written at a later stage of studying the same subject. For example, if you major in the social sciences it may be appropriate to use newspaper and magazine articles as sources for papers you write during your first year or two of college. However, when you write papers for social science courses during your junior and senior years, it may be wise to use such sources sparingly or not at all.

You should also select materials that are authoritative. Books and articles are said to be **authoritative** when they are written by people who have expert knowledge about the subject matter discussed in them. However, you may find it difficult to judge who are the experts in subjects that you have just started to study. In general, articles indexed in specialized periodical indexes of the kinds described in Section 27.1 are considered to be written by authorities. Also, since books are expensive, college libraries make an effort to purchase only authoritative books—libraries usually have no money to waste buying unauthoritative books. When you are uncertain how to find authoritative books or articles, ask an instructor or a librarian for suggestions.

27.5   Borrow or photocopy materials

When you locate books that you believe will be useful to you for writing a paper, borrow the book if it is one that circulates. If the book is a reference book and there are only a few pages in it that interest you, you may find it convenient to photocopy the pages to which you wish to refer. For instance, if you find a useful article in an encyclopedia, it may be convenient to have a copy of the article to refer to when you are at the place where you usually study.

When you find journal, magazine, or newspaper articles that are good sources of information, photocopy them as well. When writing, it is often better to refer to actual sources than to information about them in notes.

The photocopying machine is a great boon to researchers and writers; a small investment in photocopying can save hours of work. For instance, if you take notes on a magazine article, you may recall while writing a paper that the article contains some useful information that you did not record in notes. You will either regret that you did not take more complete notes, or you will spend time in the library that you would not have needed to spend if you had made a photocopy of the article.

27.6   Take the notes you need

When you collect information to write a research paper, you will need to make detailed notes about the sources of your information so that you can write footnotes or endnotes and bibliographic entries. The types of notes you need to make are explained in Section 28.1.

Also, no matter what type of paper you write, you will need notes about the information that you want to include in the paper. This is true whether you collect information by reading books and articles, by interviewing people, or by any other means. Suggestions for making the notes that are needed to write papers are given in Section 28.2, and methods for organizing them to write papers are explained in Section 24.5.

Use What You've Learned

1. Select a topic that could be used to write a ten-page paper for one of the subjects you are studying. Visit a library and make bibliographic notes (Section 28.1) for the following sources of information that could be used to write the paper: (a) four articles in popular magazines, (b) two articles in journals, (c) two articles in newspapers, (d) three books, and (e) an article in a general encyclopedia.

2. Select a well-known person who lives or who has lived in this century and make bibliographic notes (Section 28.1) on five sources that may be used to write a paper about him or her. Refer to a biographical dictionary or encyclopedia, and consult *Current Biography* or the *Current Biography Yearbook* and the *Biography Index*.

3. Select a book about which you might write a summary, report, or review for one of the courses you are taking. Find information about the book by consulting the *Book Review Digest*, the *Book Review Index*, and *The New York Times Index*.

Prepare Effective Research Papers

Papers that are written using information that is collected by doing careful and patient investigation are called **research papers.** The research is usually done by studying in a library (Chapter 27), but it may also be done by interviewing people (Section 26.4); by attending events, such as concerts; by visiting schools, hospitals, museums, businesses, governmental agencies, or other institutions; or by conducting scientific experiments in a laboratory.

There are two important reasons why your teachers will require you to write research papers:

1. You will learn a great deal about specific aspects of topics that pertain to the subjects they teach.
2. You will learn what journals, indexes, and other reference materials are used to study the subjects they teach.

These reasons that teachers require you to write research papers can guide you to write good ones. For example, if you write a research paper for a psychology course, write one that makes it clear that you learned a great deal about some aspect of a psychology topic. Also, when you do research, consult the journals, indexes, and other reference materials that are used by students of psychology.

Research papers are different from other types of papers in that they must include footnotes or endnotes to document the sources of information used in them. For example,

[1]Barbara Westbrook Eakins and R. Gene Eakins, <u>Sex Differences in Human Communication</u> (Boston: Houghton Mifflin Co., 1978), p. 7.

This footnote or endnote refers to something written on page 7 of the book identified in the reference. Footnotes are identical to endnotes except that footnotes are typed at the bottoms of pages (Figure 28c), while endnotes are typed on a page or pages at the end of a paper (Figure 28f). Formats for footnotes and endnotes are explained in Section 28.7 and Section 28.9.

Research papers must also include a bibliography, which is a list of all the sources of information referred to in a paper. Following is an example of a bibliographic entry:

```
Eakins, Barbara Westbrook, and R. Gene Eakins.   Sex

     Differences in Human Communication.   Boston:

     Houghton Mifflin Co., 1978.
```

Formats for bibliographic entries are explained in Section 28.8 and Section 28.9.

When you write a research paper, *use the suggestions in this chapter together with the suggestions in Chaper 24*. For example, make notes for the bibliography and take notes on information (Section 28.1 and Section 28.2) at the same time you select a topic and prepare an outline for a paper (Section 24.3 and Section 24.4). Also, however, keep in mind that you should prepare papers in the formats that your teachers require (Section 24.1). If a teacher states that you must use a special form for footnotes, endnotes, or the bibliography, use the form that the teacher specifies.

28.1   Make notes for bibliography

When you collect information for a research paper in a library, make notes so you can write footnotes or endnotes and bibliographic entries (Section 28.7 and Section 28.8). The types of notes to make are illustrated in Figure 28a. The notes may be written on notebook paper rather than on cards; however, there are advantages to writing them on 3 x 5 inch cards. For one thing, notes on cards can be arranged easily in correct

Figure 28a **Bibliographic Notes for a Book.**

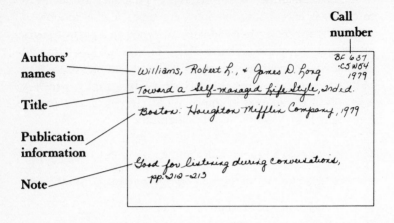

alphabetical sequence to facilitate preparation of a bibliography.

The following list summarizes the most important types of
information to include in bibliographic notes:

1. The name of an author or names of authors
2. The title of a book or article
3. The name of the publisher of a book
4. The name of a periodical
5. The date a book or periodical was published
6. The page numbers on which selections in periodicals are
   printed.
7. The edition number of a book that is published in more
   than one edition
8. The volume number of a journal or encyclopedia
9. The call number for a book

You may find it helpful to copy this list so that you can take it
with you when you make bibliographic notes in a library.

The following discussions give more detailed information

about making bibliographic notes for books and articles in magazines, journals, and newspapers.

Books. Bibliographic information for books is printed on the title page and on the copyright page. The title page is usually one of the first two or three pages in a book; the copyright page is the page that follows immediately after a title page. When you take bibliographic notes for a book, record

1. the name of the author or names of the authors (or editor or editors).
2. the title of the book.
3. the edition number of the book, if an edition number is stated.
4. the city where the book was published. Record the first city if more than one city is listed.
5. the name of the publisher.
6. the year the book was published. This date is on the page that follows the title page; if more than one year is listed, record the most recent year.
7. the call number for the book (see Section 27.2).

A call number will help you locate a book in case you do not borrow it from a library or in case you want to refer to it after you return it to a library.

If you are interested in only a specific article, essay, poem, or other selection in a book, also record

8. the author of the selection.
9. the title of the selection.
10. the page numbers on which the selection is printed.

The page numbers will help you locate the material quickly when you want to refer to it.

Magazine articles. Some bibliographic information for a magazine article may be in notes you make when you refer to a periodical index (Section 27.1). Figure 27b illustrates how to translate bibliographic information printed in periodical indexes. If the information is not in notes, it will be printed on the front cover or on one of the first few pages of a magazine. When you make bibliographic notes for a magazine article, record

1. the author or authors of the article.
2. the title of the article.
3. the name of the magazine.
4. the month, day (if one is given), and year the magazine was published.
5. the page number or numbers on which the article is printed in the magazine.

Sometimes no author is given for a magazine article. For instance, no author is given for many of the articles published in *Time* magazine.

Journal articles.   Make bibliographic notes for journals that are identical to the ones you make for magazines, except also record the volume number of a journal. In addition, the date for a journal may be a season and a year rather than a month and a year. Some journals are published four times a year: spring, summer, winter, and fall.

Newspaper articles.   The bibliographic information for a newspaper article is printed on the page on which the article is printed. Record

1. the author of the article, if an author is given.
2. the headline or title for the article.
3. the name of the newspaper.
4. the month, day, and year the article was published.
5. the page number or numbers on which the article is printed.

Figure 28b **Notes on Information for
Writing a Paper.**

**Cross-reference
to outline for a
paper**

**Cross-reference
to bibliographic
note**

**Information for
paper**

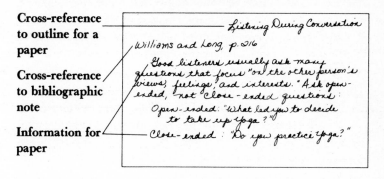

If a letter such as *A, B,* or *C* appears in front of a page number, record it with the page number; it refers to a section of the newspaper. For instance, if a page number is *B6,* write *Section B, page 6* in your notes.

If an article appears in a magazine section of a newspaper, make the same kind of bibliographic notes that you make for magazines.

28.2   Take notes on information

In addition to bibliographic notes, you also need to take notes on the information you will use to write a research paper.

Notes on the information you use in a paper are absolutely essential. They are used to prepare outlines, organize information in papers, state central themes, and draft the bodies of papers (Section 24.4 through Section 24.7). Figure 28b illustrates notes for information that was used to write a paper on the topic *listening.* Use the following procedures when you take notes:

1. *Write notes on cards, not on notebook paper.* Use 3 x 5 inch cards for notes, or, if your handwriting is unusually large, use 4 x 6 inch cards.

2. *Write only one piece of information or one quotation on each card.* A book or article may include information that is relevant to two, three, or more points you make in a paper. It is essential that each piece of information be on a card by itself. If a card contains two unrelated pieces of information, one of them cannot be placed where it belongs when notes are organized to write the draft of a paper.

3. *Write references on cards so you will know the exact sources of the information on them.* In Figure 28b, *Williams and Long, p. 216* is a cross-reference to the book for which bibliographic information is recorded in Figure 28a. This cross-reference is necessary when writing a footnote or an endnote.

4. *Leave spaces at the tops of cards to make notes about the places in your paper where you will use the information on cards.* In Figure 28b the words *Listening During Conversation* in the right, top corner refer to a place in the outline for a paper where the information will be used. It is a good idea to write this type of information in pencil so it can be erased if necessary. In the course of writing a paper you may change your mind about exactly where you want to use a piece of information or a quotation.

5. *Summarize or paraphrase information whenever possible.* Summarizing and paraphrasing are explained in Section 28.4 and Section 28.5.

6. *If you copy a writer's words exactly, enclose them in quotation marks.* Notice in Figure 28b that a phrase and two sentences are enclosed in quotation marks; they are the exact words in the book from which the information was taken. The quotation marks are a reminder that the words must be shown as a quotation or paraphrased when they are used in a paper. Methods for showing quotations in research papers are explained in Section 28.6.

The first suggestion in this list is an emphatic statement that all notes should be written on cards rather than on notebook paper. There is, however, at least one logical exception to this general rule. If a major portion of a paper will be a fairly lengthy summary of a book or article, it may be better to write the summary on a sheet of paper rather than on cards. For example, if part of a paper will be a five-paragraph summary of a seventy-five-page article or section of a book, it would probably be better to write the summary on notebook paper than on several cards.

28.3   Organize before you write

Before you write any part of a paper, prepare an outline, organize the information in the paper, and state a central theme (Section 24.4 through Section 24.6). Also, study Chapter 25 and Chapter 26 for ideas about how to present information and how to support statements and conclusions in papers.

When you write a draft (Section 24.7), a major problem may be to decide how to report facts, ideas, and other information that you have collected as a result of research. These decisions are frustrating to many students, but they need not be troublesome to you if you use the following guidelines:

1. Summarize whenever possible.
2. Paraphrase when you cannot summarize.
3. Use quotations sparingly.

Methods for summarizing, paraphrasing, and quoting are explained in Section 28.4 through Section 28.6.

Also, *write footnotes or endnotes at the same time you write a draft.* It may seem easier to write footnotes and endnotes after a paper has been written, but it is not because it is easy to forget the sources of information. You will save yourself many unnecessary problems if you write footnotes or endnotes when you write a draft, rather than later.

28.4   Summarize whenever possible

Information in research papers should usually be summarized rather than paraphrased or quoted. **Summaries** are condensed presentations of information. Use these procedures when you summarize:

1. Read articles or sections of books to find the important facts, ideas, or other information presented in them.
2. Take notes about the important content.
3. Use your notes to write a condensed version of the original material.

The following paragraph is a summary of a six-page journal article.

The first investigation of the frequency with which the various prefixes appear in English words was reported by Russell G. Stauffer in 1942.   In studying 20,000 common words, he found that 24 percent of them include a prefix.   Stauffer reported that, in decreasing order of their frequency, the ten most common prefixes in English words are com-, re-, ad-, un-, in-, dis-, ex-, de-, en-, and pro-.[1]

---

[1]Russell G. Stauffer, "A Study of Prefixes in the Thorndike List To Establish a List of Prefixes That Should Be Taught in the Elementary School," Journal of Educational Research, 30 (February 1942), 453-458.

This paragraph condenses the information in a six-page journal article to three sentences, and it accurately summarizes the important information in the article. The footnote identifies the source of the information.

Additional suggestions for writing summaries are given in Section 25.3.

28.5   Paraphrase when you can't summarize

Paraphrases are rewordings of the written or spoken statements of others; when you paraphrase you use your own words and phrasings to restate what others wrote or said. Following are a passage from a history book and a proper and improper paraphrase of the passage.

> Although the discipline of women's history is new, the first book examining the role of women in the American past appeared in 1848, when Elizabeth Fries Lummis Ellet, author of numerous books and magazine articles, published her two-volume work, *The Women of the American Revolution.* (She subsequently added a third volume.) Elizabeth Ellet, dismayed by the lack of attention to women's contributions to the war effort found in standard histories of the time—a flaw that continues to our own day—carefully researched her study by talking to the children and grandchildren of her subjects and by gaining access to private family correspondence.

Compare this passage to the following *proper* paraphrase of it to observe that the informational content of the two are similar but that the writing styles are very different.

> The first history of famous American women was
> published in 1848.   The two-volume book, The Women
> of the American Revolution, was written by Elizabeth
> Fries Lummis Ellet out of the conviction that other
> books about the Revolution did not give proper
> attention to the contributions of women.   She
> researched the lives of famous eighteenth-century

women by interviewing their descendants and by
studying their families' letters.[3]

---

[3]Carol Ruth Berkin and Mary Beth Norton, <u>Women
of America</u> (Boston: Houghton Mifflin Co., 1979),
p. 5.

Now, compare the passage from the history book to the following *improper* paraphrase of it.

Although the study of women's history is new,
the first book to examine the role of women in
American history appeared in 1848, when Elizabeth
Fries Lummis Ellet, author of many books and magazine
articles, published her two-volume work, <u>The Women
of the American Revolution</u>.   The author, dismayed
by the lack of attention to the contribution of women
to the war effort in other books of her time,
carefully researched famous women by talking with
their children and grandchildren and by reading
their private family correspondence.[3]

---

[3]Carol Ruth Berkin and Mary Beth Norton, <u>Women
of America</u> (Boston: Houghton Mifflin Co., 1979), p.
5.

This paraphrase of the history book passage is not proper
because it adheres too closely to the wordings and phrasings of

the original. It was written by deleting and rearranging phrases, and by changing a few words.

When you write paraphrases, you must write them using your own words and phrasings. The information you collect for papers will be written by people who have many different writing styles. However, your papers must be written using one consistent style—your style. Paraphrasing is one method for writing papers in a consistent style. Use the following procedures to write paraphrases:

1. Read a passage you want to paraphrase as many times as is necessary for you to completely understand the information in it.

2. Without looking at the passage, recite the information in it aloud or silently using your own words and phrasings.

3. Refer to the passage to determine if your restatement is an accurate representation of the information presented in it.

4. If it is, write your paraphrase; if it is not, continue in this way until you are able to state the information using your own words and phrasings.

Write footnotes or endnotes to indicate the sources of paraphrases, just as you write them for all sources of information in research papers.

28.6   Use quotations sparingly

A **quotation** is the exact written or spoken words of another person. There are three good reasons to quote statements rather than to summarize or paraphrase them:

1. They are forceful or dramatic proof of statements or conclusions in a paper.

2. They are so succinct, apt, or precisely stated that it is impossible to state them in better words.

3. They are statements you evaluate or criticize in a paper.

Whatever you do, use quotations sparingly. Some students believe that a research paper should be a string of quotations linked together with a few sentences; this is incorrect. Summarize or paraphrase information unless you are convinced that a quotation serves your purpose much better.

When quotations are three typewritten lines, or less, integrate them into the text of a paper. For example,

There is growing indignation about the short

prison terms criminals receive.   The mother of a

brutally murdered sixteen-year-old girl told a New

York audience: "Time and again we see short-term

sentences given to criminals while we, the victims,

serve lifetime sentences of fear, grief and

violation."[8]

---

[8]Molly Ivins, "Victims Say Lives Echo With Grief," New York Times, 21 April 1981, Section B, p. 1.

When quotations are longer than three typewritten lines, do not enclose them in quotation marks. Instead, write introductions to them and set them off from the text in the following manner:

G. D. Lillibridge identified four types of work

that must be done by those who want to weld themselves

into a nation.

Any people seeking to become a nation are thus

found working hard to preserve and protect

```
their independence, to build unity, to create

and promote a common identity, and to emphasize

the special quality of that identity.¹¹
```

```
    ¹¹G. D. Lillibridge, Images of American
Society, Vol. I. (Boston: Houghton Mifflin Co.,
1976), p. 154.
```

Quotations may be shortened by using three spaced periods (. . .) to indicate material that has been intentionally omitted. Following is an example of how three spaced periods, called *ellipses,* are used to indicate that the first part of a sentence is omitted.

```
Lillibridge summarized that nationalism

causes people to feel that the way they do things is

". . . special and superior."¹⁴
```

```
    ¹⁴Lillibridge, p. 154.
```

In the following example, ellipses are used to show that words have been purposely omitted from the end of a sentence.

```
If we are fully alive, we do not live in the past

or in the future, we live now:   "True beings are

lived in the present. . . ."¹⁷
```

```
    ¹⁷Martin Buber, I and Thou, trans. Ronald Gregor
Smith (New York: Charles Scribner's Sons, 1957),
p. 13.
```

Notice the quotation ends with four periods; one is a period to end the sentence and three are ellipses to indicate that the end of Martin Buber's sentence is not quoted.

Ellipses may also be used to indicate that the middle portion of a sentence has been purposely omitted.

My interest in knowing where happiness is to be found was stimulated by a teacher who stated: "Happiness is waiting for you . . . on the other side of pain."[19]

---

[19]Margot Walther, personal interview, 31 January 1981.

Include quotations in your research papers, but do not overuse them. When quotations are less than three typewritten lines long, enclose them in quotation marks and integrate them into paragraphs. When quotations are longer, write introductions to them, use indentation to set them off, and do not enclose them in quotation marks. Also, proofread quotations carefully to make certain that they are identical to what others wrote or said.

28.7   Write footnotes or endnotes

This section explains how to write the **footnotes** or **endnotes** that are necessary to document the sources of information that you summarize, paraphrase, quote, reproduce, or otherwise include in a research paper. Footnotes and endnotes are identical except that footnotes are listed at the bottoms of pages (Figure 28c) while endnotes are listed on a page or pages at the end of a paper (Figure 28f, which is located toward the end of this chapter).

Figure 28c **Page of a Research Paper
with Footnotes.**

During an interview, Lyman L. Steil, a
nationally known authority on communication, stated
that poor listening complicates relations among
people and sometimes even has fatal consequences:

> The sinking of the <u>Titanic</u>, Pearl Harbor . . .
> and some recent airplane disasters are classic
> examples of a breakdown in communication and
> judgment.   A message was sent, and listening
> broke down.[1]

Fortunately, good listening habits can be
learned.   This paper explores the characteristics
of poor listening and the remedies for it.

<u>Poor Listening Habits</u>

Studies have found that within two days after
listening to a ten-minute oral presentation,
average listeners remember only about one-fourth of
what was said, and poor listeners remember even
less.[2]

_____

[1]"Secrets of Being a Better Listener", <u>U.S.
News & World Report</u>, 26 May 1980, p. 65.

[2]<u>Your Personal Listening Profile</u> (New York:
Sperry Corp., 1980), p. 5.

Write footnotes or endnotes to specify the exact sources of facts, opinions, and other information you include in research papers unless the fact is general knowledge. For instance, if you state that San Francisco will break away from the mainland and slide into the Pacific Ocean, you must document the source of this information, but you do not need to document that San Francisco is located in California. Similarly, if you state that cigarette smoking decreases life expectancy by ten years, you must document the source of this information, but you do not need to document that there is a health warning from the Surgeon General of the United States on each packet of cigarettes sold in this country.

The first footnote or endnote for a source is more complete than second or later references to the same source. Therefore, the discussion about first footnotes and endnotes is followed by an explanation of how to write second and later footnotes or endnotes.

First footnote or endnote for a source.   To write footnotes or endnotes, you must have all the types of information that are explained in Section 28.1. Also, you must follow the formats in this section *exactly* as they are illustrated.

The following information may be helpful to you in case you have difficulty interpreting the examples:

1. Underlining is used to indicate titles of books and names of periodicals and other publications.

2. Quotation marks are used to indicate titles of articles, essays, poems, and other selections in books and periodicals.

3. Days of months are indicated with the day first; for example, "27 March 1982" rather than "March 27, 1982."

4. Page numbers are included in footnotes and endnotes for books, periodicals, and other publications.

For page numbers, *p.* indicates "page" (as in *p. 104*), and *pp.* indicates "pages" (as in *pp. 98–101*). However, the abbreviations *p.* and *pp.* are not used to indicate page numbers for journals and encyclopedias.

The names of authors, books, periodicals, and other information in the following examples are fictitious to help you grasp quickly the similarities among footnotes and endnotes for various sources of information.

1. Book by one author

[1]John Smith, <u>Loving</u> (New York: Shep Press, 1982), p. 39.

2. Book by two authors

[2]John Smith and Mary Smith, <u>Loving</u> (New York: Shep Press, 1982), pp. 101–104.

3. Book by three authors

[3]John Smith, Mary Smith, and Joan Green, <u>Loving</u> (New York: Shep Press, 1982), pp. 97–98.

4. Book by more than three authors

[4]John Smith, and others, <u>Loving</u> (New York: Shep Press, 1982), pp. 9–11.

5. Book by an editor rather than by an author

[5]Frank Jones, ed., <u>Love and Hate</u> (New York: Shep Press, 1982), p. 379.

6. Book that has been translated

[6]Jean LaPorte, <u>Love in France</u>, trans. John Smith (New York: Shep Press, 1982), pp. 209–214.

7. Book by an organization rather than by an individual

⁷Students for Love Society, <u>Loving More</u> (New York: Shep Press, 1982), pp. 39-46.

8. Book with no author given

⁸<u>Loveworks</u> (New York: Shep Press, 1982), pp. 8-12.

9. Book in an edition other than the first

⁹John Smith, <u>Loving</u>, 2nd ed. (New York: Shep Press, 1985), p. 20.

10. Article, essay, poem, or other selection in an edited book

¹⁰John Smith, "Try Love," in <u>Love and Hate</u>, ed. Frank Jones (New York: Shep Press, 1982), pp. 102-103.

11. Encyclopedia article, signed (the volume number precedes the page numbers)

¹¹John Smith, "Hugging," <u>Encyclopedia of Love</u>, 1980 ed., VII, 432-436.

12. Encyclopedia article, unsigned (the volume number precedes the page numbers)

¹²"Hugging," <u>Encyclopedia of Love</u>, 1980 ed., VII, 432-436.

13. Journal article (the volume number precedes the date)

¹³John Smith, "Love is All," <u>Journal of Love</u>, 14 (January 1982), 77-84.

14. Magazine article, signed

   [14]John Smith, "Love Me," <u>Kisses</u>, October 1982, pp. 33-34.

15. Magazine article, unsigned

   [15]"Love Me," <u>Kisses</u>, October 1982, pp. 33-34.

16. Newspaper article, signed

   [16]John Smith, "Love Wins," <u>Daily Love News</u>, 17 October 1982, Section A, p. 11.

17. Newspaper article, unsigned

   [17]"Love Wins," <u>Daily Love News</u>, 17 October 1982, Section A, p. 11.

18. Book review in a periodical

   [18]Fred White, "Love Ten, Hate Zero," review of <u>Loving</u>, by John Smith, <u>Kisses</u>, May 1983, p. 21.

19. Interview

   [19]John Smith, personal interview, Walla Walla, Washington, 18 October 1982.

20. Television or radio program

   [20]ABC, "John Smith's Talk Show," 30 February 1988, a conversation with Fred White.

If you do not find an example you need, use one of the formats for books when you need to document printed material. Use the format for interviews when you need to document personal letters, class lectures, visits to museums, and other sources such as these.

Second and later footnotes or endnotes.   Second and later references to sources are abbreviated, usually using authors' names. For instance, this is the first reference to a book:

[7]Kevin Ryan and James M. Cooper, <u>Those Who Can</u>, <u>Teach</u>, 3rd ed. (Boston: Houghton Mifflin Co., 1980), pp. 110-113.

Following is a second or later reference to the same book:

[15]Ryan and Cooper, p. 249.

Use the following guidelines when you write second and later footnotes or endnotes.

1. Usually use the last name of an author or the last names of the authors.

2. If you refer to two authors who have the same last name, include their first names in second and later references.

   [14]Josephine Ives, pp. 332-333.

   [17]Sumner Ives, p. 117.

3. If you refer to more than one work by the same author or authors, include abbreviated titles of the works in second and later references.

   [19]Muntz, <u>Divorce</u>, pp. 123-124.

   [23]Muntz, "Househusband," p. 174.

<u>Divorce</u> refers to a book entitled *The Divorce Rites of the Middle Class* and "Househusband" refers to a magazine article entitled "A Househusband for Twenty Happy Years."

4. If no author is given for an article, use the name of the publication in second and later references.

   [28]<u>Time</u>, pp. 97-98.

When writing abbreviated second or later references for sources, be guided by the principle that they must be worded so that there is no confusion as to which sources they refer.

28.8   Write bibliographic entries

Research papers end with a bibliography of the type that is illustrated in Figure 28g, which is located near the end of this chapter. A **bibliography** is a list of books, articles, interviews, and other sources of information that are referenced by footnotes or endnotes in a paper. The fictitious names of authors, books, periodicals, and other information in the following examples of bibliographic entries are the same ones used in the examples of footnotes and endnotes in Section 28.7.

1. Book by one author

Smith, John.   <u>Loving</u>.   New York: Shep Press, 1982.

2. Book by two authors

Smith, John, and Mary Smith.   <u>Loving</u>.   New York:

    Shep Press, 1982.

3. Book by three authors

Smith, John, Mary Smith, and Joan Green.   <u>Loving</u>.

    New York: Shep Press, 1982.

4. Book by more than three authors

Smith, John, Mary Smith, Joan Green, and Frank
    Jones. <u>Loving</u>. New York: Shep Press, 1982.

5. Book by an editor rather than by an author

Jones, Frank, ed. <u>Love and Hate</u>. New York: Shep
    Press, 1982.

6. Book that has been translated

LaPorte, Jean. <u>Love in France</u>. Translated by John
    Smith. New York: Shep Press, 1982.

7. Book by an organization rather than by an individual

Students for Love Society. <u>Loving More</u>. New York:
    Shep Press, 1982.

8. Book with no author given

<u>Loveworks</u>. New York: Shep Press, 1982.

9. Book in an edition other than the first

Smith, John. <u>Loving</u>. 2nd ed. New York: Shep
    Press, 1985.

10. Article, essay, poem, or other selection in an edited book

Smith, John. "Try Love." In <u>Love and Hate</u>, edited
    by Frank Jones. New York: Shep Press, 1982.

11. Encyclopedia article, signed

Smith, John. "Hugging." Encyclopedia of
    Love. 1980 ed.

12. Encyclopedia article, unsigned

"Hugging." Encyclopedia of Love. 1980 ed.

13. Journal article (the volume number precedes the date)

Smith, John. "Love is All." Journal of Love, 14
    (January 1982), 77-84.

14. Magazine article, signed

Smith, John. "Love Me." Kisses, October 1982,
    pp. 33-34.

15. Magazine article, unsigned

"Love Me." Kisses, October 1982, pp. 33-34.

16. Newspaper article, signed

Smith, John. "Love Wins." Daily Love News, 17
    October 1982, Section A, p. 11.

17. Newspaper article, unsigned

"Love Wins." Daily Love News, 17 October 1982,
    Section A, p. 11.

18. Book review in a periodical

White, Fred, "Love Ten, Hate Zero," review of <u>Loving</u>,

    by John Smith.   <u>Kisses</u>, May 1983, p. 21.

19. Interview

Smith, John.   Personal Interview.   Walla Walla,

    Washington, 18 October 1982.

20. Television or radio program

ABC, "John Smith's Talk Show," 30 February 1988, a

    conversation with Fred White.

If you do not find an example you need, use one of the formats for books when you need to document printed material. Use the format for interviews when you need to document personal letters, class lectures, visits to museums, and other sources such as these.

28.9   Type the final paper

Figure 28d through Figure 28g, located toward the end of this chapter, illustrate how to type a research paper. Use the following guidelines to type or supervise the typing of the final copy of a research paper:

1. Use heavy, white, bond paper that measures 8½ x 11 inches.
2. Use a typewriter that has a new black ribbon and clean type.
3. Leave a 1½-inch margin on the left and top and a 1-inch margin on the right and bottom of each page. A 1½-inch

margin at the top is nine spaces down from the top edge of a page.

4. Type only on one side of a sheet of paper.

5. Number pages consecutively beginning with *1* on the first page of text (Figure 28e). Do not number the title page (or an outline, if one is included in a paper).

6. If you use endnotes, double space the entire paper (except for the special directions that follow for headings).

7. If you use footnotes, double space the entire paper except for footnotes (and for the special directions that follow for headings). Single space footnotes, but leave a double space between footnotes.

8. Indent paragraphs five spaces.

9. When a quotation is longer than three typewritten lines, set it off from the text by indenting all lines of the quotation five spaces.

10. Leave two spaces after periods, question marks, and exclamation marks. Leave one space after all other punctuation, including colons; except leave two spaces after a colon when it is followed by a complete sentence.

11. Make clean erasures.

12. When teachers permit some handwritten corrections, make them neatly and make no more than two corrections on a page.

Also, make a carbon copy or photocopy of a paper so that you will not need to rewrite it in case it is misplaced or lost.

Title page and outline.   Prepare a title page in the format that is illustrated in Figure 28d. If you are required to include an outline, type "Outline" in the center of a page 1½ inches (nine spaces) from the top. Triple space between the heading and the first line of the outline. Use the format for outlines that is explained in Section 24.4, and place the outline immediately following the title page.

Headings in the text.   Include headings in the text of a paper to indicate the major divisions; they are likely to be the major divisions of your outline. A page of text with a major-division heading is illustrated in Figure 28e; triple space before typing a heading of the kind illustrated in Figure 28e.

Footnote and endnote numbers in the text.   Place footnote and endnote numbers in papers one-half space above the line *following* the facts, quotations, or other information to which references apply. Number footnotes or endnotes consecutively, beginning with *1* for the first reference (Figure 28c and Figure 28e).

Footnotes.   Use endnotes unless you are required to use footnotes; endnotes are much easier to type.

Before you type a page of text, estimate how much space you will need at the bottom for footnotes and a 1-inch margin. Then allow at least one-half inch more space than you estimate you need. Before you type anything on a page, mark, in pencil, where you must stop typing in order to have space for footnotes and a 1-inch margin at the bottom. Placement of footnotes is illustrated in Figure 28c. The line above the footnotes in Figure 28c was typed by striking the underscore key ten times.

Formats for footnotes are explained in Section 28.7. Indent the first line of a footnote five spaces and type the number of the note one-half space above the line. Single space footnotes, but double space between them.

Endnotes.   Place endnotes immediately following the last page of the text of a paper. Type "Notes" in the center of a blank sheet of paper 1½ inches (nine spaces) from the top. Triple space between the heading and the first line of the first endnote. List endnotes using the same numbers that are used in the text of the paper (compare Figure 28e and Figure 28f).

Formats for endnotes are explained in Section 28.7. Indent the first line of an endnote five spaces, type the number of the note one-half space above the line, and double space the note.

Bibliography.   When you use endnotes, place the bibliography immediately following endnotes; when you use footnotes, place the bibliography immediately following the last page of text. Type "Bibliography" in the center of a blank sheet of paper 1½ inches (nine spaces) from the top. Triple space between the heading and the first line of the first bibliographic entry.

Formats for bibliographic entries are explained in Section 28.8. Type the first line of an entry at the left margin, indent other lines five spaces, and double space the entry (Figure 28g).

Arrange the entries alphabetically, using the first words of each entry. If there is more than one reference for an author, do not repeat the author's name; indicate the name by typing ten hyphens and a period. For example:

Bott, Elizabeth.   <u>Family and the Social</u>

     <u>Network</u>.   New York: Free Press, 1971.

Groffman, Erving.   <u>The Presentation of the Self in</u>

     <u>Everyday Life</u>.   New York: Doubleday, 1959.

----------.   <u>Relations in Public</u>.   New York: Basic

     Books, 1971.

President's Commission on Obscenity and

     Pornography.   <u>Report of the President's</u>

     <u>Commission on Obscenity and Pornography</u>.   New

     York: Bantam Books, 1970.

Smith, Geroal R., Thomas B. Gregory, and Richard C.

     Pugh.   "Meeting Students' Needs."   <u>Phi Delta</u>

     <u>Kappan</u>, 62 (April 1981), 561-564.

Figure 28d **Title Page for a Research Paper.**

REMEDIES FOR POOR LISTENING

Erika Steffer

Speech 301

Professor Leonard Martin

April 20, 1982

1

During an interview, Lyman L. Steil, a nationally known authority on communication, stated that
poor listening complicates relations among people
and sometimes even has fatal consequences:

> The sinking of the <u>Titanic</u>, Pearl Harbor . . .
> and some recent airplane disasters are classic
> examples of a breakdown in communication and
> judgment. A message was sent, and listening
> broke down.[1]

Fortunately, good listening habits can be learned.
This paper explores the characteristics of poor listening and the remedies for it.

<u>Poor Listening Habits</u>

Studies have found that within two days after
listening to a ten-minute oral presentation,
average listeners remember only about one-fourth of
what was said, and poor listeners remember even
less.[2]

Any speaker can quickly identify the poor
listeners in an audience. They don't look at the
speaker, they slouch, they shift around in their

Notes

[1]"Secrets of Being a Better Listener," U.S. News & World Report, 26 May 1980, p. 65.

[2]Your Personal Listening Profile (New York: Sperry Corp., 1980), p. 5.

[3]John A. Blubaugh, "Effects of Positive and Negative Audience Feedback on Selected Variables of Speech Behavior," Speech Monographs, 36 (June 1969), 133.

[4]George DeMare, Communicating at the Top (New York: John Wiley & Sons, 1979), pp. 102-106.

[5]U.S. News & World Report, p. 66.

[6]Blubaugh, 135-136.

[7]Paul W. Keller, Monologue to Dialogue (Englewood Cliffs, N.J.: Prentice-Hall, 1973), pp. 87-91.

[8]Sara W. Ludsteen, Listening: Its Impact on Reading and Other Language Arts (Urbana, Ill.: National Council of Teachers of English, 1971), p. 34.

[9]Blubaugh, 137.

[10]Ludsteen, pp. 51-52.

14

Bibliography

Blubaugh, John A.   "Effects of Positive and
    Negative Audience Feedback on Selected
    Variables of Speech Behavior." Speech
    Monographs, 36 (June 1969), 131–137.

DeMare, George.   Communicating at the Top.   New
    York: John Wiley & Sons, 1979.

Keller, Paul W.   Monologue to Dialogue.   Englewood
    Cliffs, N.J.: Prentice-Hall, 1973.

Ludsteen, Sara W.   Listening: Its Impact on Reading
    and Other Language Arts.   Urbana, Ill.:
    National Council of Teachers of English, 1971.

"Secrets of Being a Better Listener." U.S. News &
    World Report, 26 May 1980.

Weaver, Carl H.   Human Listening.   Indianapolis:
    The Bobbs-Merrill Co., 1972.

Williams, Robert L., and James D. Long.   Toward a
    Self-managed Life Style.   2nd ed.   Boston:
    Houghton Mifflin Co., 1979.

Your Personal Listening Profile.   New York: Sperry
    Corp., 1980.

The ten hyphens followed by a period indicate that the third book was written by the same person who wrote the second book; the publication dates (1959 and 1971) were used to decide which book should be listed first. If an entry begins with *a, an,* or *the,* use the second word in the entry to place it in alphabetical sequence. For instance, if the next-to-the-last entry were written by "The President's Commission on Obscenity and Pornography," the name of the commission would be typed including the word *the,* but the entry would be placed in the list as though the word *the* were not in the title.

28.10   Check a paper before you submit it

Use the following statements as a checklist to evaluate a research paper before you submit it to an instructor. Each statement should describe a paper accurately.

1. The central theme is clearly stated in an interesting introduction (Section 24.6 and Section 24.8).
2. The paper is an informative explanation of the central theme *or* it provides convincing evidence for the conclusion that is stated in the central theme.
3. All statements or conclusions are supported using sufficient and convincing evidence (Chapter 26).
4. All facts, opinions, and other statements made by writers or speakers are accurately and fairly represented (Chapter 26.1).
5. The paper is written as well as you are able to write.
6. The paper is free of all spelling, punctuation, and other writing errors (Section 24.10).
7. The paper is neatly typed (Section 28.9) and it is in the format that the teacher specified (Section 24.1).
8. References are up to date (Section 26.1 and Section 27.4).
9. References include primary sources (Section 27.4).
10. Facts, opinions, and other information from references are

mostly summarized and paraphrased rather than quoted (Section 28.4 through Section 28.6).

11. All quotations are presented in correct formats (Section 28.6).

12. There are no statements in the paper that are likely to antagonize those who read it (Section 25.8).

13. The sources of all facts, opinions, and other information are referenced by footnotes or endnotes (Section 28.7).

14. All footnote or endnote numbers in the text are placed *following* the information to which they refer (Section 28.9).

15. All footnotes or endnotes are written in correct formats (Section 28.7 and Section 28.9).

16. All bibliographic entries are written in correct formats (Section 28.8 and Section 28.9).

17. The paper is securely stapled in the upper left corner.

Also, make certain that you have a carbon copy or photocopy of a paper before you submit it to a teacher so that you will not need to rewrite it in case it is misplaced or lost.

Use What You've Learned

1. Submit a photocopy of a one- or two-page article from a magazine or journal and the following:

a. A summary of the information in the article

b. A paraphrase of two paragraphs in the article

On the photocopy of the article, indicate which portion of it you paraphrased and also indicate one sentence or more that would be appropriate to use as a direct quotation in a paper.

2. Write a two-page research paper on any subject you choose.

a. Include as references at least one book, one magazine article, one journal article, and one newspaper article.

b. Include at least six endnotes in the paper.

c. Include a title page, a page of notes, and a bibliography.

Type the paper in the format that is described in Section 28.9.

Give Good Oral Reports

The methods for planning the organization and content of oral reports are the same ones that are used to write papers (see Chapter 24 through Chapter 28). This chapter gives practical hints you may use to give effective oral reports for your college courses.

29.1   Prepare a brief report

When you are not given a time limit for an oral report, plan a report that is as brief as possible. For example, if you can say everything that is important to say in five minutes or in ten minutes, say it in five minutes.

If a teacher specifies the length for an oral report, observe the time limit as closely as you can. For instance, when you have a five-minute time limit, your report should be between four and six minutes long. It is better to speak for too little rather than too much time; when you have a ten-minute time limit, it would be better to speak for eight minutes than for fourteen minutes.

Most people speak within the range of 100 to 150 words per minute; the average rate of speech is about 125 words per minute. As a result, on the average, five-minute oral reports consist of about 625 words (5 x 125 = 625). The number of words in an average five-minute speech is equivalent to about two type-written, double-spaced pages. Of course, you may speak more slowly or quickly than the average.

29.2   Plan no more than four major points

Oral reports should usually include two or three major points; they should seldom include more than four major points. Many speakers consider three major points to be the ideal number for oral presentations. The following skeleton outline illustrates the basic organization that might be used for a five-minute oral report given by a person who speaks at the rate of 135 words per minute.

   I. Introduction (125 words)
  II. Body (450 words)
     A. Major point (150 words)
     B. Major point (150 words)
     C. Major point (150 words)
III. Conclusion (100 words)

A five-minute report prepared using this plan consists of five paragraphs—one for the introduction, three for the major points, and one for the conclusion. Most paragraphs range from 100 to 150 words.

29.3   Decide how to interest your audience

The topics for the oral reports that are given for college credit are usually assigned by instructors. As a result, your problem will usually not be to select an interesting topic, but to decide how you can make a topic that you have been assigned interesting to your audience.

One way to develop a topic so that you can present it in an interesting way is to ask the following questions about it:

1. *Can I state interesting or surprising facts that might intrigue my audience?* This question is answered by doing research—usually in a library (Chapter 27).

2. *Can I explain how the information about the topic may*

benefit my audience? If what you say will benefit people in some way, they are more likely to be interested in your report.

3. *Can I evaluate the subject matter of my report for my audience?* When you give an evaluation (Section 25.7), your audience learns how your mind works; members of your audience may be interested in learning how your mind works even if they are not interested in the subject matter of your report.

4. *Can I persuade my audience that they should change a belief, opinion, or point of view they hold about my topic?* If you present a persuasive argument (Section 25.8) that requires members of your audience to reconsider opinions they hold, you may capture their attention. We tend to listen when our opinions or beliefs are challenged.

Also *include a variety of evidence* to support the statements you make or the conclusions you draw. Consult Chapter 26 for ideas. Include whatever personal experiences you have had that are appropriate to share (Section 26.3). If your audience is not interested in knowing about your topic, they may be interested in knowing about you.

Finally, decide whether you can provide your audience with something to observe other than you speaking. Decide if your topic lends itself to doing one or more of the following:

1. Drawing or writing something on the chalkboard
2. Displaying a picture or drawing
3. Showing an object
4. Giving a demonstration

Charts, tables, graphs, and diagrams are among the types of things that might be drawn or written on a chalkboard or displayed in a drawing prepared on heavy paper. Objects to show include works of art, machines, tools, utensils, and models (for instance, a model of the parts of a human eye or a model of a setting for a theatrical production). If you explain a method or way of doing something, a demonstration is likely to be appropriate.

29.4   Practice giving the report

The organization and content of oral reports are planned using the same procedures that are used to write papers, but oral reports are not written. Rather, they are developed from outlines (Section 24.4).

After you state the central theme for an oral report (Section 24.6), develop your draft of the body of the report by speaking it rather than by writing it. Use the procedures that are explained in Chapter 17 to recite and learn the basic outline of the body of the report. Then, use the same procedures to recite the supporting evidence that you will include for each major point. You may find it helpful to pace around a room or to walk outdoors when you rehearse what you will say.

When you have a fairly good grasp of what you will say in the body of a report, outline in detail what you will say for the introduction and conclusion (Section 24.8). The opening and closing statements for an oral report should be worked out more carefully than the statements made in the body of the report. After you have decided exactly how you want to begin and end, recite the entire report as many times as is necessary so that you could give the report without referring to notes if you had to. If you know exactly what you will say, you will be more confident when you stand up in front of a class to give a report.

However, you may refer to notes when you speak. Make a brief outline of a report on 3 x 5 cards. Make one card for the introduction, one for each major point, and one for the conclusion. If you are well prepared, the cards should give you absolute confidence that you will say all the things you want to say in the well-organized way you planned to say them. Also, the cards will give you something logical to do with your hands in case you are self-conscious about what to do with them when you are speaking in front of a group

29.5   Relax and speak to the individual

Section 6.3 gives some suggestions that may be helpful to you in case you experience apprehension when you must make an oral presentation before a class. As you await your turn to speak, think the thoughts that are suggested in that section:

1. If you are nervous, think "It is normal for me to be nervous—my classmates are nervous when they give reports too."

2. If you are concerned about how you will appear to others, think "If I concentrate on what I want to say I will speak intelligently and look good to others."

3. If you resent that you must give an oral report, think "By giving this report I will gain experience that may benefit me in other classes or when I take a responsible job."

As you think positive thoughts such as these, do the breathing exercise that is suggested in Section 18.1; it will help you to relax.

When you rise to give your report, take time to find some friendly faces in various parts of the room. Instead of faces, you may see tops of heads; you may see people playing with books or pens, or you may notice some people talking to one another. If so, do not worry; these types of behaviors are normal for some people. Accept that some people do not know how to behave when you are in front of them and about to speak.

When you give your report, make it your goal to communicate with your audience. An audience is a group of individuals who all happen to be in the same place at the same time. In our culture, we look at individuals when we speak to them. Therefore, look into the eyes of a friendly face and begin with the introduction that you have planned. As you continue your report, find attentive faces in various parts of the room, and, as often as possible, make your statements while looking directly into the eyes of an audience member.

If the thought of looking into people's eyes when you speak to them in a group is frightening to you, observe yourself when you speak to people one at a time. You should find that it is natural for you to look into people's eyes when you speak to them. When you speak to people in a group, do what you naturally do when you speak to them one at a time. If you do, you will appear more natural and relaxed to your audience.

Use What You've Learned

1. Prepare a one-minute oral report about a successful or unsuccessful experience you had using one of the suggestions that is given in this handbook. You will give the report seated at your desk.

2. Prepare a two-minute oral report about an interesting article you read in a newspaper or magazine recently. You will give the report seated at your desk.

3. Prepare a two-minute oral report about any topic that you believe may be interesting to your classmates. You will give the report standing in front of the class.

4. Prepare a five-minute oral report about a topic that is related to one of the courses you are now taking. You will give the report standing in front of the class.

Answer Key

This answer key contains suggestions for notes for some text-book excerpts in Chapter 13 and Chapter 14. It is not likely that the notes you take will be identical to the ones that are illustrated here. Use the model notes to judge the completeness and accuracy of your notes.

Section 13.2 (Figure 13b)

Stages of Pregnancy

* Normally lasts 240–300 days, average is 266 days
1. First trimester (1–3 months)
    * Women adjust to "owning" the pregnancy
    * Mixed feelings about being pregnant
2. Second trimester (4–6 months)
    * Uterus weight increases 20 times (mostly before 20th week)
    * Heartbeat of fetus heard (4th–5th month)
    * Fetus moves (6th month)
    * Woman's breasts ready for nursing
3. Third trimester (7–9 months)
    * Stomach and other organs are crowded
    * Frequent urination needed
    * Woman may want to nap
    * Baby moves

Section 13.4

Types of Families

1. Nuclear family—married couple and their children
   * Family of orientation (mother, father, brothers, sisters)
   * Family of procreation (spouse, sons, daughters)
2. Extended family—in U.S., parents, children, and relatives who live with them or nearby
3. Monogamous family—one husband and one wife
4. Polygamous family—more than two marriage partners
   * Polygyny (one husband and two or more wives)
   * Polyandry (one wife and two or more husbands)

Section 13.5

Eye Behavior

* *Oculesics* (eye behavior) is expected to conform to certain norms.
1. We expect those who pay attention to us to look into our eyes (but eye contact is not necessary for paying attention).
2. We believe sustained eye contact is an invitation to communication.
3. We believe those who look at us find us physically attractive (but it's not necessarily so).

Section 14.1 (Figure 14a)

The Impact of the Civil War on the South

1. Crops and homes destroyed; cities and towns occupied
2. Southern economy ruined and lives of people made miserable (poverty led to disease)
3. Intellectual and cultural life devastated (libraries, publishers, schools, etc., all suffered greatly)

Section 14.2

Pretension, Jargon, and Cliché

1. Pretension—use words to impress rather than to express thoughts clearly ("perambulate" for walk)
2. Jargon (gobbledygook)—use words to obscure meaning ("anti-personnel detonating device" for bomb)
3. Cliché—overused, tired phrases ("clear as day")

Section 14.3

Types of Social Mobility

1. Horizontal—a person goes from one status to another roughly equivalent status (from plumber to carpenter)
2. Vertical—person goes from a status to a higher or lower status (plumber to corporation president, or vice versa)
3. Intergenerational—change in status of family members from one generation to the next (plumber's child becomes corporation president, or vice versa)

Section 14.6

The Causes of Rapid Population Growth

1. Change in the ratio of births to deaths (birth rate remains high and people live longer)
2. Populations were large before change in ratio of births to deaths
3. Large families are valued by the poor (children needed to work)
4. Religious teachings promote large families
   * Judeo-Christian—"Be fruitful and multiply"
   * Arabs—"many children . . . blessed by Allah"
   * Islam—opposes birth control
   * Catholic Church—opposes contraceptives

Section 14.7

The information in the sample notes is arranged in a different sequence than it is presented in the passage.

Effects of Early and Late Maturing

1. Early maturing
   * Boys
     * Treated as adults—don't need to strive for status
     * Tend to be leaders in high school
   * Girls
     * May be embarrassed or self-conscious (about breasts)
     * May be pressured to date too early
     * May be expected to act like an adult
2. Late maturing
   * Boys
     * Immature behavior
     * Feel inadequate or inferior
     * Compensate by striving for attention
     * May be personally or socially maladjusted
     * Problems may carry over into adulthood
   * Girls
     * May be anxious or shy

Section 14.8

The Middle Class

* Dominant morality in the U.S.; its attitudes and tastes are respected by politicians, advertisers, schools, etc.
1. Upper-middle (high-income business and professional families)
   * White, Protestant, Anglo-Saxon (mostly)
   * Respectable, but not society
   * Tend to live comfortably in suburbs
   * Active in politics and community organizations
   * Concerned with career advancement
   * High goals for children (most go to college)

2. Lower-middle (have less money than upper-middle)
   * Do not do manual labor
   * Small business operators, salespersons, teachers, etc.
   * Concerned with respectability
   * Value hard work
   * Politically and economically conservative

Glossary

Words within the definitions that are printed in *italics* are defined in this glossary.

Acronym. A word made from the initial letters of other words. "Scuba" is an acronym made from the initial letters of the following words: s(elf)- c(ontained) u(nderwater) b(reathing) a(pparatus).

Analysis. A discussion that uses specific *categories* to organize observations about a topic.

Anxiety. A feeling of uneasiness or uncertainty that is often induced by worry about what may happen in the future. See *test anxiety*.

Appendix. The part of a book that contains any supplementary materials or information; usually located in the back of a book, immediately following the last chapter.

Aptitude. A talent or ability.

Assistant professor. A rank for a college teacher that is lower than the rank of *associate professor* but higher than the rank of *instructor*.

Associate degrees. *Degrees* that are usually offered by two-year colleges, often the A.A. (Associate of Arts), A.S. (Associate of Science), or A.A.S. (Associate of Applied Science).

Associate professor. A rank for a college teacher that is lower than the rank of *professor* but higher than the rank of *assistant professor*.

Authoritative. Said of information that is written by people who are experts on the subjects about which they write.

Bachelor's degrees. *Degrees* offered by four-year colleges and universities, usually the B.A. (Bachelor of Arts) or B.S. (Bachelor of Science).

Bar graph. A drawing in which broad, straight lines are used to show differences in amounts. A bar graph may be used to show differences in the amounts of tar content of various brands of cigarettes.

Base word. The English word in a *derivative*. The word "kind" is the base word in "unkindness."

Bibliography. A list of books, articles, and other sources of information that are referred to by a writer.

Bluebook. A booklet, not necessarily blue, that contains lined paper on which may be written answers to *essay questions*.

Bulletin. A booklet published by a college or university that includes information about *curriculums,* courses, and other important facts; a *catalogue.*

Bursar. The title of a person at a college who is responsible for money transactions; a treasurer.

Catalogue. Same as a *bulletin*.

Categories. Divisions created to organize facts and concepts so they are more easily understood; same as *types*. Biology textbooks explain the categories or types of animals and plants.

Causes. Explanations that help us understand why things are as they are; same as *reasons*. Psychology textbooks explain the causes or reasons people behave in the ways they do.

Comparison. An explanation of similarities and differences. See *contrast*.

Context. A sentence, paragraph, or longer unit of writing that may reveal the meaning of an unfamiliar word.

Contrast. An explanation of differences. See *comparison*.

Course outline. A paperback book that summarizes the information that is usually taught in a college course, such as an introductory business or psychology course. Also, a summary of the topics for a course that is distributed by a teacher.

Credits. Units given for completion of any study that applies toward a college *degree*.

Curriculum. The courses required to earn a particular *degree*.

Deans. Members of the administration of a college who are in charge of specified aspects of the school's activities such as dean of students, dean of faculty, dean of instruction, or dean of a *school* or *division* within a college or university.

Degrees. Ranks given to students who have successfully completed specified courses of study, usually *associate degrees, bachelor's degrees, master's degrees,* or *doctoral degrees.*

Derivative. A word that contains a *base word* and at least one *prefix* or *suffix.* The derivative "unkindness" includes the prefix "un-," the base word "kind," and the suffix "-ness."

Diagram. A drawing that explains something by outlining its parts and by showing the relationships among its parts. For example, a diagram may show the parts and relationships among the parts of an automobile engine.

Direction word. A word in an *essay question* that informs test-takers what type of answer they are to give. The direction word "diagram" usually indicates students are to draw a picture and label its parts.

Distractor. An *option* for a *multiple-choice question* that is not the correct answer.

Division. In some colleges, departments are organized under larger groups called divisions. For example, the social sciences division of a college may include a psychology department, sociology department, anthropology department, and other departments.

Doctoral degrees. The highest *degrees* offered by colleges and universities. Many college teachers earn a Ph.D. (Doctor of Philosophy) or Ed.D. (Doctor of Education).

Effects. The consequences of actions, events, or circumstances; same as *results.* Ecology textbooks explain the effects or results of pollution on the environment.

Endnote. A *footnote* located in a list that follows written material rather than at the bottom of a page.

Essay questions. Test items that require students to give written answers that are usually one paragraph or more in length.

Evaluate. To consider the positive and negative aspects of something and come to a conclusion about its merits.

Example. Something selected to show the general characteristics of something else. Spaghetti is an example of pasta, and nose-picking in public is an example of bad manners.

Exposition. Written or spoken language that states facts and explanations. Mathematics, sociology, and most other college books contain mostly exposition.

Fact. A statement that represents reality.

Footnote. A reference printed at the bottom of a page. The reference is usually to a book, article, or other source of information.

Freshmen. Students in their first *undergraduate* year of study at a college or university.

Glossary. A list of words and their definitions; usually located in the back of a book just in front of the *index*. This is a glossary.

Grade point average. A number that usually ranges from 0.00 to 4.00 and indicates a student's average course grade.

Grade point values. Values given to *letter grades* so that *grade point averages* may be computed. The following values are used at many colleges: A, 4.00; B, 3.00; C, 2.00; D, 1.00; and F, 0.00.

Graduate students. Students who have earned *bachelor's degrees* and are continuing study, usually for *master's degrees* or *doctoral degrees*.

Highlighting. The act of marking important words or sentences in a book using a pen that contains water-color ink. This is done so important statements will stand out clearly and not be overlooked while *studying*.

Incomplete (INC). A grade given at many colleges when students are doing passing work but have not completed all course requirements. Usually an INC grade is changed to F or some other grade if incomplete work is not completed within a specified time.

Index. An alphabetically arranged listing of subjects and the page numbers on which they are discussed in a book; usually located at the very end of a book.

Infer. To use known facts or evidence to arrive at an opinion or conclusion. For instance, if you have thirty-year-old classmates, you may infer that they were high school students about fifteen years ago.

Instructor. A title for college teachers who have the rank lower than *assistant professor*. Also, a general term to refer to any teacher.

Interest inventory. A kind of test that gives people opportunities to state their preferences for participating in specific activities. Trained counselors can use responses to interest inventories to help people understand what their interests are.

Interview. A conversation engaged in to collect information.

Glossary

Introduction. The part of a book that gives the author's explanations of why the book was written. It often includes a summary of the purposes, philosophy, or contents of the book; usually located right after the *table of contents*. This information may also be located in a *preface*.

Juniors. Students in their third *undergraduate* year of study at a college or university.

Lecturer. A title sometimes applied to college teachers who do not have the rank of *professors* or *instructors*, and sometimes to distinguished visiting teachers.

Letter grades. Grades such as B+, C, and D— that designate the quality of work students do. Letter grades have the following meanings at many colleges: A, excellent; B, good; C, satisfactory; D, passing; and F, failing.

Line graph. A drawing in which lines are used to show increasing or decreasing amounts. A line graph may be used to show increases or decreases in the numbers of students enrolled at a college over a period of years.

Lower division. The first two years of college study; the *freshman* and *sophomore* years.

Master's degrees. Degrees that rank higher than *bachelor's degrees* but lower than *doctoral degrees,* usually the M.A. (Master of Arts) or M.S. (Master of Science).

Matching questions. Test items that present two lists and require test-takers to associate words or statements in one list with words or statements in the other list.

Matriculation. A classification for individuals who are currently accepted by colleges or universities to study for *degrees.*

Methods. The procedures, processes, or ways of doing something. Mathematics textbooks explain methods for solving mathematical problems.

Mnemonic device. Any method used to aid memory. "Use *i* before *e* except after *c*" is a mnemonic device that is a rhyme for remembering a spelling principle.

Multiple-choice questions. Test items written in a format that requires test-takers to select the correct answer from among four or five possible answers that are listed.

Number grades. Grades such as 91, 85, and 68 that designate the quality of work students do. Many colleges agree on the following correspondences among number grades and letter grades: A, 90–100; B, 80–89; C, 70–79; D, 60–69; and F, 0–59.

Open-book test. A test during which students may refer to books, and sometimes notes, as they write the answers to questions.

Opinion. A point of view about which equally knowledgeable and informed people may argue or debate: "No American citizen should have to pay for health care."

Option. In a *multiple-choice question,* one of the choices from which a correct answer is selected; one option is a correct answer and the others are *distractors.*

Orientation. A period of time or a series of events planned to help new students satisfactorily adjust to college or university life.

Outline. A summary of information that lists important points. In the traditional outline format, major points are labeled with Roman numerals and details are labeled with capital letters.

Paraphrase. To use one's own wordings and phrasings to restate the written or spoken words of another person.

Pass/fail. A grading system that permits students to receive only passing or failing grades. *Letter grades* such as A, B, and C are not given when courses are taken on a pass/fail basis.

Preface. See *introduction.*

Prefix. A word part that appears in front of *base words* in *derivatives.* The prefix "un-" appears in "unkindness."

Prerequisite. A requirement that must be completed before a course may be taken. For example, the prerequisite for an intermediate algebra course may be a course in elementary algebra.

President. At a college or university, the chief administrative officer who has ultimate responsibility for all aspects of the functioning of the school.

Preview. To quickly examine introductory paragraphs, headings, pictures, tables, and other features of a chapter or article to learn what major topics it discusses.

Primary source. A first-hand source of information. A motion picture starring Marilyn Monroe is a primary source for information about her appearance on screen. Contrast with *secondary source.*

Probation. A classification into which students are put while they attempt to raise low *grade point averages* or to remove other academic deficiencies.

Professor. The highest rank for college teachers, also sometimes called full professor to distinguish from *associate professor* and *assistant professor*.

Program. The courses one takes during a *term* of study at a college or university.

Quarter system. A system that divides a school year into three parts, usually a fall, a winter, and a spring *term* of ten weeks each.

Quotation. The exact written or spoken words of another person.

Reading. The process used to understand information that is presented in writing. Contrast with *studying*.

Reading flexibility. The difference between the rate at which one reads easy material rapidly and difficult material slowly. See *reading rates*.

Reading rates. The numbers of words per minute people read. A slow reading rate is used to read material that is very difficult to understand, a moderate reading rate is used to read material carefully that is of average difficulty, and a fast reading rate is used to read easy material quickly.

Reasons. See *causes*.

Reciting. The act of repeating information silently or aloud to learn it and to be able to recall it.

References. See *bibliography*.

Registrar. The title of a person at a college who is responsible for registering students in courses and maintaining their academic records on *transcripts*.

Registration. A period of time during which students register for the courses they will take.

Regressions. When reading, the tendency for the eyes to look back at something that has already been read.

Research paper. A paper written using information that is collected by doing careful and patient investigation, usually in a library. The papers are typed in a special form that includes *footnotes,* or *endnotes,* and a *bibliography*.

Results. See *effects*.

School. A division within a college or university, such as a school of medicine.

Secondary source. A statement made about a *primary source*. A motion picture review describing Marilyn Monroe's appearance on screen is a secondary source about her appearance.

Section. One of two or more classes for the same course. For instance, a large university may offer many classes (or sections) of a freshman writing course.

Sentence completion questions. Statements that have deleted portions that test-takers must supply: "There are _____ letters in the English alphabet."

Semester system. A system that divides a school year into two parts, usually a fall and a spring *term* of fifteen to sixteen weeks each.

Seniors. Students in their fourth *undergraduate* year of study at a college or university.

Sequence. The order in which things follow each other in time, space, rank, complexity, or some other dimension. History textbooks explain the historical sequences in which important events occurred.

Skill. An ability acquired as a result of training and practice. Reading and writing are skills.

Skim. To read quickly to find the main thoughts in written material. Similar to *previewing*.

Sophomores. Students in their second *undergraduate* year of study at a college or university.

Statistics. Numerical data. The populations of cities in the United States are examples of statistics.

Stem. The part of a *multiple-choice question* that comes before the first *option*. The first option is usually preceded by the letter "a."

Study guide. A paperback book that summarizes the information that is usually taught in a college course, such as an introductory business or psychology course.

Studying. The process used to remember and recall information. Contrast with *reading*.

Subject label. In a dictionary, a term printed in italic type to indicate the field of knowledge or activity to which a definition for a word applies. The word "Botany" printed in italic type just before a definition indicates the definition applies to the word when it is used to discuss botany.

Suffix. A word part that appears at the ends of *base words* in *derivatives*. The suffix "-ness" appears in "unkindness."

Summary. A condensed presentation of information.

Summer session. A period in the summer during which students may take courses for academic *credit* but which is usually not considered a *semester* or *quarter* for the purposes of a school's business.

Syllabus. A *summary* or *outline* distributed by an instructor that states the main topics to be discussed in a course.

Table. A presentation of *statistics* arranged in well-organized columns and rows.

Table of contents. A list that shows the page numbers on which chapter headings and subheadings of a book appear; usually located in the front of a book, right after the *title page*.

Take-home test. A test for which students are given questions that they answer at home, or study at home before they answer them in class.

Term. A period of study in a college. A term may be a *semester*, a *quarter*, or a *summer session*.

Terminology. Words or phrases that are used with specific meanings when a subject is discussed. *Stem, option,* and *distractor* are terminology that is used to discuss the subject of multiple-choice questions.

Test anxiety. Uneasiness or apprehension experienced because of the need to prepare for or take a test. See *anxiety*.

Title page. The page of a book that gives information about the title, author, and publisher; usually the first or second page of a book.

Transcripts. Official records of courses taken, grades received, and *grade point averages*. Transcripts are maintained by a *registrar*.

True-false questions. Test items that are statements that test-takers must decide are either true or false.

Tutor. A person who gives individual instruction to students.

Types. See *categories*.

Undergraduates. College students who have not yet earned *bachelor's degrees*.

Underlining. The act of drawing lines under important words or sentences in a book so they stand out clearly and will not be overlooked while *studying*.

Upper division. The third and fourth years of study in a four-year college or university; the *junior* and *senior* years.

Visualization. An image that can be pictured in the mind and used to recall information. If you picture in your mind the room where you sleep, you can use the image to recall information about the room.

Withdrawal grade (W). A grade given at many colleges so that students may drop courses when they have good reasons for doing so. Usually W grades do not lower *grade point averages* when they are requested within specified time limits or when students are doing passing work at the time of withdrawal.

Credits

The following figures, tables, or excerpts are used with permission. The word *adapted* usually indicates that a phrase or a sentence was deleted, words were underscored, or a heading for an excerpt differs from the original.

Part opening page backgrounds and other dictionary entries: The following credit line applies to the dictionary entries reproduced on pages 1, 35, 117, 215, 289, and 313 of this text: Copyright © 1980 by Houghton Mifflin Company. Reprinted by permission from *The American Heritage Dictionary of the English Language.*

Chapter 5:   Page 46, Figure 5a: From James F. Shepherd, *RSVP: The Houghton Mifflin Reading, Study, and Vocabulary Program.* Copyright © 1981 by Houghton Mifflin Company. Adapted by permission.

Chapter 9:   Page 83, Figure 9b and excerpt: From Gary S. Belkin and Ruth H. Skydell, *Foundations of Psychology.* Copyright © 1979 by Houghton Mifflin Company. Adapted by permission. *Page 89,* top: From Barbara Westbrook and R. G. Eakins, *Sex Differences in Human Communication.* Copyright © 1978 by Houghton Mifflin Company. Reprinted by permission. *Page 89,* bottom: From G. D. Lillibridge, *Images of American Society,* Volume I. Copyright © 1976 by Houghton Mifflin Company. Adapted by permission. *Page 93,* Figure 9d: From James F. Shepherd, *RSVP: The Houghton Mifflin Reading, Study, and Vocabulary Program.* Copyright © 1981 by Houghton Mifflin Company. Reprinted by permission. *Page 97,* Figure 9e: From James F. Shepherd, *RSVP: The Houghton Mifflin Reading, Study, and Vocabulary Program.* Copyright © 1981 by Houghton Mifflin Company. Adapted by permission. *Page 99:* From Alfred R. Stone and Stuart M. DeLuca, *Investigating Crimes.* Copyright © 1980 by Houghton Mifflin Company. Reprinted by permission.

Chapter 11:   Page 122, Figure 11a; *Page 123,* Figure 11b: From Gary S. Belkin and Ruth H. Skydell, *Foundations of Psychology.* Copyright © 1979 by Houghton Mifflin Company. Adapted by permission.

Chapter 12:   Page 132, Figure 12a: From Alan Sherman, et al., *Basic Concepts of Chemistry,* 2nd ed. Copyright © 1980 by Houghton Mifflin Company. Reprinted by permission. *Page 133:* From Robert Kreitner, *Management: A Problem-Solving Process.* Copyright © 1980 by Houghton Mifflin Company. Reprinted by permission. *Pages 135 and 139:* From Gary S. Belkin and Ruth H. Skydell, *Foundations of Psychology.* Copyright ©

418

1979 by Houghton Mifflin Company. Reprinted by permission. *Page 137,* Figure 12b: From Ronald J. Waldron, et al., *The Criminal Justice System,* 2nd ed. Copyright © 1980 by Houghton Mifflin Company. Adapted by permission. *Page 138,* Figure 12c: From Robert A. Lynn and James P. O'Grady, *Elements of Business.* Copyright © 1978 by Houghton Mifflin Company. Adapted by permission.

Chapter 13: Page 144, Figure 13b: From Joann S. DeLora, Carol A. B. Warren, and Carol Rinkleib Ellison, *Understanding Human Sexuality.* Copyright © 1980 by Houghton Mifflin Company. Reprinted by permission. *Page 145:* From James F. Shepherd, *RSVP: The Houghton Mifflin Reading, Study, and Vocabulary Program.* Copyright © 1981 by Houghton Mifflin Company. Adapted by permission. *Page 146:* From Michael D. Scott and William G. Powers, *Interpersonal Communication.* Copyright © 1978 by Houghton Mifflin Company. Reprinted by permission. *Page 147,* Figure 13c: From Kevin Ryan and James M. Cooper, *Those Who Can Teach,* 3rd ed. Copyright © 1980 by Houghton Mifflin Company. Adapted by permission.

Chapter 14: Page 158, Figure 14a: From G. D. Lillibridge, *Images of American Society,* Volume I. Copyright © 1976 by Houghton Mifflin Company. Adapted by permission. *Page 160:* From James F. Shepherd, *RSVP: The Houghton Mifflin Reading, Study, and Vocabulary Program.* Copyright © 1981 by Houghton Mifflin Company. Adapted by permission. *Pages 161, 162, 170, and 176:* From Ian Robertson, *Sociology,* Worth Publishers, New York, 1977. *Page 164:* From Robert L. Williams and James D. Long, *Toward a Self-managed Life Style,* 2nd ed. Copyright © 1979 by Houghton Mifflin Company. Adapted by permission. *Page 167:* From Robert Kreitner, *Management: A Problem-Solving Process.* Copyright © 1980 by Houghton Mifflin Company. Adapted by permission. *Page 173,* From Gary S. Belkin and Ruth H. Skydell, *Foundations of Psychology.* Copyright © 1979 by Houghton Mifflin Company. Adapted by permission. *Page 175:* From Joann S. DeLora, Carol A. B. Warren, and Carol Rinkleib Ellison, *Understanding Human Sexuality.* Copyright © 1980 by Houghton Mifflin Company. Adapted by permission.

Chapter 15: Page 186: From Ian Robertson, *Sociology,* Worth Publishers, New York, 1977.

Chapter 16: Page 197, Figure 16c; *Page 201,* Figure 16f: From James F. Shepherd, *RSVP: The Houghton Mifflin Reading, Study, and Vocabulary Program.* Copyright © 1981 by Houghton Mifflin Company. Adapted by permission. *Page 199,* Figure 16d: From Robert Kreitner, *Management: A Problem-Solving Process.* Copyright © 1980 by Houghton Mifflin Company. Adapted by permission. *Page 200,* Figure 16e: From Joann S. DeLora, Carol A. B. Warren, and Carol Rinkleib Ellison, *Understanding Human Sexuality.* Copyright © 1980 by Houghton Mifflin Company. Adapted by permission.

Credits

Index

Index